ACCOUNTABILITY, INVESTIGATION AND DUE PROCESS IN INTERNATIONAL ORGANIZATIONS

NIJHOFF LAW SPECIALS

VOLUME 63

The titles published in this series are listed at the end of this volume.

Accountability, Investigation and Due Process in International Organizations

Edited by

Chris de Cooker

International Institute of Administrative Sciences

MARTINUS NIJHOFF PUBLISHERS
LEIDEN/BOSTON

A C.I.P. Catalogue record for this book is available from the Library of Congress.

Printed on acid-free paper.

ISBN 90-04-14793-4

Published by Koninklijke Brill NV, Leiden, The Netherlands

Koninklijke Brill NV incorporates the imprints Brill Academic Publishers, Martinus Nijhoff Publishers and VSP.
http://www.brill.nl

Printed and bound in The Netherlands

CONTENTS

ANNEXES

PREFACE

The IIAS Supranational Administration Working Group, formerly the Permanent Working Group on International Administration and Civil Service, has been active for more than 25 years. The group has met on average once a year and of course over the years its participants have changed – in fact, it now appears that there are few of the original group left and the present writer is pleased to be counted among them. The aim of the group has, however, remained constant: to bring together a number of experts, mostly senior and active international civil servants, but also some retired staff and academics, to analyse topics of common interest to international organisations. It is evident that international organisations have much in common even if they differ in size, purpose and the available means at their disposal. Over the years, the group has benefited greatly from this free and informal exchange of information and ideas. Initially and for the first twenty years, the group was under the stimulating leadership of Alain Plantey, *Membre de l'Académie des Sciences Morales et Politiques (France)*, who was a leading force in the IIAS. Generally, the results of discussions have remained discreet and confidential among the members of the group, but on two occasions the group published the members' reflections together with relevant documentation.[1]

This might be considered a meagre result in a "publish or perish" environment, but this would not do justice to the work done. It should be remembered that the results of some of the group's work can be found in other publications. More importantly, most discussions have been – and continue to be – concerned with confidential matters or even issues that are unresolved, thereby making a common position difficult, a publication unthinkable. However, the overall result today is that the IIAS has created a group which is well-established with a broad membership from all over the world, including universal and regional organisations alike. The group is quite unique.

In the early 1980s the group discussed, amongst other topics, dispute resolution mechanisms in international organisations, paying particular attention to pre-litigation procedures.[2] Being convinced that much had changed

[1] See, *The Pensions of International Civil Servants*, and *La couverture médicale dans la fonction publique internationale*, published respectively in 1993 and 1998.

[2] As acknowledged, both the information and the views exchanged were used in Chris de

in the interval, the group chose, in the second half of the 1990s, to have another look at this issue.

The group met for a first meeting in Brussels, in October 1997. The topic of the meeting was "Internal Justice Reform". Major efforts had been made in several organisations in this respect. The United Nations (UN) had initiated such a reform only to be blocked by budgetary considerations in the General Assembly;[3] it was only some years later that the Ombudsman's Office was established in the UN. The World Bank was more successful; it managed a major overhaul of its internal justice system.

However, what struck the group most was that many organisations had created specific procedures in the 1980s and 1990s to tackle, in particular but not exclusively, the problem of (sexual) harassment. These new complaint procedures were in general introduced in parallel to existing pre-litigation procedures, adding to the confusion of how to proceed; how to ensure that one's voice is heard. Even more strikingly, these procedures often went hand in hand with new codes of conduct, the purpose of which was to provide guidelines for correct conduct with a view, amongst others, to avoiding (pre-)litigation. Staff received detailed and positive guidelines on how to behave; this was quite different from receiving a sudden message that a particular conduct was in violation of (non-defined) professional obligations. Thus, a step forward.

Several organisations went so far as to create (or strengthen) the function of an ethics officer. This officer generally had the almost impossible dual task of explaining and guiding staff collectively or individually through the codes of conduct, on the one hand, and of enforcing the code and (the rest of) the law of the organisation, on the other. In short, counsellor and prosecutor at the same time.

In this respect it should also be remembered that in the 1980s and 1990s there was a call from some quarters, more than from others, for strict(er) implementation. Anti-corruption and anti-fraud initiatives were introduced or improved. In consequence, special oversight and control bodies were set up; other bodies received increased/improved powers and additional instructions.

In a positive sense these new codes of conduct (and some were still in the process of being drafted and colleagues benefited from exchanges in our group!) were instrumental in avoiding disputes, since staff knew more

---

Cooker, "Pre-Litigation Procedures in International Organisations", in *International Administration, Law and Management Practices*, V.6.

[3] As will be explained *infra*, a new exercise is underway at the moment of writing this book. One can only hope that this undertaking will not again meet the same budgetary considerations. Accountability, investigation, and dispute resolution do have a price.

clearly what was expected of them. On the other hand, the enforcement mechanisms raised new questions concerning procedures and due process.

In November 1999 a major conference on dispute resolution (CEDRIO) was organised by the World Bank. A large number of our members attended. During the conference alternative dispute resolution methods (ombudsman, mediation, arbitration, etc.) were discussed in detail. Also during the conference attention was given to the major new developments concerning codes of conduct for the (new) European Commissioners. The fall of the previous Commission had caused more than a stir in Europe and in the world of international administration. Then, in 2000, another major event was the publication of a white paper on administrative reform by the new European Commission.

The topic was presented and discussed in the margin of the First Regional International Conference of the IIAS, held in Bologna in June 2000.

When the group met again in 2001 – it had only met briefly in 2000 in the margin of the conference celebrating the 20th anniversary of the World Bank's Administrative Tribunal – it identified many new regulatory initiatives concerning the behaviour of senior staff (such as financial disclosure). It also acknowledged the first negative outcomes before international administrative tribunals; these related to "solid" fraud or corruption cases that were lost by international organisations because of a lack of due process. The group then began to wonder what the real purpose of these codes was: to avoid disputes or create new law (through soft law) with new implementation and enforcement mechanisms that could not always pass rule-of-law standards.

In 2002 the group held a unique meeting in Paris. For the first time the administrative lawyers had an open debate with the investigators/prosecutors. It was clear that all were working towards making their organisations better, e.g. more transparent, corruption free, respecting the highest standards – including those of due process, showing to the world that every Dollar/Euro spent was well spent; in other words, international organisations were becoming increasingly accountable.

This book is a reflection of these exchanges of views and information. It brings to light the issues and questions that were – and are – at stake. These are the questions that we have been struggling with and will continue to examine, including the need to respect basic rules of due process when things go wrong. Nonetheless the primary goal remains the same: dispute avoidance through better education and information.

As noted, many relevant texts have been published in recent years and it looks as if we have not yet seen the end of it. These have all been honest efforts to improve the situation in various organisations. It is also clear that the members of the group have not been alone in taking note of several (press) reports about particular events in one or the other organisation. It is quite evident that much is left to be done.

This book simply provides an indication of the ideas exchanged and experiences shared by a group of people who, because of their employment by and commitment to international administration, have been – and most of them still are – taking part in a more general process of change in the public service, national and international alike. Accountability and transparency have now become the rule. Only recently have international organisations been looking for common values. It is not clear what triggered the process. Was it the call for empowerment of the (international) public service? Was it an anti-corruption drive, as we have witnessed almost simultaneously in some of the major contributor countries? Has it resulted from the movement of citizens and the press calling for greater transparency, a new approach, "introducing" the concept of governance? It may be a mixture of all the above as well as a number of other factors. Nonetheless the fact remains that at the end of the previous century and at the beginning of the current one most international organisations were entangled in complicated internal debates, drafting codes of conduct and designing new and more dynamic mechanisms of control – and the procedures that go with it.

The purpose of this collective reflection is to take stock of what has happened in international administration in recent years. Although new developments continually arise, it is clear that the major "outburst" is over. This book brings together the thoughts, reflections and comments made by some, and sometimes by all members of the group. The book does not aim to cover each and every development in each organisation.

The most recent years have been very difficult for a number of our organisations. Negative (press) reports have come out and, unfortunately, most of them are correct. It shows that a lot remains to be done and we hope that this book can contribute to the discussion.

We are very grateful for the members' frank contributions and for their participation in the exchange we had in the meetings. Obviously, only those who took the risk of writing contributions for this book are responsible for what is written here, not the organisations for which they work. It must be emphasised, however, that this book could not have been published without the contributions of other members of the group. This is indeed a collective exercise.

We stopped collecting information for inclusion in the book in the beginning of May 2005.

Chris de Cooker

ONE

Ethics and Accountability in the International Civil Service

Chris de Cooker[1]

The problem, of course, was that people did not seem to understand the difference between right and wrong. They needed to be reminded about this, because if you left it to them to work out for themselves, they would never bother. They would just find out what was best for them, and then they would call that the right thing. That's how most people thought.

Alexander McCall Smith, The No. 1 Ladies' Detective Agency, 1998

I. Introduction

Public Administration has in the last decades of the 20th century gone through major changes, and continues to do so in the 21st. International Administration is no exception to this. It has been following this trend, sometimes slower, sometimes faster, which is logical in view of its specificities (and the differences between the respective organisations).

Public administrators have, at all levels, made considerable efforts to shake off the old image, which had for so long been associated with the civil and public service: that of lack of efficiency, of being excessively costly for the services they rendered, and of their reliability on authority rather than on the concept of service. New concepts were embraced, generally coming from the private and commercial sectors: notions like "efficiency" and "value for money" became trendy. These latter notions, however, when taken to their extreme – and they were at times – risk to put in jeopardy the basic notions underlying public administration, such as equal treatment, proportionality, consistency, respect for the rule of law, and standards of ethical behaviour.

This process was, and is, a reaction to the outside pressure on public administration: administrations have become accountable to a more and

[1] The views expressed in this article are those of the author, and do not necessarily represent the views of the European Space Agency. I am grateful to Giancarlo Vilella, former Director General of IIAS, for shaping my mind on this topic.

Numerous references are made to specific rules and codes in different organisations. Unless otherwise indicated, these are given as examples only and without any preference. The aim of this contribution is, moreover, not to cover each and every statute or code that may exist.

more demanding public. This growing demand for transparency requires governments to ensure high standards of conduct in the public office, or as the IIAS itself puts it: "Accountability is a core value for the Institute. Those who exercise authority must account for its use to those on whose behalf they use it. Public Administration is the key activity that connects between the power-holders and the citizen. We believe it should be effective, efficient and economical in its execution of the duties and rights of the state. We support modern governance and proper public administration and believe these should be carried out in a way that actively acknowledges diversity, that is respectful of identity and serious belief and that reflects balance."

Every society governed by the principle of the rule of law has a system of checks and balances. It is then the classical role of the representatives of the citizens, such as parliament or local councils, to execute these control functions. But in the more and more open democratic societies that we have today, the public often takes an active part in this process, through the press, through action groups, etc. Relevant information can only be kept from the public in very exceptional cases. Transparency has become the rule rather than the exception. Must one conclude that the citizen has come closer to the administration, or was it the other way around?

It must also be emphasised that over the same period of time one could also witness the trend that public servants (or civil servants – both notions are used here without distinction) have, at all levels, been more and more empowered to answer questions directly, i.e. at their level of responsibility without resorting automatically to a higher level of authority, and to take decisions themselves and, where appropriate, explain and/or justify them.[2] A new level of transparency, of trust between the civil servant and "his" public, has emerged. A public servant must now be able to answer, i.e. be accountable, both internally (vis-à-vis his superiors) and externally (vis-à-vis his direct "client" or the public at large). He can no longer hide behind the institutional fact that he has a superior.

Such a new level of responsibility is tempting and represents a challenge. It usually also goes hand in hand with new types of performance appraisals and corresponding tokens of merit recognition.

Civil servants must then also be clearly explained what is exactly expected from them in most of the circumstances. The old-fashioned approach of rather undefined "professional obligations" enforced by disciplinary proce-

[2] The Charter of Values of the European Space Agency (ESA), for example, underlines that the aim is "to highlight personal responsibility as the fundamental and most effective element in the functioning of an organisation." See also Annex VI.

dures can no longer be applied to an official who is standing more and more independently in the front-line. Hence the requirement to give guidelines and to describe in more detail the conduct that is expected from an official, described in a positive way: the "do's" rather than the "don'ts". This approach resulted initially in general codes of conduct. But they have over the last few decades been complemented with more detailed codes concerning specific situations, such as harassment, relations with the public, relations with the business community, financial disclosure, etc.[3] These codes undoubtedly assist the officials in better structuring their conduct, and in enhancing their integrity and service responsiveness to the public. It also helps the employer to show to the outside world that it has taken all steps to see to it that its staff is functioning properly and that the administration is a respectable one and can be trusted.[4]

This is an essential element: the citizen must have confidence both in the public servant who is dealing with his/her individual case and in the overall "system". Measures must be taken in order to conserve and enhance public confidence and trust in integrity, objectivity and impartiality of government. Or as the Public Management Service of the Organisation for Economic Cooperation and Development (OECD) put it:

> Citizens trust public institutions if they know that public offices are used for the public good.[5]

In this latter respect one can observe another tendency, in many countries and international organisations alike: a stronger commitment to combat fraud and corruption, or even the suspicion of it. In many cases the public (or the politicians) are not satisfied with a general assurance that there is no corruption. It wants the assurance that all measures have been taken that, ideally, corruption cannot or can no longer take place. This anti-corruption drive has often blurred the evolution described above towards

---

[3] Many guidelines have in this respect been prepared at international level, e.g. the 1998 OECD Principles for Managing Ethics in the Public Service, the 2000 Recommendation of the Committee of Ministers of the Council of Europe on codes of conduct for public officials, the 2003 OECD Recommendation on Guidelines for Managing Conflict of Interest in the Public Service, the 2003 United Nations Convention against Corruption, etc.

[4] Or as the IMF put it in its Financial Certification and Disclosure Policy: "While management has full confidence in the integrity of staff, it attaches the utmost importance to ensuring and being able credibly to demonstrate that the IMF has in place internal control measures to prevent conflicts of interest." (*cf.* http://www. imf.org/external/hrd/fdiscl.htm). The Charter of Values of ESA stipulates: ". . . adopting a code of ethics constitutes a public affirmation of *bona fides* that gives confidence to the public at large regarding the organisation's integrity and honesty."

[5] Building Public Trust: Ethics Measures in OECD Countries, PUMA Policy Brief No. 7, OECD, 2000; http://www.oecd.org/dataoecd/60/43/1899427.pdf.

a more modern (international) civil service,[6] or as the president of the World Bank put it in a letter prefacing the World Bank's code of conduct:

> (o)ur commitment to ethics extends well beyond issues of corruption.

One other element should not be forgotten in this respect. Norms and standards, and in particular ethical norms, change over time. What was maybe accepted as acceptable behaviour yesterday, is no longer so today; and tomorrow may bring again new norms and values. Accountability is a living concept.

As another study of the OECD summed it up, public servants operate in a changed and changing environment. They are subject to greater public scrutiny and increased demands from citizens, yet they are also facing stricter limits on resources. They are having to assume new functions and responsibilities as a result of: devotion and greater managerial discretion; increased commercialization of the public sector; a changing public/private sector interface; and changing accountability arrangements. In short, they are having to adopt new ways of carrying out the business of government. While public management reforms have realized important returns in terms of efficiency and effectiveness, some of the adjustments may have had unintended impacts on ethics and standards of conduct. This is not to suggest that changes have caused an increase in misconduct or unethical behaviour. But they may place public servants in situations involving conflicts of interest or objectives where there are few guidelines as to how they should act. There may indeed be a growing mismatch between the traditional values and systems governing the behaviour of public servants and the roles they are expected to fulfil in a changing public sector environment.[7]

Another side to the medal is the risk that elected officials in local or national governments may no longer assume their end-responsibility for the acts of their public servants, thus entailing a loss in trust in the governments. This is an important element: in a democratic society public administration, with all its internal and necessary checks and balances of administrative accountability, is ultimately subject to parliamentary accountability.

It would appear that International Administration is very similar to national public administration. Many parallels can be drawn but also differences

[6] The Council of Europe's Code of Conduct for (national) public officials was, for example, prepared by the Multidisciplinary Group on Corruption.

[7] Public Management Occasional Papers, No. 14, Ethics in the Public Service, Current Issues and Practice, OECD, 1996, p. 5 (http://www.oecd.org/dataoecd/59/ 24/1898992.pdf).

can, of course, be identified. International Administration is, first of all, very young compared to national administration. International society is, not only in legal terms, still rather primitive, even in its most civilised form, that of international organisation. And it is only since the last 50 years that citizens, to some extent, can feel the influence of international organisations in their daily lives. To a large extent, however, the real stakeholders in international organisations are the member States. The organisations are set up to assist member States in achieving common goals. The stakeholders, represented on the governing boards, also finance the organisations and fix, in the budgets, the priorities in the respective activities. The executive powers of the Heads of the organisations, and of their staff, are thus very limited compared to national administrations. Many organisations could do much more, as could national administrations, if only the resources were provided. As is the case with national administrations, international organisations are critically followed by the stakeholders, but also by "organised" citizens. This may be the press; this may be action groups.

It is also true that international organisations differ between themselves, in purpose, in membership, in size, in resources, and in power. There are, however, enough common elements that justify a common analysis.

Like most administrations, international administrations tend to be slow. Most organisations have, moreover, a complex decision making process, often requiring unanimity or consensus. Delegations in the organisations are, in addition, generally specialists in the particular field of activity for which the organisation was set up. They are not necessarily experts in the evolution of the public service. They tend to be more interested in technical results rather than in administrative matters. This entails a special responsibility for the Heads of the organisations to see to it that the organisations are run adequately.

One can over the last decade notice two trends in international administration regarding accountability. One trend is the introduction of improved control mechanisms with a larger remit than the classical financial control or internal audit function. This concerns closer checks on book-keeping and accounts, checking integrity, and the fight against fraud and corruption.

The second trend is the proactive one. Detailed codes of conduct are being enacted concerning ethical behaviour as it is expected from staff within the larger concept of the organisation's mission statement.

When analysing questions of accountability and ethics in international organisations, one can observe that, generally, the organisations operate in a responsive mode. As will be demonstrated below, only a few organisations have codes of conduct that were introduced without any apparent pressure from either inside or outside these organisations. Most of the codes of the organisations are, however, a reaction to particular events.

As will be shown below, the European Union (EU) lived, in the 1990s, a genuine battle between institutions, particularly between the European Commission and the more recently established Court of Auditors, about management practices and accountability. The debate became blurred when specific allegations of favouritism and nepotism came to light. As is well-known and as will be explained in some detail below, the Commission resigned and their successors initiated major work in terms of working methods, accountability and codes of conduct.[8] Other organisations in Europe have wisely followed the example.

The European Central Bank (ECB) only came in existence during the same period. Its code of conduct may therefore be inspired by unfortunate events elsewhere, but not by allegations of improper behaviour within the organisation.

The beginning of the new millennium brought many headaches for the United Nations' (UN) top management in the field of ethics and accountability. Reports came out on fee-splitting arrangements between counsel and detainees at the International Tribunal for Rwanda and the International Tribunal for the Former Yugoslavia.[9] Peacekeepers of the North Atlantic Treaty Organisation (NATO) and the UN in Bosnia and Herzegovina, and Kosovo, have been accused of involvement in sexual trafficking and in prostitution rings.

The code of conduct of the United Nations High Commissioner for Refugees (UNHCR), which came out in 2003, was, also in its contents, a reaction to the delicate situation it found itself in following serious charges that came out in early 2002 of sexual exploitation of refugees and displaced children in West Africa.[10] Local employees of several governmental and non-governmental organisations, i.e. not only UNHCR staff (!), have been accused of using their positions to solicit and obtain sexual favours from children, primarily adolescent girls. In Kenya similar cases of bribery and extortion of refugees, seeking to be resettled, came to light. They were investigated by the UN's Office of Internal Oversight Services (OIOS) resulting in a number of arrests by the Kenyan authorities. The implementation, and acceptance, of the code of conduct in 2003 and 2004 became, moreover, more delicate in the context of allegations of sexual harassment by the High Commissioner himself. The investigation concerning the latter case resulted in a letter by the UN Secretary General

---

[8] This didn't keep the Prodi Commission from problems. See, for example, the "Eurostat" issue in 2003.

[9] See, for example, doc. A/56/836.

[10] See, for example, General Assembly resolution 57/306 of 15 April 2003.

to the UNHCR staff, saying he had written to the High Commissioner conveying in the strongest terms his concerns about the incident. When, in early 2005, the results of the same 2004 investigation were leaked to the press, the High Commissioner was obliged to resign.

The UN was in 2004 also plagued by reports of charges of sexual exploitation and abuse by civilian and military personnel serving in the UN Organization Mission in the Congo (MONUC). The allegations include criminal activity, paedophilia, rape and solicitation of prostitution. The UN Secretary General has in November 2004 indicated that there was "clear evidence that acts of grave misconduct have taken place." An OIOS report came out in January 2005.[11] In February 2005 the Moroccan mission to the United Nations announced that its Government had decided to arrest six of its soldiers.

In 2004 also a major investigation started concerning the oil-for-food programme in Iraq. The Independent Inquiry Committee into the United Nations Oil-for-Food Programme issued an interim report on 3 February 2005[12] and a second interim report on 29 March 2005.[13]

In a reaction to the first report the Secretary-General of the United Nations immediately initiated disciplinary actions against one staff member still on active duty and against the former head of the Office of the Iraq Programme, who had in the meantime retired but had been kept on staff at a token salary to ensure his availability to the inquiry. He also announced a number of corrective measures aiming at a greater accountability and transparency throughout the Organisation and an improvement of the performance of the management team.

The second report mainly dealt with the role of the Secretary-General of the United Nations and particularly his relationship with a company that employed his son. The report, however, also revealed that the Under-Secretary-General for Internal Oversight Services had used oil-for-food money to employ one senior staff to work under him but who did not work on the oil-for-food issues. On 30 March 2005, i.e. some three weeks before the end of his non-renewable 5-year term, a so-called charge letter was issued against the Under-Secretary-General.

The OIOS itself, UN's oversight and investigating body, came also under attack and was accused of favouritism and sexual misconduct. After an investigation by the Undersecretary-General for Management, the Secretary General concluded that no rules had been violated. Following issues raised

---

[11] Document A/59/661 of 5 January 2005.
[12] http://www.iic-offp.org/documents/InterimReportFeb2005.pdf.
[13] http://www.iic-offp.org/documents/InterimReportMar2005.pdf.

in this respect by the Staff Council the investigation was re-opened in the beginning of 2005.

It must be emphasised that these are examples of incidents and that they do not reflect normal practice. They do, however, show the context in which several organisations must operate, under difficult circumstances, with limited resources and in the absence of an infrastructure *sur place* which would normally accompany a more "static" administration (such as ethics advisers, counsellors, mediators, etc.). They also show that serious measures must be taken to correct situations, to punish those who are guilty of misconduct and to ensure that similar situations will not recur. They explain the measures taken to improve the situation, as will be described below. Only this way can the image of the UN and other organisations be restored. It must be underlined that these events have been widely reported by the press and have been used, and often abused, by groups that have declared themselves openly to be anti-UN. This is clearly not the purpose of the current contribution.

II. Staff Regulations and General Codes of Conduct

Staff, when joining an international organisation, accept the staff regulations and rules which generally contain a loyalty clause to the effect that they must "act with the interest of the organisation always in mind".

Staff Regulation 1.1 of the UN, for example, provides that staff members are international civil servants and that their responsibilities as staff members are not national but exclusively international. UN staff must, in addition, make the following written declaration, witnessed by the Secretary-General or his/her authorized representative, which is placed in his/her official status file:

> I solemnly declare and promise to exercise in all loyalty, discretion and conscience the functions entrusted to me as an international civil servant of the United Nations, to discharge these functions and regulate my conduct with the interests of the United Nations only in view, and not to seek or accept instructions in regard to the performance of my duties from any Government or other source external to the Organization.

The Council of Europe also requires staff, on the basis of Staff Rule 25, paragraph 1, to sign, on the taking up of duties, the following declaration in the presence of the Secretary General:

> I solemnly declare that . . . I will refrain from any action which might reflect upon my position as a member of the staff of the Council or which might be prejudicial morally or materially to the Council.

The statutes of most organizations provide that in their recruitment they apply the standards of the highest ability and efficiency. Many organisations add "integrity" as a further requirement (UN, Council of Europe, European Patent Office, etc.). The staff regulations of the International Monetary Fund (IMF) provide that:

> Persons on the staff of the Fund shall maintain standards of conduct compatible with their position as international civil servants and shall avoid any action or pronouncement, either in their own country or elsewhere, that would not be in keeping with their position as international civil servants. They shall bear in mind the reserve and tact incumbent upon them by reason of their international functions, and they shall exercise the utmost discretion in matters of official business. (Rules and regulations, N-4)[14]

In almost every organisation discussions have taken place over the last two decades about the introduction of ethical standards They have resulted in the adoption of mission statements, codes of conduct or charters of values. Only in a few organisations have these discussions resulted in the introduction of more detailed provisions in the Staff Regulations themselves.

The new Staff Regulations of Interpol, for instance, go in much more detail and describe, unlike the texts one normally sees, duties and obligations in a more positive way. This renders the introduction of a code of conduct less urgent. It provides, for example, in Regulation 1.1(3):

> Superiors shall. . . . set an example and offer guidance to the persons placed under their responsibility. They shall be impartial, objective and fair to their subordinates. The latter are entitled to express their views on the work they are given to perform and for which they are answerable to their immediate superiors . . .

Regarding conduct Regulation 1.3(1) stipulates:

> Officials of the Organization shall conduct themselves under all circumstances in a manner befitting their status as international officials. They are not expected to give up their national sentiments, or their religious, political or philosophical convictions, but they shall at all times proceed with the reserve and tact incumbent upon them by reason of their international status.[15]

---

[14] See also the contribution of Joan Powers, *infra*. IMF's General Administrative Order No. 33 on conduct of staff members describes in more detail the types of misconduct for which disciplinary measures may be imposed.

[15] Rule 1.7.2(2) stipulates that "No mention of the political, philosophical or religious convictions of an official may appear in his personal file."

The same can be said of part 1.2 of the Staff Rules of the European Central Bank (ECB) containing the rules on professional conduct and professional secrecy, which will be dealt with below.[16]

Most organisations have, however, opted for the issuing of separate codes of conduct, which are issued to staff in post and joined with the letter of appointment to new staff. [17]

Also the *members of Governing Bodies* of, mainly, financial institutions have adopted a code of conduct for themselves. The IMF Executive Board did this, for example, on 14 July 2000.[18] The ECB followed in 2002.[19] Similar codes exist in the World Bank, the European Bank for Reconstruction and Development (EBRD), etc.

Staff regulations and codes of conduct naturally apply only to serving staff. The obligation of loyalty, however, continues, to some extent, for *former staff.* Almost all staff regulations are clear on this. Staff members leaving the Council of Europe must sign a declaration:

> I declare that I have been informed that. . . . I remain bound after the end of my employment to maintain the utmost discretion in respect of facts and information which may have come to my notice in or in connection with the performance of my duties. I have taken note in particular that I am obliged to restore to the Council before my departure any document or paper forming part of the files or unpublished documents of the Council of Europe. Moreover I have noted that I may not without the consent of the Secretary General, mention in legal proceedings nor communicate under any form to any person not qualified to receive it, any document or information which has not been made public.

This is, obviously, even more important, or at least more visible, for the most senior officials. The Code of Conduct for members of the Commission of the EU, for example, provides that:

> whenever Commissioners intend to engage in an occupation during the year after they have ceased to hold office, they shall inform the Commission in good time. The Commission shall examine the nature of the planned occupation. If it is related to the content of the portfolio of the Commissioner during his/her full term of office, the Commission shall seek the opinion of an ad hoc ethical committee. In the light of the committee's findings it will

---

[16] See p. 26.

[17] It is perhaps more than just an anecdote: the partners in the International Space Station have, in 2000, agreed on a Crew Code of Conduct for the International Space Station, which has been signed by all astronauts and has to be signed by each newly recruited astronaut.

[18] See the contribution of Joan Powers *infra*.

[19] Code of Conduct for the Members of the Governing Council, OJ C 123, 24.5.2002, p. 9.

> decide whether the planned occupation is compatible with the last paragraph of article 213(2) of the Treaty.

Directors of the European Space Agency (ESA) may not, within 18 months of leaving the Agency, take up employment with any enterprise which has been awarded one or more large contracts from any department under their responsibility at any time during the year preceding their departure. Also here an Ethics Committee will give a ruling on whether the restriction in this clause is to be applied in a particular case.

The obligations of ECB staff provided for in Staff Rules 1.2.14 and 1.2.15[20] continue to apply beyond the termination of their employment with the ECB for six months. The External Auditor may continue to request information during this period.

Enforcement of these provisions is admittedly not easy and would generally require procedures before national instances, whereby the organisation would implicitly waive the protection of the immunities it would normally enjoy.

Many organisations these days also expect from *non-staff who participate in the activities*, including contractors, high ethical standards, and not only for "security" reasons. For example, contractual appointment letters of the IMF contain the following clauses:

> You are expected to observe the highest standards of ethical conduct in carrying out your duties for the Fund. You should strive to avoid even the appearance of impropriety in your conduct and avoid behavior that would reflect adversely on you or the Fund. In conducting your work, you are expected to treat others with courtesy and respect, and to comply with the Fund's policy on harassment; you are also expected to act with tolerance, sensitivity, respect and impartiality toward other persons' cultures and backgrounds.
>
> ......
>
> You may not accept any favor or gift from any government or from any other authority or person external to the Fund for, or with respect to, services rendered by you on behalf of the Fund.
>
> While the Fund's Code of Conduct is not directly applicable to you as a contractual employee of the Fund, you may find it useful in helping you consider ethical issues with which you may be presented."

The introduction to the UNHCR code of conduct provides:

> Persons holding a UNHCR consultant contract and interns will also receive the Code and be requested to confirm that they uphold its standards as

[20] See below, p. 26.

> far as applicable to their status. Governmental and non-governmental organisations and companies which, through their employees, work for UNHCR, will be requested to make the principles contained in the Code known to those persons in an appropriate manner.

Section 6 of the UN's Special measures for protection from sexual exploitation and sexual abuse[21] deals also with cooperative arrangements with non-United Nations entities or individuals. When entering into such arrangements relevant UN officials must inform those entities or individuals of the standards of conduct contained in these Special measures. They must receive a written undertaking from those entities or individuals that they accept these standards:

> 6.2 The failure of those entities or individuals to take preventive measures against sexual exploitation or sexual abuse, to investigate allegations thereof, or to take corrective action when sexual exploitation or sexual abuse has occurred, shall constitute grounds for termination of any cooperative arrangement with the United Nations.

The Council of Europe's instruction on the protection of human dignity[22] provides that its provisions also apply to persons who are not Council of Europe staff members who participate in the organisation's activities. Where the sexual or psychological harassment is carried out by a person who is not a member of staff, the measures taken by the Secretary General to ensure the effective protection of the victim may include denying the harasser access to the Council of Europe premises, ceasing collaboration between the Council of Europe and the person concerned and informing his or her employer.

The first code of conduct was, within the framework of the UN System, prepared between 1952 and 1954 by the International Civil Service Advisory Board, the predecessor of the International Civil Service Commission (ICSC). The code was entitled "Standards of conduct in the international civil service".[23] The code had a large distribution and has for almost half a century served as a guidance for international civil servants. It explains the basic requirements of integrity, loyalty, independence and impartiality. It gives guidelines for conduct within a Secretariat, for the relations with

---

[21] ST/SGB/2003/13 of 9 October 2003.

[22] Instruction No. 44 of 7 March 2002 on the protection of human dignity at the Council of Europe.

[23] See Report on Standards of Conduct for the International Civil Service: 1954 (COORD/CIVIL SERVICE/5). See also the contribution of Thanassis Aghnides, at the time Chairman of the ICSAB, in Revue Internationale des Sciences Administratives, 1953, No. 1.

governments and with representative bodies of the organization, for political activities, for relations with the public, for conduct of staff members serving away from Headquarters, for outside activities, and for the private life of the staff member.

The standards were re-issued in 1982 with a new preface. The preface acknowledges the changes international organisations have gone through: the role of secretariats is no longer limited to conventional servicing functions. Moreover, staff of many organisations are more and more serving away from Headquarters often cooperating in projects for which the host country is responsible. The preface also recognised the changing role of elected staff representatives. The preface closed by saying:

> What has not changed is the need for the highest standards of efficiency, competence and integrity in the international civil service; without those qualities, the organisations could no longer fulfil the purposes for which they were established. The pressures which threaten the independence and impartiality of international civil servants are, however, greater today than ever; it is then all the more important that staff members, for their part, conduct themselves in a way which will enhance the image of their service and will give no foothold to attempts to influence them improperly in the performance of their duties . . .

In 1998 the Secretary General, pursuant to the request of the General Assembly[24] and in order to assist staff members in understanding their status, basic rights and duties issued a special bulletin on "Status, basic rights and duties of United Nations staff members."[25] It contains a new staff regulation concerning financial disclosure, and provisions from the UN Charter and the Convention on the Privileges and Immunities on basic rights and duties, together with the texts of, and commentary to, relevant staff rules. The bulletin also included the 1954 standards of conduct.[26]

In 1998 the General Assembly also requested a review of the standards. A draft was presented by the UN Secretary General to the ICSC, which then undertook a review which lasted until 2001. The standards were reviewed as to their formulation and new sections were added on gender equality, harassment, conflict of interest and protection of confidential information.[27] They were welcomed by the General Assembly in its resolution

[24] GA Resolution 52/252 of 8 September 1998.

[25] ST/SGB/1998/19 of 10 December 1998.

[26] The Secretary-General's Bulletin on 'Use of information and communication technology resources and data' uses the notion of the "*highest* standards of conduct for international civil service" (emphasis added). *Cf.* ST/SGB/2004/15 of 29 November 2004.

[27] Document A/56/30. See also Annex I. The Secretary General of the UN re-issued the special bulletin on "Status, basic rights and duties of United Nations staff members." *Cf.* ST/SGB/2002/13 of 1 November 2002.

56/244. The review was not without controversy. In particular some staff representatives felt that they should have more freedom of expression. They also feared the impact of the clause that "at times, international civil servants may be required to disclose certain personal assets if this is necessary to enable their organizations to make sure that there is no conflict." Some even argued that since organisations aim to recruit and retain staff of the highest calibre, there was no need for a code of conduct.

The Code of Conduct adopted by the IMF in 1998 is another example of a general code, which clearly aims to provide guidelines for staff conduct. In addition, it contains a chapter with detailed examples.[28]

The World Bank reviewed in 1999 its Code of Professional Ethics and replaced it with a new one, entitled "Living our Values."[29] The code, first of all, recalls the World Bank's mission statement, its guiding principles ("Client centered, working in partnership, accountable for quality results, dedicated to financial integrity and cost-effectiveness, inspired and innovative,") and "our core values" (Personal honesty, integrity, commitment; working together in teams – with openness and trust; empowering others and respecting differences; encouraging risk-taking and responsibility; enjoying our work and our families."). The code then deals with staff relations and conflicts of interest. Under the item "World Bank Group Operations" topics such as accuracy of books and records, procurement, use of Bank assets, community and environmental commitment, kickbacks and bribery. The code does not stop with these guidelines. It also gives a list of helpful resources, where staff can turn to for help or advise. This includes the manager, Human Resources, the Staff Association, the Ombudsman Office, the Mediation Office, the Offices of the Senior Advisers on Gender Equality and Racial Equality, the Professional Ethics Office, or the Appeals Committee. There is also a special hotline to report any allegation of fraud, corruption, financial irregularities, or violations of law. For those feeling uncomfortable calling this hotline, an ethics helpline is available.

The European Central Bank issued its Code of Conduct on 10 October 2000.[30]

Most of the codes that have been issued over the last decade are responsive, however. They are sometimes an implementation of a policy statement made by the Head of the organisation, but more often they are a reaction to a particular situation or event.

---

[28] http://www.imf.org/external/hrd/code.htm. See also Annex II.
[29] http://wbln0018.worldbank.org/crn/ope/ethics.nsf/(BillboardPictures)/code/ $FILE/code.pdf
[30] OJ C 76, 8.3.2001, p. 11. See also Annex IV.

The European Union. Following a number of conflicts between the Court of Auditors and the Commission on control and procedures, a major clash occurred in the Autumn of 1998 between The European Parliament and the Commission. This led, in January 1999, to the establishment by the European Parliament of a Committee of Independent Experts. Both the creation of the Committee and its terms of reference were accepted by the Chairman of the Commission, Jacques Santer. The Committee was chaired by a former President of the Court of Auditors. The Committee produced a first report on 15 March 1999 on allegations regarding fraud, mismanagement and nepotism in the European Commission.[31] Eleven of the 146 pages dealt with allegations of favouritism and nepotism, on which, in fact, the Committee in most cases[32] concluded that he allegations were unfounded or that the conduct of a Commissioner was void of irregularity (although in some cases it felt that a different procedure should have been followed in cases of employment of family members). These eleven pages, however, received the most attention in the press.

In the rest, and major part, of the report the Committee analysed a number of the activities of the Commission: Tourism, the MED programmes, the ECHO affair – the Humanitarian Office –, the Leonardo da Vinci programme (on vocational training), the Security Office, and nuclear safety. The Committee concluded that the Commission did not have an adequate mechanism to deal rapidly and adequately with irregularities and establish responsibilities. In particular with regard to the responsibilities, the Committee concluded:

> The responsibility of individual Commissioners, or of the Commission as a body, cannot be a vague idea, a concept which in practice proves unrealistic. It must go hand in hand with an ongoing process designed to increase awareness of that responsibility. Each individual must feel accountable for the measures he or she manages. The studies carried out by the Committee have too often revealed a growing reluctance among the members of the hierarchy to acknowledge their responsibility. It is becoming difficult to find anyone who has even the slightest sense of responsibility. However, that sense of responsibility is essential. It must be demonstrated, first and foremost, by the Commissioners individually and the Commission as a body. The temptation to deprive the concept of responsibility of all substance is a dangerous one. That concept is the ultimate manifestation of democracy.

---

31 http://www.europarl.eu.int/experts/report1_en.htm. A second report on "Reform of the Commission, Analysis of current practice and proposals for tackling mismanagement, irregularities and fraud" was published on 10 September 1999 (http:// europa.eu.int/comm/anti_fraud/reports/sages/2_en.pdf).

32 The case of Commissioner Mrs. Cresson and her special adviser is the well-known exception.

The whole Commission resigned the day the report came out. Needless to say that this was a major event having its impact also on other organisations in Europe. Many of them reviewed internally, often with outside help, the validity of their systems and control procedures in place.

When the new Commission, the "Prodi Commission", arrived, it immediately adopted a set of codes of conduct: the Code of Conduct for Commissioners,[33] a Code of Conduct for the relations between Commissioners (their Offices) and Departments,[34] and Rules of Conduct for appointment to senior posts.

The Code of Conduct recalls that:

> (t)he Treaty articles on the Commission make special reference to the complete independence enjoyed by the Members of the Commission, who are required to discharge their duties in the general interest of the Community. In the performance of their duties they must neither seek nor take instructions from any government or from any other body. In addition, the general interest requires that in their official and private lives Commissioners should behave in a manner that is in keeping with the dignity of their office. Ruling out all risks of a conflict of interests helps to guarantee their independence.

As far as outside activities are concerned the Code provides that Commissioners may not engage in any other professional activity, whether paid or unpaid. (For example, writing a regular column is regarded as a professional activity whereas giving courses free of charge in the interest of European Integration on the other hand is permitted). Royalties from copyright in a work published in connection with their duties must be given to charity. Commissioners may not accept any form of payment for delivering speeches or taking part in conferences. Commissioners may hold honorary, unpaid posts in political, cultural, artistic or charitable foundations or similar bodies. They may also hold such posts in educational institutions. "Honorary posts" means posts in which the holder has no decision making power in the management of the body concerned. These must be declared. Commissioners may be active members of political parties (including participation in election campaigns) or trade unions, provided that this does not compromise their availability for service in the Commission. Commissioners standing for election to public office shall also inform the President of their intended level of participation in the election campaign. If their intention is to play an active role in the election campaign, they

[33] http://europa.eu.int/comm/reform/formation/commiss_en.pdf.
[34] http://europa.eu.int/comm/reform/formation/commdep_en.pdf.

must withdraw from the work of the Commission for the duration of the campaign. They may not hold any public office of whatever kind.

They must also declare their spouses' professional activities. Commissioners may not accept gifts with a value over € 150.

As far as collective responsibility and confidentiality is concerned the Code provides that:

> Out of respect for the collective responsibility, Commissioners shall not make any comment which would call into question a decision taken by the Commission. They shall also refrain from disclosing what is said at meetings of the Commission.

Lastly, the Code provides details for official missions, receptions and official representation.

The Committee of Independent Experts was, in its second report of 10 September 1999, critical of the Codes of Conduct. It observed:

> (t)he Committee considered that the codes of conduct elaborated by the Commission remain insufficient and are not yet backed up by the necessary legal framework. The attribution of responsibilities and chain of delegation between the Commission, single commissioners and the departments are ill-defined and ill-understood by those concerned. Finally, the concepts of political responsibility and accountability remain unclear and the mechanisms for their practical application inadequate.

It in particular recommended that:

> the code of conduct for commissioners should redefine the concept of collective responsibility to encompass not only a prohibition on calling into question decisions adopted by the college, but also the right and the obligation of each commissioner to keep him/herself fully appraised of the activities of every commissioner and to take action in this respect as necessary, for example by having frank and open discussions with other commissioners both inside and outside the college.

The Prodi Commission did, however, embark on a major overhaul of its administrative systems and procedures in order to create an administration based on the principles of efficiency, transparency and accountability.[35]

The current, Barroso, Commission adopted, at its first meeting on 24 November 2004, a new Code of Conduct.[36] It consists of two parts. The first part is similar to the Prodi Code of Conduct, giving some more details concerning the information to be provided about financial interests.

---

[35] See below, p. 22.

[36] http://europa.eu.int/comm/reform/2002/code_conduct_en.htm

The second section is based on the principle that the general interest also requires that Commissioners establish good working relations, based on loyalty, trust and transparency, with their departments. The Code then provides the following:

> To this end, the Commission acts collectively on the basis of the political guidelines set by the President. The chain of responsibility runs from the level of the College to the level of the Commissioner, who is answerable to the College for his/her activities and those of his/her departments. The Commissioner lays down, in the light of the guidelines and work programme of the Commission and the principle of collegiality, the policy guidelines and priorities relating to his/her portfolio. He/she shall ensure that it is implemented by his departments, supervising the management of his/her Director-General or Head of Service (hereinafter the Director-General) and giving him/her, where necessary, the guidelines or general instructions to put these policies and priorities into practice.
>
> The chain of responsibility continues down to department level in the person of the Director-General, who is answerable to the Commissioner and the College for the proper implementation of the guidelines set by the College and the Commissioner and, in particular, for the management of the Directorate-General or Service in line with the distribution of powers as defined by the Staff Regulations, the Financial Regulation, the Rules of Procedure and the rules laid down as part of the administrative and financial reform of the Commission.
>
> In order to exercise his/her political responsibility and play his/her supervisory role, the Commissioner must receive the appropriate information from his own departments and the central departments, including information with regard to the quality of internal control put in place in his/her departments. This exercise does not in any way release the Director-General from his/her duty of informing specifically the Commissioner of any fact, situation or matter relating to the management, in particular, financial management, which could have a serious impact on his/her responsibility or that of the College.
>
> The working arrangements made by each Commissioner in agreement with his/her departments and the methods for circulating information between them are transmitted, by way of information to the Head of the President's cabinet and to the Secretary-General. Either of these may ask for further information and/or clarification.

The Prodi Commission had already given guidelines on the Private Offices of the Commissioners (the *Cabinets*). The Barroso Code goes much further in describing the role of the Cabinets, and of those of the Departments. It also lays down the basic rules on the organisation of work and the management of resources. Lastly, the Code gives the rules concerning travel on official missions for Commissioners.

Other European organisations enacted codes of conduct in the same period. The European Space Agency, which is increasingly cooperating with the European Union, published, for example, a "Charter of Values" in 2002, but reviewed it in 2004, since staff representatives had not formally approved the initial text.[37] It was stated by the Director General when issuing the Charter that:

> by describing the fundamental values and principles that guide the Agency's actions and appealing to each person's sense of individual responsibility, the Charter aims to strengthen the bonds of trust that exist between staff members, the Agency, Member State delegations and external partners.

The Charter also emphasises that:

> by officially promulgating a Charter of Values, the Agency is able to make a solemn declaration of its profound attachment to the ethical principles and values that have continuously inspired its activities. The Charter initiative puts in writing what are already commonly considered as central standards of conduct. In so doing, the Charter seeks to reaffirm the very identity of the European Space Agency and brings greater transparency to its activities.

The Charter then covers ESA's principles and values, interpersonal relations, commitments and responsibilities (on the part of the Agency and of the staff), and conflicts of interest and outside activities.

The Agency has also produced a document entitled "the Values of the European Space Agency". This document, "directed at the public at large, recalls the fundamental values (ethics, European identity, investment in people, professionalism and technical innovation) that go to make up ESA's identity, rooted in our mandate to serve European citizens and guide our future activities. Although directed at different audiences, the Charter of Values and the Values of the European Space Agency form a common philosophy, through which the Agency's ethical standards and values are given expression."

In September 2002 senior management of the UNHCR signed a code of conduct. All staff have been requested to countersign it. The code is designed to "better understand the obligations placed upon their conduct by the Charter of the United Nations and the Staff Regulations and Rules, which remain the only legal instruments that determine acceptable conduct in UNHCR." In order to avoid any misunderstanding the code in its introduction states: "while acknowledging that local laws and customs may differ from one country to another, the Code of Conduct is based on international legal standards. For example, children are defined as those under the age of 18." The most outspoken, and in some respects apparently also the most controversial, clause, is the last one:

[37] For text see Annex VI.

> I will not engage in or tolerate any form of harassment in the workplace, including sexual harassment and abuse of power. As a manager/supervisor, I will not solicit favours, loans or gifts from staff, nor will I accept unsolicited ones that are more than token value. I recognise that there is an inherent conflict of interest and potential abuse of power in having sexual relations with staff under my supervision. Should I find myself in such a relationship, I will resolve this conflict of interest without delay.

A. Legal Character

As was shown, the codes of conduct are guidelines and are in general a mere operational reflection of the basic rules of public administration. They, however, do explain in detail what the professional obligations are. This has entailed discussion on the question of the legal character of these codes, often inspired by the fear expressed by staff that new norms or obligations are imposed on them. It may indeed be true that in some organisations the codes were developed and introduced rather rapidly and perhaps without the necessary consultations.

A study by the OECD on ethics in the public service observed that "a code of conduct can be either a legal document or purely administrative statement prescribing the expected levels and quality of performance of the employees it covers. It outlines the ethical principles applying to either the public service generally or to a particular department or agency specifically. A code of conduct for an organisation may contain a combination of a statement of its values, a description of its role, including responsibilities of and to its employees (in some cases also specifying relationships to the constitution, the public, the government of the day, elected officials and legislative assemblies), and a list of its employee's legal obligations (such as declaring conflicts of interest, restraints in making public comments, and restrictions on political activities)."[38]

As was, however, indicated above, in several organisations norms of behaviour have been introduced in the staff regulations themselves. The same norms are in some organisations given in the regulations and in other organisations in the codes of conduct, for example on the conduct in the staff's private lives.

It is also clear that, if a particular ethical norm laid down in a code of conduct is violated, this constitutes misconduct which is liable to disciplinary action. Also the OECD Principles for Managing Ethics in the Public Service, adopted in April 1998, provide that ethical standards should be

---

[38] Public Management Occasional Papers, No. 14, Ethics in the Public Service, Current Issues and Practice, OECD, 1996, p. 33 (http://www.oecd.org/dataoecd/ 59/24/1898992.pdf).

reflected in the legal framework: "The legal framework is the basis for communicating the minimum obligatory standards and principles of behaviour for every public servant. Laws and regulations could state the fundamental values of public service and should provide the framework for guidance, investigation, disciplinary action and prosecution."[39]

This being said, many organisations underline the guideline character of the codes, i.e. that the codes are not binding. For example, the General Introduction to the Charter of Values of ESA states:

> By its very nature as an ethical document, the Charter of Values does not provide for new rules or legal obligations, neither does it in any way supersede or amend the contractual obligations of staff members under the Staff Regulations . . . Unlike the Staff Regulations . . ., the Charter of Values is not legally binding, as its sole purpose is to set common standards for ethical behaviour.[40]

The UNHCR code stipulates "It is a moral code that does not have the force of law." It adds that "signing the Code does not take away any acquired rights of UNHCR Staff."

IMF's Financial Disclosure Policy, on the other hand, which will be dealt with below,[41] provides: "As with other aspects of the Code of Conduct, staff members are expected to comply . . ."[42] And the ECB's Code stipulates:

> The Code makes explicit the ethical conventions and standards by which the ECB considers it necessary for the Addressees to abide and clarifies the benchmarks against which fulfilment of the obligations already assumed by the Addressees will be measured. The Code draws on, and is without prejudice to, the terms of individual contracts of the members of the Executive Board, the Conditions of Employment for Staff of the European Central Bank . . . and all texts implementing them.

The European Commission, in its Code of Good Administrative Behaviour,[43] is clear on the matter: the guidelines are binding on its staff.[44]

---

[39] PUMA Policy Brief No. 4, OECD, 1998 (http://www.oecd.org/dataoecd/60/13/1899138.pdf).

[40] It is to be noted, however, that the Charter sometimes uses language such as: "staff are bound . . ." or "staff members are under a duty . . .", etc.

[41] See below p. 32.

[42] Joan Powers calls the IMF's Code of Conduct "not a legal document *per se*", *infra*.

[43] See below, p. 26.

[44] Also Recommendation No. R(2000)10 of the Committee of Ministers of the Council of Europe to Member states on codes of conduct for public officials, adopted on 11 May 2000, and its appendix containing the model code of conduct for public officials make it clear that the code forms part of the provisions governing the employment of (national) public officials. See also the Explanatory Memorandum which states that "(u)sually, codes of conduct describe guidelines binding employees to act in a certain manner whereas codes of practice are often addressed to clients rather than to members of the institution for whom the code is drafted. Codes of practice lay down standards that clients

B. *Privileges and Immunities*

Staff of international organisations generally enjoy a number of privileges and immunities. Most Staff Regulations (and codes of conduct) emphasise that these privileges and immunities are functional in character. As a consequence, they "furnish no excuse to the staff members who are covered by them to fail to observe laws and police regulations of the State in which they are located nor do they furnish an excuse for non-performance of their private obligations."[45] Staff are generally also reminded that they should conduct also their private lives in such a way as not to cause harm to the (image of) the organisation.[46]

III. Specific Areas of Concern

Many organisations have adopted specific provisions in their staff regulations or in dedicated codes of conduct on a number of separate issues, such as the following.

A. *(Sexual) harassment*

A major "set" of codes of conduct concern (sexual) harassment. The Council of Europe defines sexual harassment as "any physical or verbal conduct of a sexual nature infringing the dignity of women and men at work which is unwanted by or offensive to the recipient and which creates humiliating or intimidating working environment for that person."[47] It adds that the "essential characteristic of sexual harassment is that it is unwanted by the recipient. A single incident may constitute sexual harassment if it is sufficiently serious. It is for each individual to determine what behaviour is acceptable to him or her and what he or she regards as offensive. It is the unwanted nature of the conduct that distinguishes sexual harassment from friendly behaviour, which is welcome and mutual." And the UK's Human Rights Act defines harassment (at work) as "any conduct based on age, disability, HIV status, domestic circumstances, sex, sexual orientation, gender reassignment, race, colour, language, religion, political, trade

---

have the right to expect, rather than standards that members of the profession are instructed to uphold." (GMC(2000)26 Final, p. 16).

45 UN Staff Regulation 1.1(f)).

46 See below, p. 30.

47 Instruction No. 44 of 7 March 2002 on the protection of human dignity at the Council of Europe.

union or other opinion or belief, national or social origin, association with a minority, property, birth or other status that is unreciprocated or unwanted and which affects the dignity of men and women at work."

A notion that is often associated with it is bullying or mobbing, a repeated offensive behaviour seeking to humiliate individual staff or groups of staff. This is sometimes also referred to as psychological or moral harassment. The Council of Europe defines psychological harassment a "any sustained, repetitive and/or systematic abusive conduct in the workplace or in connection with work in the form of behaviour, actions, gestures, spoken or written words, threats or working organisation methods which, intentionally or otherwise, is prejudicial to a person's personality, dignity or physical or psychological integrity; which causes a deterioration in the working environment or endangers that person's employment or creates a hostile, intimidating, degrading, humiliating or offensive environment."

The WHO describes harassment as "any behaviour by a staff member that is directed at and is offensive to others, which that person knows or should reasonably know, would be offensive, and which interferes with work or creates an intimidating, hostile or offensive work environment. Harassment may include conduct, comment or display related to race, religion, colour, creed, ethnic origin, physical attributes, age, gender, or sexual orientation. It may involve a group or team and may occur among and between all levels of employees. It can take many forms, including sexual harassment." The policy then rightly observes that the most common origin of harassment is unresolved conflict in the workplace.

The Secretary General of the UN published, in October 1992, a bulletin, entitled "Promotion of equal treatment of men and women in the Secretariat and prevention of sexual harassment",[48] which lays down the UN's policy in the matter. It was supplemented by an Administrative Instruction with guidelines for dealing with sexual harassment.[49] It defines sexual harassment as any unwelcome sexual advance, request for sexual favours or other verbal or physical conduct of a sexual nature, when it interferes with work, is made a condition of employment or creates an intimidating, hostile or offensive work environment. It adds that it is particularly serious when behaviour of this kind is engaged in by any official who is in a position to influence the career or employment conditions (including hiring, assignment, contract renewal, performance evaluation or promotion) of the recipient of such attentions.

---

[48] ST/SGB/253 of 29 October 1992.
[49] ST/AI/379 of 29 October 1992.

In 2003, for example, the Secretary General of the UN, in an information circular, reminded staff that the Organization's core values prohibit discrimination and harassment. These core values require respect for the diversity and the dignity of all staff and that all forms of discrimination and harassment are prohibited. He recalled Staff Regulation 1.2(a) and Staff Rule 101.2(d) in this respect. He underlined that the UN cannot tolerate discrimination and harassment in any form and that any infraction will be taken very seriously. He called on all managers to take or initiate prompt and appropriate action whenever an infraction occurs. Depending on the facts of the case, action may take the form of clear and specific guidance to the individuals concerned or other type of managerial action, sensitivity training and awareness raising, and/or disciplinary proceedings.[50]

On 7 March 2002 the Secretary General of the Council of Europe issued an instruction on the protection of human dignity at the Council of Europe.[51] The Instruction recalls that the respect for human dignity is enshrined in the Convention for the Protection of Human Rights and Fundamental Freedoms and in the Social Charter. Article 26 of the latter contains provisions on the right to dignity at work which is designed to ensure the effective exercise of the right to protection against sexual and psychological harassment in the workplace or in relation to work. These principles should also underlie the Council of Europe's own legal system. Article 1 of the Instruction reads as follows:

> All conduct infringing the dignity of men and women in the workplace and/or in connection with work at the Council of Europe shall be prohibited.

Article 2 then provides:

> Everyone at the Council of Europe, regardless of status or employment contract has the right to effective protection[52] against sexual and psychological harassment, irrespective of the person perpetrating such conduct.
>
> The provisions of this Instruction shall apply to all staff members of the Council of Europe whether or not carrying out their functions, and wherever they are called upon to work.
>
> These provisions also apply to persons who are not Council of Europe staff members who participate in the Organisation's activities, wherever they may be held.[53]

---

[50] ST/IC/2003/17 of 11 March 2003.

[51] See footnote 47.

[52] "Effective protection shall be taken to mean compliance with the measures provided for in this Instruction in accordance with Council of Europe policy."

[53] "Members of the Parliamentary Assembly, of the Permanent Representations, experts, employees of outside companies, etc."

The Instruction then lays down informal and formal procedures that can be followed in order to solve the problem.[54]

The WHO published a Policy on Harassment in March 2001.[55] It states that the WHO recognizes the right of all staff to be treated with dignity and respect. Harassment being an abrogation of that right, it is entirely unacceptable. The WHO policy on harassment seeks to provide (a) a harassment-free work environment in which staff at all levels avoid behaviour that may create an atmosphere of hostility and intimidation; (b) support for persons subject to harassment and (c) due process for all concerned. The policy, which regularly refers to the Standards of Conduct in the International Civil Service, observes that the definition of harassment concerns not only intent but effect: "if a specific action by a person or group is reasonably perceived as offensive by another person(s), that action might constitute harassment, whether intended or not. Offensive comments or behaviour could amount to harassment if repeated or pervasive."[56]

In 2002 the OECD, on the one hand, inserted new provisions in its staff regulations and, on the other hand, issued a decision of the Secretary General concerning the policy to prevent and combat harassment.[57]

B. Relations with the Public and Business Community

Not many organisations have direct contacts with the citizens of their member States, the major exception being the EU. The contacts generally go via organised channels in the member States and are limited to specific activities. Some organisations are, however, directly "on the market" with their procurement activities. Other organisations, in particular those in the field, are in direct contact with groups of citizens (peace-keeping, refugees).

i) *Relations with the public at large*

Only a few organisations have direct contacts with the public at large. Under the Human Rights conventions, citizens can, however, lodge complaints with, for example, the United Nations or the Council of Europe system.

---

[54] See below, p. 39.

[55] Cluster Note 2001/9.

[56] The policy gives a number of examples that might constitute harassment: public outbursts directed at a staff member that degrade the staff member; deliberate and unjustified attempts to discredit a staff member; menacing comments (whether oral or written, including e-mail); malicious and/or unsubstantiated complaints of harassment; deliberate isolation of a staff member; unwelcome verbal or physical conduct of a sexual nature; unwelcome sexual advances, pressure for unwelcome social activity outside the workplace, suggestive remarks, innuendos or lewd comments, displays of pornography, suggestive gestures, written communications or objects of a suggestive nature (including e-mail).

[57] For details see the contribution of Sylvie Vanston, *infra.*

The Code of Conduct of the European Central Bank makes it clear, in its preliminary statements, that the code also serves as a reference for the public with regard to the standard of conduct that third parties are entitled to expect in their dealings with the ECB. It gives further precisions in provision 3.3.1:

> Accessibility, efficiency, correctness and courtesy should guide the addressees in their relations with the public. The addressees shall ensure, to the extent possible, that members of the public are provided with the information they request. Such information, as well as any reason not to provide the information, shall be clear and understandable.[58]

The organisation that has most direct contacts with the citizens in its member States and in a large number of activities is the supranational European Union. As indicated above[59] the Prodi Commission had undertaken a major review of its administrative system and procedures.

A major milestone in this respect was the adoption, on 13 September 2000, of a Code of Good Administrative Behaviour,[60] which is binding on the Commission staff. It provides not only a set of guidelines for Commission staff in their relations with the public, but also a mechanism under which the public may lodge complaints with the Secretariat-General of the Commission concerning a possible breach of the principles set out in this Code. The Code lays down the following general principles that the Commission respects in its relations with the pubic: lawfulness, non-discrimination and equal treatment, proportionality, and consistency. The guidelines for good administrative behaviour include objectivity and impartiality, and the duty to ensure that information concerning administrative procedures is timely provided and within the deadline fixed for the procedure in question. Staff must also ensure that parties are heard where Community law provides for this and justification for decisions must be given whenever possible, if necessary using standard replies. Where Community law so provides, measures notified to a party should clearly state that an appeal is possible and describe how to submit it. The Code gives further details on how the Commission answers enquiries (request for documentation, correspondence, telephone communications and e-mail, and requests from the media). Lastly, the Code provides that the staff respects the protection of personal data and confidential information.

---

[58] There is also a specific provision 3.8 on relations with interest groups.
[59] See above, p. 16.
[60] OJ L 267 of 20 October 2000.

Furthermore, and in implementation of the new Art. 225 which was introduced by the Amsterdam Treaty, a Regulation[61] was adopted on 30 May 2001 concerning public access to European Parliament, Council and Commission documents. The Commission has made major efforts in implementing this Regulation.[62]

ii) *Relations with specific groups*
Many organisations have in the exercise of their duties direct contacts with specific groups of the population who are beneficiaries of assistance, in particular those they protect, such as refugees, and people in areas of armed conflict or emergency aid.

One issue that has recently come up in this respect concerns *sexual exploitation and sexual abuse.*[63]

The UNHCR has taken a number of initiatives in order to reduce the risk of such misconduct and, consequently, to diminish the risk of abuse of a group of people who find themselves already in the most vulnerable of situations.

UNHCR has, as mentioned above, published its code of conduct in September 2002. The following month a list was issued of remedial measures and preventive actions taken by UNHCR and its partners in order to strengthen UNHCR's core protection function by enhancing the prevention and response to sexual and gender-based violence. Measures and actions include raising awareness, improving reporting channels and victim support, empowering refugee women and children, legal assistance and training. It has, in May 2003, issued guidelines for prevention and response concerning sexual and gender-based violence against refugees, returnees and internally displaced persons. It has also revised the terms of reference of its Inspector General Office in order to enhance, *inter alia*, its role as the focal point for investigating allegations of misconduct. This includes not only misuse of funds, resources or facilities, but also abuse of authority and other forms of workplace harassment, and mistreatment of refugees.

The UN Secretary General published a bulletin on 9 October 2003[64] with special measures for protection from sexual exploitation and sexual abuse. This bulletin applies to all UN staff, including staff of separately administered organs and programmes of the UN. It recalls that UN forces

---

[61] Regulation 1049/2001, OJ L 145 of 31 May 2001.
[62] See, for example, the citizens' guide for access to Commission documents in http://europa.eu.int/comm/secretariat_general/sgc/acc_doc/docs/en.pdf.
[63] See above, p. 6.
[64] ST/SGB/2003/13 of 9 October 2003.

conducting operations under UN command and control are prohibited from committing acts of sexual exploitation and sexual abuse, and have a particular duty of care towards women and children. It refers in this respect to the 1999 bulletin on "Observance by United Nations forces of international humanitarian law."[65] It defines "sexual exploitation" to be any actual or attempted abuse of a position of vulnerability, differential power, or trust, for sexual purposes, including, but not limited to, profiting monetarily, socially or politically from the sexual exploitation of another. "Sexual abuse" means the actual or threatened physical intrusion of a sexual nature, whether by force or under unequal or coercive conditions.

The measures then provide that sexual exploitation and sexual abuse constitute serious misconduct and are grounds for disciplinary measures, including summary dismissal. In particular sexual activity with children, i.e. under the age of 18,[66] is prohibited. Exchange of money, employment, goods or services for sex, including sexual favours or other forms of humiliating, degrading or exploitative behaviour, is prohibited. Sexual relationships between UN staff and beneficiaries of assistance, since they are based on inherently unequal power dynamics, undermine the credibility and integrity of the work of the UN and are strongly discouraged. Section 4 of the measures deals with the duties of the Heads of Department, Offices and Missions who have a special responsibility in this respect.

Also the UN Department of Peacekeeping Operations (DPKO) has taken major steps in order to improve the situation. It has, in 2003, issued a Directive on Sexual Harassment in UN Peacekeeping and Other Field Missions (for military members of national contingents, military observers and civilian police officers),[67] Directives for Disciplinary Matters Involving Civilian Police Officers and Military Observers,[68] and a similar one for military members of national contingents.[69]

The most recent peace-keeping operation, the one in Burundi (ONUB), began operations in June 2004. It could benefit from the experience elsewhere and has its own code of conduct, and an infrastructure including a code of conduct unit and a gender adviser.

---

65 ST/SGB/1999/13.

66 Section 4.4 provides that this does not apply where a staff member is legally married to someone under the age of 18 but over the age of majority or consent in their country of citizenship. This point was also an issue of debate when the UNHCR code was being adopted.

67 DPKO/MD/03/00995, DPKO/CPD/DSHCPO/2003/002.

68 DPKO/CPD/DDCPO/2003/001, DPKO/MD/03/00994.

69 DPKO/MD/03/00993.

iii) *Relations with the business community*

Several organisations have major contacts with the business community. They procure goods and services on a large scale. In those organisations where staff are likely to have many direct contacts with companies, specific clauses are inserted in the Staff Regulations outlining the limits of commercial activities that staff may have. In the European Space Agency, for example, Staff Regulation 3.4 provides: "A staff member, or his spouse, may not directly or indirectly hold such interests in a commercial firm as could, by their nature, compromise his independence in the discharge of his duties in the Agency." The Staff Rules then explain that "a staff member must declare any interest held by himself or his spouse, as well as any active participation by either of them in any firm which he knows or can normally assume to have or to be likely to have commercial dealings with the Agency . . ."

Staff Regulation 1.6(b) of the World Intellectual Property Organization provides: "Apart from their duties with the International Bureau, staff members shall not engage in any activity or have any financial interest whatever in any enterprise concerned with intellectual property. They may not accept any gratuities or favors from firms or private individuals concerned with intellectual property or having commercial relations with the International Bureau."

Several organisations go much further than that and require concrete reporting on assets and transactions.

Organisations also more and more establish guidelines that commercial firms should meet in order to be acceptable partners.

On 17 July 2000 the Secretary General of the UN issued Guidelines for the Cooperation between the United Nations and the Business Community.[70] These indicate that business partners should demonstrate responsible citizenship by supporting UN causes and core values as reflected in the UN Charter and other relevant conventions and treaties. They must have demonstrated a commitment to meeting or exceeding the principle of the Global Compact – an overall value framework for cooperation with the business community[71] – by translating them into operational corporate practice. Business entities that are complicit in human rights abuses, tolerate forced or compulsory labour or the use of child labour, are involved in the sale or manufacture of anti-personnel mines or their components, or that otherwise do not meet relevant obligations or responsibilities by the UN, are not eligible for partnership.

---

[70] http://www.un.org/partners/business/guide.htm.

[71] www.unglobalcompact.org.

The UNHCR has also adopted a Corporate Code of Conduct. It sets clear minimum criteria for cooperation. It excludes companies that are, or have been, engaged in weapons sale or manufacture, systematic and sustained forced labour or child labour, tobacco sale or manufacture, or operating in countries subject to UN sanctions.

The EBRD's Office of the Chief Compliance Officer is also in charge of setting the standards of integrity that the EBRD expects of its business partners. The EBRD has also made an "anti-terrorist statement" to the effect that it performs extensive due diligence on the integrity of all prospective clients. Integrity checks undertaken before committing any funds now include verification that no client or prospective client is on the UN Security Council lists of entities and individuals suspected of supporting terrorist activities.

C. Personal Conduct

As the Standards of conduct in the international civil service indicate, "the private life of international civil servants is their own concern and organizations should not intrude upon it. There can be situations, however, in which the behaviour of an international civil servant can reflect on the organization. International civil servants must therefore bear in mind that their conduct and activities outside the workplace, even if unrelated to official duties, can compromise the image and the interests of the organization."

Most staff regulations and codes of conduct lay down ground rules for outside employment and activities that staff may have, including (limits on) the gifts, honours and remuneration they may receive. These should, on the one hand, confirm that the staff member almost exclusively devote their energies to their organisations and guarantee that there is no conflict of interest and that the staff is working in all independence. Special aspects of these are the interest that staff may have in companies that may do business with the organisation, or the knowledge they may have through their employment and which could influence their private financial transactions. This will be dealt with below.

The consequences of certain types of personal conduct are more delicate since they touch on the privileges and immunities of the organisation. International organisations are immune from jurisdiction and execution. This immunity can be waived by, depending on the convention setting up the organisation, the Head of the organisation or the governing body. Some conventions provide that there is a duty to waive the immunity in all cases where reliance upon it would impede the course of justice and it can be waived without prejudicing the interests of the organisation.[72] It is now generally recognised that international organisations have an obligation to cooperate with national authorities to facilitate the proper administration of justice.

The Standards of conduct in the international civil service underline that the privileges and immunities that international staff enjoy are functional in character and that staff must observe local laws and must respect legal or financial obligations. Cases at hand are non-compliance with family support orders or other private legal obligations (banks, rent, etc.).

In 1999 the UN Secretary General published a bulletin on Family and child support obligations of staff members.[73] It was, in 2000, followed by an administrative instruction concerning private legal obligations of staff members.[74] They recall the obligations of the staff members and that abuse of the privileges and immunities in order to avoid service of process may result in disciplinary action. It underlines that if a staff member persists in not complying with family support orders that the sums due may be directly deducted from his emoluments. This has now become the practice in most organisations. In the case of non-compliance with other private legal obligations the staff member is requested to take prompt action. If no prompt action is taken all correspondence goes in the official status file and disciplinary action may be initiated. Legally established indebtedness to third parties may be withheld from any final payments.

D. Financial Disclosure, Inside Information and Trading

Several organisations now require their senior officials to disclose any interests they may have. When Dr. Brundtland took up duty as WHO's Director General in July 1998, she immediately implemented a new code of conduct for financial disclosure. High-level WHO officials have to disclose and, if judged necessary by the Director-General on the advice of the Legal Counsel, divest themselves of financial and other interests if these interests affect their independence from external authorities. These interests include shareholdings, bond holdings, patent interests and directorships.

Starting with the Prodi Commission, in 1999, Commissioners of the European Union must declare any of their or their spouses' financial interest

---

[72] See, for example, Annex I to the Convention for the establishment of ESA. For the United Nations this is laid down in the Convention on the Privileges and Immunities of the United Nations.

[73] ST/SGB/1999/4.

[74] ST/AI/2000/12 of 25 October 2000.

or assets which might create a conflict of interests in the performance of their duties. These are made public.

The Staff Regulations of the IMF are rather vague on the matter of conflicts of interest. It contains the general loyalty clauses in Rules N-3 ("... shall owe their duty entirely to the Fund ...") and N-7 ("... shall not ... engage in occupation, business activity, or profession, that, in the opinion of the Managing Director, is incompatible with these Rules or the proper performance of their official duties or inconsistent with their position as international civil servants."). IMF's Code of Conduct, on the other hand, contains a specific chapter V on "Conflicts of Interest, including Personal Financial Affairs." Paragraph 24 provides: "you should avoid any situation involving a conflict, or the appearance of a conflict, between your personal interests and performance of your official duties." It explains that "if you are engaged in Fund procurement activities and if you have, or are considering having, any direct or indirect outside interests, financial or otherwise, which might conflict or appear to conflict with the interests of the Fund, you should make this situation known to your supervisor ...", and also that one must be extremely careful with prospective employers outside the Fund.

As far as personal financial affairs are concerned IMF staff are, under paragraph 25, free to conduct their personal financial affairs with two exceptions: 1. because of the Fund's role in exchange rate surveillance, all staff are prohibited from engaging in short-term trading in gold, foreign currency and closely related financial instruments, and 2. staff members are prohibited from using, or providing to others, confidential information to which they have access for purposes of carrying out private financial transactions. Details are given in paragraph 26.[75]

Paragraphs 27 and 28 of IMF's Code of Conduct then provide that staff should disclose any financial or business interests that he/she or immediate family members have that might be in actual or apparent conflict with Fund duties and that all staff members must certify that hey have read the policy on conflicts of interest and that they are in compliance.

In 2000, and amended in 2003, a Financial Certification and Disclosure Policy was introduced on the basis of the provisions of IMF's Code of Conduct.[76] It stipulates that all staff regardless of grade level will be required to submit an annual financial certification form in which they declare that they have read the policy on conflicts of interest and that they are in com-

---

[75] For text, see Annex II.

[76] See for further details: http://www.imf.org/external/hrd/fdiscl.htm.

pliance with it. Senior staff (grade level B1 and above) must also every year complete, on a confidential basis, a form with information on relevant financial assets and liabilities, as well as selected financial transactions for the relevant period, of the staff and his/her spouse or dependants. The forms, which go in much more detail than the ones for the EU Commissioners, are submitted to and reviewed by an external Compliance Officer.

Part 1.2 of the ECB Staff Rules contains the rules on professional conduct and professional secrecy. The most recent version was published in the Official Journal of the European Union in April 2004.[77] Rule 1.2.9 provides that:

> Members of staff are prohibited from using, whether directly or indirectly via third parties, inside information to which they have access, irrespective of whether such information is used in any kind of private financial transaction conducted at their own risk and for their own account, or at the risk and for the account of third parties. The term 'third party' shall include, but is not limited to, spouses, recognised partners, parents, children, other family members, colleagues, and legal persons.

ECB staff are in particular prohibited from using their position or information by acquiring or disposing of assets (such as foreign currency and gold) or rights (rights under derivative contracts or other elated financial instruments) to which that information is related. This prohibition applies to any kind of financial transactions, such as investment in securities (or index contracts based on such securities), interest rate transactions, foreign exchange and commodity transactions. Short-term trading for speculative purposes is forbidden.

The Executive Board of the ECB determines, in accordance with Staff Rules 1.2.14, which staff members have, by virtue of their functions, access to inside information concerning financial operations and concerning monetary and exchange rate policies. Staff concerned must, at the request of the Director General of Administration provide a list of bank accounts, including custody accounts and accounts with stock brokers, directives that they may have given to third parties for managing an investment portfolio and powers of attorney that may have been conferred on them. At the annual request of the ECB's External Auditor must provide documentation on sale or purchase of assets or rights, statement of bank accounts, including the conclusion or amendment of mortgages or other loans, and dealings in relation to retirement plans.

In 1998 the UN General Assembly approved a new Staff Regulation 1.2(o) to the effect that all senior staff at ASG level and above "shall be

[77] OJ C 92, 16.4.2004, 31. See also Annex V.

required to file financial disclosure statements upon appointment and at intervals . . ., in respect of themselves and their dependent children, including any substantial transfers of assets and property to spouses and dependent children from the staff member or from any other source that might constitute a conflict of interest, after knowledge of the appointment or during its tenure, to provide certification stating that there is no conflict of interest with regard to the economic activities of spouses and dependent children, and to assist the Secretary-General in verifying the above mentioned certification on his special request."[78]

E. Informatics and Internet

Many organisations have set up rules for the use of IT technology and of the Internet.

The Council of Europe's user charter for the use of computer resources and of Internet services, which must be signed by each user, stipulates that access by users to information and documents stored on computer systems shall be limited to their personal files and those that are public or shared. It is forbidden to obtain knowledge of information held by other users, even when the latter have not explicitly protected it. This also applies to private e-mail communications where the user is not the recipient. All users are responsible for the proper use of the computer resources and the Council of Europe's network and they may not effect operations that may be detrimental to the system. Each user undertakes not to deliberately cause any perturbations to the IT systems, including the introduction of viruses. Each user must protect his/her data. Staff may make use of Internet services exclusively in the context of their professional activities.

The OECD, in Staff Instruction 103/1, also underlines that the organisation's equipment, supplies and systems are furnished for the performance of their official functions. Nevertheless, officials may, if the need arises, make an occasional telephone call, e-mail communication, or visit an internet site for personal reasons while at the office. Officials are expected to use common sense and judgement in doing so.[79]

Staff of ESA must ensure that their use of the Internet is wholly consistent with their job responsibilities and access to files not related to their duties should be exceptional. The use of the Internet should not bring ESA into disrepute.

[78] General Assembly Resolution 52/252 of 8 September 1998.
[79] See also the contribution Sylvie Vanston, *infra*.

In the UN staff are permitted limited personal use of information and communication technology (ICT) resources, provided such use: (a) is consistent with the highest standard of conduct for international civil servants (among the uses which would clearly not meet this standard are use of ICT resources for purposes of obtaining or distributing pornography, engaging in gambling, or downloading audio or video files to which a staff member is not legally entitled to have access, (b) would not reasonably be expected to compromise the interests or the reputation of the UN, (c) involves minimal additional expenses to the UN, (d) takes place during personal time or, if during working hours, does not significantly impinge on such working hours; (e) does not adversely affect the ability of the authorised user or any other authorised user to perform his/her official functions, and (f) does not interfere with the activities or operations of the UN or adversely affect the performance of ICT resources. Personal use is a privilege that may be modified or withdrawn at any time. Users bear full responsibility and liability in connection with their personal use. OIOS has the authority to access all ICT resources and data remotely without informing the staff member.[80]

F. Anti-fraud and anti-corruption

The World Bank defines "fraudulent practice" or "fraud" as a "misrepresentation of facts in order to influence a procurement or selection process or the execution of a contract to the detriment of the borrower, and includes collusive practices among bidders or consultants (prior to or after submission of bids or proposals designed to establish prices at artificial, non-competitive levels and to deprive the borrower of the benefits of free and open competition." It defines "corrupt practice" or "corruption" as "the offering, giving, receiving or soliciting of any thing of value to influence the action of a public official in the procurement or selection process or in contract execution." The World Bank has undertaken a large number of initiatives in its anti-corruption campaign.

The EBRD, in its statement "about compliance" emphasises that "(c)orruption and fraud result in the erosion of public confidence in political institutions and legal systems. They distort the allocation of resources, inflate spending on public procurement and undermine competition. They weaken the very institutions that he Bank is mandated to strengthen: market economics, pluralism and democracy. The EBRD combats corruption and

[80] ST/SGB/2004/15 of 29 November 2004.

fraud, as well as misconduct of Bank officials, employees and consultants, or any other activity, which might compromise the integrity of the Bank and its partners."

It is recalled that the report of the Committee of Independent Experts reviewing the functioning of the EU Commission[81] made it clear that it had not encountered cases where a Commissioner was directly and personally involved in fraudulent activities. It found, however, instances where Commissioners or the Commission as a whole bear responsibility for instances of fraud, irregularities or mismanagement in their services or areas of special responsibility. Furthermore, the Committee found no proof that a Commissioner had gained financially from any such fraud, irregularity or mismanagement.[82]

IV. Implementation and enforcement

Almost all organisation have made major efforts in bringing the ethical standards to the attention of their staff. Awareness is the first step of implementation. Brochures and circular notes have been published, information sessions are being held, etc. Special offices have been created where staff can receive advise, including via help lines.

Many of the staff who are associated with the implementation of the standards and control mechanism receive special training.

A. Ethics officers

Many organisations have created a special office where staff can seek confidential advise about the interpretation to be given to the ethical standards in a particular situation they find themselves in. This can be a work situation, this may also concern a situation in their private lives that may have an impact on their professional life.

The ECB has created the function of Ethics Adviser.[83] The Adviser provides guidance on all aspects of professional conduct and professional secrecy. He/she gives direct advice and adopts interpretative ethical criteria. He/she is subject to an obligation of strict confidentiality. Advice and criteria are published in a generalised format on ECB's intranet. The Adviser must in particular ensure a consistent interpretation of the ECB's inside trading rules and keep the External Auditor informed.

[81] For reference, see footnote 31.
[82] Paragraph 9.2.3.
[83] Staff Rule 1.2.1. See Annex IV.

ESA has appointed a Custodian of the Agency Charter of Values. In addition, it has set up a Joint Panel to assist the Custodian, consisting of four staff members, two appointed by the staff association and two by the Administration. The Panel's role is to "1. advise the Custodian on specific points concerning individual requests submitted to him and for which he feels clarifications are required, notably in relation to the internal functioning of the Agency. The confidentiality of the request and the anonymity of the parties concerned are rigorously safeguarded and under no circumstances does the Panel examine the request itself; 2. advise the Custodian on the themes of the investigations he wishes to carry out on his own initiative; and 3. support the Custodian as he seeks to further develop the Charter of Values."

The EBRD has created the Office of the Chief Compliance Officer, which promotes good governance and ensures that the highest standards of integrity are applied to all activities of the EBRD. In particular, it deals with conflicts of interest, corruption, confidentiality and money laundering. It is responsible for procedures governing the ethical behaviour of EBRD officials, employees and consultants, and its conducts investigations on alleged staff misconduct.

In some organisations the ethics officer has a delicate double role. He/she not only gives informal advise, but is also in charge of enquiries and investigations of allegations of misconduct. The IMF is a good example of this.[84]

B. Complaints by staff of misconduct of which they are or have been the victim

All organisations have (disciplinary) procedures once a particular misconduct has been reported to the Administration.[85] Most organisations have,

[84] See contribution of Joan Powers, *infra*.

[85] The UN issued Revised disciplinary measures and procedures. *Cf.* ST/AI/371 of 2 August 1991. It provides that conduct for which disciplinary measures may be imposed includes, but is not limited to:

(a) acts or omissions in conflict with the general obligations of staff members set forth in article 1 of the Staff Regulations and the rules and instructions implementing it;
(b) Unlawful acts (e.g. theft, fraud, possession or sale of illegal substances, smuggling) on or off United Nations premises, and whether or not the staff member was officially on duty at the time;
(c) Misrepresentation or false certification in connection with any United Nations claim or benefit, including failure to disclose a fact material to that claim or benefit;
(d) Assault upon, harassment of, or threats to other staff members;
(e) Misuse of United nations equipment or files, including electronic files;
(f) Misuse of office; abuse of authority; breach of confidentiality; abuse of United Nations privileges and immunities;
(g) Acts or behaviour that would discredit the United Nations.

however, set up informal and formal procedures to deal with the cases at hand. In addition, several organisations have created special procedures for staff that have been (sexually) harassed.

The special UN procedure for dealing with sexual harassment[86] first of all encourages staff members to notify the offender that his or her behaviour is unwelcome. It admits, however, that power or status disparities or other considerations may make direct confrontation difficult. In such a case, the individual is encouraged to discuss the matter with a colleague or friend. The staff member may also seek (informal and discreet) help from supervisors, the Staff Counsellor, an HR or Personnel Officer, a member of the panel of Counsel, a member of the Panel on Discrimination and other Grievances, staff representatives, one of the Departmental Focal Points for Women, or, since its creation at the end of 2001, the Ombudsman.[87] In the case a staff member seeks advice and help from his/her Personnel Officer, and the latter considers that the incident may constitute misconduct, it will be reported to the Office of Human Resources Management (OHRM).

Under the formal procedure the staff member must make a written complaint to OHRM, upon which an initial investigation and fact-finding will be conducted, in accordance with the Revised disciplinary measures and procedures.[88] The alleged offender then receives copy of the complaint. He/she has the opportunity to answer the allegations. Upon this OHRM decides a. to close the case, b. should the facts appear to indicate that misconduct has occurred, refer the matter to a joint disciplinary committee for advice, or c. to propose to the Secretary General summarily dismissal, if the seriousness of the misconduct warrant immediate separation from service.

Also the WHO emphasises, in its policy on harassment, that complaints can often be resolved informally. If it is not possible to defuse the situation by talking to the individual concerned, help may be sought from the supervisor and/or the Ombudsman. The WHO has a month after publishing the policy on harassment issued details of the formal process for the investigation of harassment allegations for Headquarters which includes the establishment of a Grievance Panel,[89] which is to examine and make recommendations to the Director General.

---

86 Procedures for dealing with sexual harassment, ST/AI/379 of 29 October 1992.

87 A 2004 Information circular on Conflict Resolution in the UN Secretariat gives more details, ST/IC/2004 of 12 January 2004.

88 ST/AI/371 of 2 August 1991.

89 Cluster Note 2001/13 dated 26 April 2001.

In ESA staff can, in each establishment, contact colleagues, who have been appointed by the Director General on the recommendation of the Custodian, following consultations with the staff representatives. These points of contact act as interfaces between staff members and the Custodian and are bound by a specific duty of discretion and confidentiality in discharging their duties. Any matter concerning the Charter of Values can be submitted. It can also be referred to the Custodian directly by e-mail. One may conclude that anonymous complaints are not possible.[90]

In the Council of Europe persons confronted with a conflict situation or who believe themselves to be victims of sexual or psychological harassment may, in an informal procedure, request the assistance of a "counsellor" among those appointed in the Secretariat. The counsellors are appointed by the Secretary General on the basis of parity and on the proposal of the HR Directorate and the Staff Committee. They are chosen on a voluntary basis; they are given special training. They provide support, inform about the procedures and, if necessary accompany and help staff in the steps they will take to resolve the problem. Staff may also address themselves to the HR Directorate, the Equality Administrator, specialists in the medical, psychological and social team, or the Mediator. Where the informal efforts have failed, the formal procedure may be followed which starts with a written complaint to the Director of HR, who will seize a commission responsible for dealing with complaints and inform the alleged perpetrator. This commission consists of four members, two appointed by the Secretary General and two by the Staff Committee. The commission hears the parties, separately. It may decide, in agreement with both parties, to seek a solution via mediation. Where this is not advisable or possible, the commission may ask for an official enquiry which is carried out under the authority of the Directorate of HR. The results of the enquiry are communicated to the commission, which will assess the facts and express an opinion on the facts behind the complaint and make a recommendation to the Secretary General on the measures to be taken, including, depending on the seriousness of the case, that disciplinary proceedings are initiated.

C. Reporting by staff concerning misconduct of one or more colleagues

Public servants are not only accountable for their own acts, but they are also, or may be, confronted with the situation that some of their colleagues

[90] Although the procedure was designed for complaints by staff concerning cases concerning them directly, it does, on the other hand, not expressly prohibit staff to report on alleged misconduct not directly affecting them.

may not respect the norms and rules in force, raising the question of the duty to report misconduct.

A system can, in fact, only validly operate if it allows for the reporting of misconduct. There are several ways of achieving this. One may establish the duty to report misconduct, a heavy burden on colleagues. Procedures, internally, must then be established for dealing with such reports. Those who report must be protected, but inappropriate reporting must be punished. Those "accused" are entitled to a fair dealing with the case at issue. People are afraid to report, afraid of reprisals, as if it is against the *esprit de corps*, and afraid of an impact on their career. This should also be seen in the context of the increasing use by organisations of short-term contracts. Most organisations have not, however, established ways and means for dealing with anonymous reporting, which is almost essential for an optimal functioning. The duty of confidentiality of an Ombudsman, for example, can only be considered a partial solution. It is, after all, not the role of Ombudsmen to be the go-between on issues of misconduct.

In the EU, if staff believe that they have significant evidence of possible fraud, corruption, any other illegal activity, or serious unprofessional behaviour, they are expected to report this. The Staff Regulations now include a new article 22a which places a duty on all staff to report such concerns either within the Commission or directly to OLAF (or another institution, in the case the Commission or OLAF have not taken appropriate action on an initial complaint). New article 22b protects officials disclosing information on serious wrongdoings.[91] Also those who are accused are entitled to a certain protection and to due process.

OECD Staff Instruction 103/3 provides:

> In the event an official becomes aware of fraud, corruption or misuse of the Organisation's resources, he must bring it to the attention of the Secretary General.

In the UN staff can use the hotline to make reports directly (to the OIOS) of any waste, fraud and mismanagement in the UN. The UN Special measures for protection from sexual exploitation and sexual abuse[92] provide in section 3.2(e):

> Where a United Nations staff member develops concerns or suspicions regarding sexual exploitation or sexual abuse by a fellow worker, whether in the

---

[91] A Commission communication (SEC/2004 /0151) of 6 February 2004 from Vice-President Kinnock, provides for specific measures to ensure a maximum of protection for staff making proper use of the whistle-blowing procedure.

[92] See above, p.

> same agency or not and whether or not within the United Nations system, he or she **must**[93] report such concerns via established reporting mechanisms.

The most recent Information Circular to the UN staff[94] is now very clear concerning all misconduct. Its paragraph 5 provides that staff members have the duty to report cases of suspected misconduct either to a higher-level official whose responsibility it is to take appropriate action, or to the OIOS (without the need for prior consultation with their supervisor or the head of department).

Paragraph 4 of the circular stipulates that no retaliatory action is permitted against a staff member for submitting in good faith a report of suspected misconduct or for cooperating with investigations subsequent to such a report. Staff are, on the other hand, also reminded that the submission of information or reports with knowledge of their falsity or with wilful disregard for their veracity would be inconsistent with the concept of integrity.

The circular further outlines the different avenues, official and non-official, for reporting cases of suspected misconduct.

In the EBRD anybody, within or outside the bank, may report fraud, corruption and misconduct. Suspected fraud and corruption in the EBRD and EBRD-financed projects, as well as allegations regarding misconduct of bank officials, employees or consultants can be reported by calling a hotline or submitting a written report. All matters reported will be handled by the EBRD's Office of the Chief Compliance Officer for follow-up.

In the Council of Europe, the counsellors mentioned above may also be contacted by anyone who has witnessed harassment and who wishes to discuss it in order to understand more readily how to deal with the situation without, at this stage, wishing to reveal the names of the people concerned.

Whistle blowing *to the outside world*, in particular the press, is a very delicate issue. It can only be acceptable if serious misconduct is at stake and if previously all efforts have been made to report the matter internally and management has not followed up on it – or there must be compelling reasons not to follow the internal procedure first. Non-compliance with these ground rules may entail disciplinary procedures.[95]

There have obviously been a number of famous, or notorious, cases of whistle blowing, which will not be further discussed here. It appears, however, that the administrations concerned reacted in most of these cases rather defensively. Major effort seems to have been spent on the whistle

---

[93] Emphasis added.

[94] ST/IC/2005/19 of 24 March 2005. For text see Annex X. See also contribution of Loriot *infra*.

[95] See, for example, the UK's Public Interest Disclosure Act of 1998.

blowing itself, and on the whistle blower him/herself, resulting in disciplinary sanction, suspension, non-renewal of contract,[96] or removal from office. It appears that also press agencies that publish information are not exempt from pressure.[97]

D. Complaints by the public

Under the Code of Good Administrative Behaviour of the European Commission, members of the public may lodge complaints concerning a possible breach of the principles set out in this Code. The complaint is to be lodged with the Secretariat-General of the Commission.[98] Complaints can also be lodged with the European Ombudsman.[99]

Anybody, within or outside the EBRD, may report (suspected) fraud and corruption in the EBRD and EBRD financed projects, as well as allegations regarding misconduct of EBRD officials, employees or consultants. This can be done in writing or by calling a special hotline. Matters are followed up by the Chief Compliance Officer.

The World Bank has similar procedures. The Department of Institutional Integrity has a 24-hour Fraud and Corruption Hotline to receive any allegation of fraud, corruption, financial irregularities, or violations of law.

V. Investigation and control

Generally investigations result from a reported complaint or suggestion. Sometimes investigations are based on an analysis of the potential for fraud. Allegation can come from both inside and outside the organisation.

As was already indicated above, the introduction, or reinforcement, of ethical standards coincided with a reinforced campaign against fraud and corruption. Where codes of conduct were seeking to limit possible misconduct, new investigation and control bodies were set up with more investigation powers than ever before.

---

[96] By the end of December 2004 the UN Secretary General decided to follow a recommendation of the Joint Appeals Board and to extend the contract of Andrew Thomson by two months in order to allow him to lodge an appeal. Thomson is co-author of the, unauthorised, book *Emergency Sex and Other Desperate Measures: A True Story from Hell on Earth*, which had come out earlier that year.

[97] For example, on 19 March 2004 the Belgian police raided the Brussels office of the weekly *Stern* and the home of one of its journalists (who was moreover taken into custody).

[98] Complaint forms can be downloaded from: http://europa.eu.int/comm/secretariat_general/code/index_en.htm

[99] http://www.euro-ombudsman.eu.int.

The OIOS defines the notion of investigation as follows: "An investigations, which is a legal, analytic process, is an inquiry by specialized professionals to determine whether a wrongful or unlawful act has occurred and, if so, the person or persons responsible for the act. The findings are based on evidence which is in a form and of a sufficiency to present to a tribunal or other decision maker. Because the findings of such an inquiry must be based on evidence, it also can lead to the clearing of those who have been maliciously or simply incorrectly accused."[100]

The UN Office of Internal Oversight Services (OIOS) was created by the General Assembly in 1994.[101] It was set up to enhance oversight functions within the UN, in view of the increased importance, cost and complexity of the UN's activities. This is achieved through intensified evaluation for the benefit of the General Assembly, auditing,[102] inspection, investigation, advise, etc. OIOS submits that it has identified potential financial benefits, savings and recoveries in the UN totalling $ 310 million, of which $ 140 million was actually recovered.

The Investigations Division investigates allegations of employee misconduct, abuse of authority, payment of kick-backs, embezzlement of funds, and waste and mismanagement of the UN's resources. The investigations are done with all confidentiality. In the ten years of existence the unit has identified a number of illicit activities and corrupt practices involving UN staff and others. A number of them have been identified in this contribution (extortion and sexual exploitation of refugees, for example). To this can be added the more "classical" types of fraud, such as theft of equipment, travel fraud and fraudulent medical claims.

It is recalled that numerous exchanges have taken place in the EU between the Commission and the Court of Auditors and internal discussions had been underway to establish an anti-fraud unit. This resulted in the replacement, at 1 June 1999, of the Unit for the Coordination of Fraud Prevention (UCLAF), which had been created in 1988, by the European Anti-fraud Office – commonly referred to as OLAF, its French acronym – as an inter-institutional body with independent powers of investigation.

OLAF carries out inquiries within the European institutions to detect serious misconduct in the exercise of professional activities, which could

[100] Rules and procedures to be applied for the investigation functions performed by the Office of Internal Oversight Services, document A/55/469 of 11 October 2000.

[101] Resolution 48/218 B of 29 July 1994. The General Assembly refined the initial mandate with its Resolution 54/244 of 23 December 1999.

[102] The previously existing, and traditional, audit function was integrated in the OIOS. It was enlarged with the management and performance monitoring audit functions.

constitute failure on the part of officials and other servants of the Community of their professional obligations. Conditions and procedures for investigations and rights and obligations of staff still appear to be unclear. In addition, and in particular, OLAF coordinates the anti-fraud activities between the institutions and the member States on activities related to the European Union.

As soon as OLAF decides to open an investigation, it has direct and immediate access to all information held in the institutions as well as direct access to their buildings. The members or officials of the institution involved must cooperate and provide all the necessary information. Information received is confidential and covered by the rules on data protection.

In the ECB the External Auditor may, in the event he has reasonable grounds to believe that the rules and interpretative ethical rules have not been respected, ask any ECB staff member for full information. This information is to be provided in a sealed envelope via the Director General Administration. The External Auditor reports any case of non-compliance to the Directorate Internal Audit. Reports by the External Auditor may be used in a disciplinary procedure and in prosecutions by external authorities regarding alleged violations of national criminal laws.

As mentioned above, the functions of the ethics officer in the IMF include investigation of misconduct by staff; he may also conduct preliminary inquiries. Requests for enquiries and investigations normally come from the Managing Director or the Director of HR. In the case the ethics officer carries out an investigation on his own initiative, for example after having received information from staff, he must seek authorisation from the Oversight Committee. Procedures provide that the respondent must be informed that an inquiry or investigation has started, unless notification seriously interferes with the inquiry, such as the risk of destruction of evidence. The respondent must also be given adequate opportunity to respond. Both the respondent and other staff have the duty to cooperate. The role of the ethics officer is clearly limited to fact-finding. The conclusions of the inquiry or investigation are communicated to the Oversight Committee and/or the Director HR.[103]

In the WHO the Office of Internal Audit and Oversight is not only responsible for reviewing WHO's accounting, administrative and operating controls, and to evaluate the responsible, efficient and economic use of WHO's resources. It is also responsible to audit, and where indicated, investigate allegations of ethical impropriety. A staff member whose con-

[103] See for details Joan Powers, *infra.*

duct is being investigated has the opportunity to provide information relevant to the case and to answer questions. If it is suspected that the alleged misconduct could lead to serious consequence, the staff member will be formally charged with misconduct under Staff Rule 1130 and has eight days to furnish a written reply.

Not every allegation is in the end confirmed by the facts. Some investigations indeed conclude that "allegations of misconduct are not supported by evidence."[104] Such conclusions should be published just as reports concluding that there is misconduct. Sometimes false allegations are intentionally made in order to damage the reputation of colleagues or staff of an organisation. Sanctions are then warranted and confidentiality can no longer be guaranteed.

A. Standards of procedure and due process

Although, generally, the procedures in international organisations provide opportunity for staff to respond to allegations and to have access to representation before a final decision is taken, much has recently been improved in terms of more detailed rules of due process. Much is still left to be done, however. It still sometimes occurs that staff are advised late that they are the subject of an investigation, and that they are not always well informed about the details of the allegations or of the evidence.

OLAF states as its basic principle that its activities will be carried out with integrity, impartiality and professionalism, and will, at all times, respect the rights and freedoms of individuals and be fully consistent with the law. It has recently awarded the International Institute of Administrative Sciences a contract to carry out a multi-national European study of the "rights of defence" in cases where there may be accusations of fraud or misuse of public funds. The research will be a survey of the rights of "defendants" to have a fair hearing in administrative proceedings in the Member States carried out with a view to protect the financial interests of the European Union.

Annex A to the Directive on Sexual Harassment in United Nations Peacekeeping and Other Field Missions for military members of national contingents, military observers and civilian police officers[105] gives detailed

[104] See, for example, the OIOS investigation into allegations of misconduct and mismanagement of the "boat project" at the United Nations Office for Drug Control and Crime Prevention, document A/56/689 of 7 December 2001, in which the OIOS concluded that there was no misconduct, but that there was mismanagement.

[105] *Cf.* footnote 67.

guidelines for investigating complaints. They cover the composition of the investigation team, the timeframe, confidentiality, the planning of the investigation, interviewing (the complainant, the subject and witnesses), the reviewing of facts, and a format of the investigation report. The directives for Disciplinary Matters Involving Civilian Police Officers and Military Observers and for Military Members of National Contingents have similar annexes.[106]

The OIOS underlines[107] that UN staff have the right to a fair, objective investigation and that the investigators are required at all times to conduct themselves in a professional manner and to operate in accordance with the applicable rules, regulations and procedures. Guidelines in this respect are the revised disciplinary measures and procedures which have been issued in 1991.[108] Basic rights of staff during a preliminary investigation include the right to respond to allegations made against them before any report is issued.

Investigations are to be conducted with regard to fairness and due process for all staff members. On the other hand, staff members are obliged to make themselves available and to provide access to all records, documents or other materials that are relevant for the investigation. Confidentiality has to be guaranteed during the investigation. Details of the OIOS investigative process are given in the document on rules and procedures to be applied for the investigative functions performed by the OIOS.[109]

As is explained in detail elsewhere in this publication,[110] the World Bank has set up an investigation function within its Department of Institutional Integrity. Guiding principles are also here to ensure professional, impartial, thorough and timely investigations while at the same time protecting the individual rights of the staff members and ensuring due process.

OIOS and the World Bank were at the initiative of Uniform Guidelines for Investigations, which have been adopted at the fourth Conference of International Investigators of United Nations Organizations and Multilateral Financial Institutions in April 2003.[111]

---

[106] *Cf.* footnotes 68 and 69.
[107] *Cf.* document A/55/469, see footnote 100.
[108] Revised disciplinary measures and procedures, document ST/AI/371 of 2 August 1991.
[109] Document A/55/469, see footnote 100.
[110] See the contribution of Howard Dean, *infra*.
[111] The text can be found in Annex III to the Report of the Office of Internal Oversight Services on strengthening the investigation functions in the United Nations, document A/58/708 of 10 February 2004.

B. Sanctions

Once misconduct is established a disciplinary procedure follows leading to disciplinary sanctions. It must be emphasised, however, that not everybody can be sanctioned by the organisation. Peacekeepers, for example, are part of national contingents. The UN can investigate, but perpetrators can only be tried by their own country. The message that the UN in the future will not accept them in a peacekeeping mission can hardly be considered a sanction.

Organisations sometimes also refer cases to national authorities for criminal prosecution. A senior former staff member of the United Nations Interim Administration in Kosovo (UNMIK) had committed several criminal offences to the financial disadvantage to the UNMIK, totalling $ 4,3 million. Following a joint OIOS/OLAF action the case was referred to the authorities of the country of citizenship of the perpetrator. He was tried and convicted and sentenced to a prison term of three years and six months. The sums involved could be recovered.[112] A senior UNCTAD staff member who had embezzled over $ 600.000, was not only summarily dismissed from the UN and ordered to repay the sums involved. He was also prosecuted by the Swiss authorities and sentenced to an 18 month suspended prison term. A staff member at the UN Mission in Bosnia and Herzegovina was convicted and is serving a 41 months sentence for travel fraud amounting to more than $ 800.000.

Section 5 of the UN's Special measures for protection from sexual exploitation and sexual abuse provides that "(i)f, after proper investigation, there is evidence to support allegations of sexual exploitation or sexual abuse, these cases may, upon consultation with the Office of Legal Affairs, be referred to national authorities for criminal prosecution."[113]

Also the Director of the Department of Institutional Integrity of the World Bank may determine that laws of member countries may have been violated and may at any time make available to the law enforcement or administrative authorities of the countries involved any information relating to such a violation. Between July 2003 and March 2004, for example, the World Bank referred 18 cases of fraud and corruption to national justice authorities. A good example is a recent judgment, in January 2004, in a Swedish district court which convicted two individuals of bribery in connection with the misuse of World Bank trust funds. The case was reported to the World Bank's hotline in 1999. In 2000 the World Bank

[112] Document A/58/592 of 13 November 2003.
[113] ST/SGB/2003/13.

terminated the employment of three of its staff members involved in the matter and referred the case to the US and Swedish authorities. Two of the former staff members have pleaded guilty in a US district court. The two individuals in Sweden were involved in firms that received World Bank contracts; they had made payments to the former World Bank staff members.[114]

The World Bank has, moreover, a procedure under which companies or individuals may be temporarily or permanently debarred. They are ineligible to be awarded World Bank financed contracts because they were found to have violated the fraud and corruption provisions of the Procurement guidelines or the Consultants guidelines.[115] Debarment is a sanction that can be imposed by a Sanction Committee following the application of a detailed procedure. This Sanction Committee was established in November 1998 to review allegations and to recommend sanctions to the President of the World Bank. In August 2001 written procedures were issued. Also in 2001 the World Bank started reviewing the debarment process which resulted in July 2004 in an overall debarment reform policy. The new Committee now consists of both internal and external members. Contractors may henceforth be temporarily suspended from eligibility for World Bank financed contracts during the sanctions procedure.

The procedure starts with a proposed Notice of Debarment Proceedings which is presented by the Director of the Department of Institutional Integrity (INT) to the Secretary of the Sanctions Committee once it has been concluded from an investigation that there is reasonably sufficient evidence to support a finding that fraud or corruption was committed. The Notice is forwarded to a subcommittee of the Sanctions Committee composed of the Chairman of the Committee and the General Counsel. Unless the subcommittee disagrees within 10 days the Notice is issued to each organisation or individual who may be subject to sanctions. The respondent has 60 days to submit written materials presenting arguments and evidence in response to the Notice. INT may within 20 days of receipt of the respondent's response submit a written reply. All written submissions and evidence are provided to both parties. The Sanctions Committee holds a hearing where both parties are heard. It subsequently deliberates *in camera*. If the Committee finds that the evidence is reasonably sufficient it determines an appropriate sanction and recommends that sanction to the

[114] See World Bank News Release No. 2004/207/S of 13 January 2004.

[115] So far more than 220 companies and individuals have been debarred. The list of debarred firms and individuals is published and can be found at http://www. worldbank.org/debarr.

President of the World Bank. A possible sanction is, as mentioned, debarment, but the Committee may also recommend any other sanction it deems appropriate under the circumstances, including a reprimand. The President of the World Bank takes a final decision within 10 days.

The Asian Development Bank (ADB) has a similar procedure. The most striking differences with the World Bank procedure are that in the ADB individuals may be debarred indefinitely, but not companies. ADB applies a maximum debarment period of 84 months (which may be extended). Secondly, ADB does not make public the list of entities on which it has imposed sanctions.

Although sanctions imposed by one organisation are public and published, it appears that there is no "blacklist" mechanism in place under which other organisations would follow the sanction and not do business with these firms or individuals (or recruit them as staff). The only clear exception to this is the provision in the World Bank's Sanction Committee's Procedures that the "Secretary of the Sanction Committee may at any time, upon approval of the Chairman of the Committee, make available materials submitted to the Committee to another international or multinational organization, including another development bank, or to an agency of a member government that promotes international development, that has agreed to make similar information available from its own files to the Bank."

C. Follow up

Lessons learned: not many organisations have an institutionalised follow-up procedure after an investigation has been brought to an end, when reports are final and when, where necessary, disciplinary procedures have been followed.

The Secretary-General of the UN has, with effect from 1 November 2000, for the purposes of strengthening accountability in the Secretariat and to advise him on matters thereon, established an Accountability Panel which is to ensure that the Secretariat addresses the findings of its oversight review bodies from a systemic perspective, and to reinforce existing accountability mechanisms.[116] The Panel consists of the Deputy Secretary-General, who is in the chair, and four members at USG level, appointed by the Secretary-General. The Panel is to review the analysis of significant management issues, together with recommendations, to be prepared annually

[116] ST/SGB/2000/14.

by the Department of Management based on the reports of the oversight bodies (including OIOS, the Board of Auditors and the JIU); identify actions required to remedy accountability issues raised; and identify actions required to remedy systemic management weaknesses, irregularities and any other matters which may have a major impact on management issues.[117]

VI. Conclusion

As an OECD study observed: "Concerns about the effectiveness of codes of ethics have arisen in both public and private management circles. Problems cited range from the codes being too specific or too general, unworkable, unused, unknown, unavailable, and even insulting to employees. But foremost among those concerns is that relatively simplistic statements of rules are not the ideal medium for answering complicated ethical questions faced by public servants. No statement of rules will address every permutation of ethical dilemmas in the public sector. Other problems surrounding codes are attributable either to a confusion about their purpose or poor implementation."[118]

On 4 June 2004 the Secretary General of the UN sent to all staff a copy of an Organizational Integrity Survey. In a five-page letter accompanying this survey he concludes that staff think that "policies, practices and guidelines which help define ethical behaviour and professional conduct are widely accessible, and used by staff." "Nevertheless," he continues, "staff believe that not enough action is taken to investigate and address instances of unethical behaviour, and that those who expose such breaches may put themselves at risk of reprisal."

---

[117] The Panel was, on 5 May 2005, replaced with the Management Performance Board. *Cf* Staff Bulletin ST/SGB/2005/13; for text see Annex 14. See also contribution of Loriot *infra*.

[118] Ethics in the Public Service, Public Management Occasional papers, No. 14, OECD, 1996, p. 34, with reference to Kernaghan in R.A. Chapman, ed., Ethics in Public Service, Edinburgh, 1993.

The present contribution was finalised at a moment when a survey in France showed that citizens were convinced that senior public (and elected) servants were corrupt, although they admitted not to have been subject to this. In the same month a survey amongst Dutch public servants, mainly at municipal and regional level, revealed that 40% had doubts about the integrity of their colleagues and 20% about the honesty of senior management. There is a great hesitation to share facts or suspicion of irregularities or misconduct with management. A third wouldn't know what to do in such situations. And a survey in the UK revealed that almost half of the women working in the Royal Air Force experienced sexual harassment last year. Only half of them made a complaint.

Staff of international organisations, and this is certainly not limited to the UN, are, with only very few, and indeed painful, exceptions, committed to applying the highest level of ethical conduct and integrity, when they aim in the execution of their duties to achieve a better world.

The codification of norms and standards, as well as the introduction of guidelines may have been helpful in achieving this, and maybe in some situations they were necessary. Many staff remain largely lost and frustrated, however. It is one of the prime duties of senior management to show the way and their staff have a legitimate expectation to be able to follow them in an impeccable behaviour. Managers should set the example. In too many an organisation can one notice, however, that the real guardians of the rules, norms and values of that organisation have been seen to apply the norms – or have been accused by their staff of applying them – differently when it concerns senior staff or when it concerns junior staff.

One of the main conclusions of the UN integrity survey, in fact, is that "(m)ost of the infrastructure to support ethics and integrity is in place; accountability is not. There are perceived weaknesses, (e.g., protection from reprisal for identifying those who violate the guidelines on professional conduct) but such weaknesses may be . . . perceptions only. More importantly, staff seems to wonder: Who can (or should) be held accountable if leaders and supervisors are not? Who can care much about ethics and organizational integrity if leaders, supervisors and staff appear to not care and not caring has little impact on career success?"[119]

An administration is only credible when it is committed, at its highest level, to the highest standards of ethics and accountability, and when priority is given to the rule of law. Also here, International Administration is no exception.

[119] The Secretary General has in January 2005 appointed a new chief of staff, who is to play a key role in carrying out a series of measures to enhance the effectiveness of the UN.

TWO

Overview of the Rules on Conduct and Ethics at the IMF

Joan S. Powers[1]

The principles of good governance and transparency apply not only to the IMF's advice to member countries but within the organization as well. This is illustrated by the rules of conduct and ethics that apply to staff members in the IMF, as well as the members of its Executive Board. This paper will examine the following aspects of ethics within the IMF:

- Reasons for having rules of conduct and ethics
- How these rules are enforced at the IMF
- Avoiding conflicts of interest and the financial disclosure process
- Special Code of Conduct for members of the IMF Executive Board

I. Background: Purpose of Rules of Conduct

All of the major public international organizations like the IMF have adopted rules regulating the conduct and ethics of their employees. These rules are considered to be part of the terms and conditions of employment, and a staff member's failure to follow them could lead to disciplinary action, including termination.

It may seem obvious that international civil servants should be honest and behave properly, and not take improper advantage of their positions. However, there are various reasons for spelling out these obligations in the staff rules. Most importantly, it is not always clear or obvious what actions are not permitted for an employee. It may not occur to someone that there is a potential conflict between his actions and the interests of the organization. For example, staff may not realize that they need permission in order to run a family business on the side while employed at the IMF, or whether they may recommend a relative's software products to the

---

[1] Ms. Powers is Assistant General Counsel of the IMF and is responsible for administrative legal matters. She has been with the Legal Department of the IMF since 1984 and was previously an associate with the law firm of Wilmer, Cutler & Pickering (Washington, DC and London). She received her A.B. from Brown University (History) and her J.D. from the University of Pennsylvania Law School. She is a member of the District of Columbia Bar. The views expressed herein are her own and are not necessarily those of the IMF. An earlier version of this article was published in IMF, Current Developments in Monetary and Financial Law, Vol. 3, IMF, 2004.

information technology staff. Likewise, it may not be obvious whether and to what extent an employee is allowed to use an office computer to do trading on the stock market during working hours, or to accept an award from a member country to which the staff member has provided technical assistance.

It is incumbent on the organization as an employer to clarify what the expectations are, so that staff can conform their behavior to these requirements. At the IMF, the Executive Board has approved a series of staff regulations known as the "N Rules", which include rules of staff conduct.[2] These rules impose on IMF staff, as international civil servants, a high standard and some rather special rules that would not typically apply in the private sector. This is a consequence of the special nature of international organizations and the fact that they must be non-political and above reproach in the manner which they and their staffs conduct themselves. For example, Rule N-4 provides that:

> Persons on the staff of the Fund shall maintain standards of conduct compatible with their position as international civil servants and shall avoid any action or pronouncement, either in their own country or elsewhere, that would not be in keeping with their position as international civil servants. They shall always bear in mind the reserve and tact incumbent upon them by reason of their international functions, and they shall exercise the utmost discretion in matters of official business.

Another N Rule (Rule N-5) prohibits staff from expressing their personal views in public e.g., by making a speech or writing a letter to a newspaper, on national political issues (e.g., criticizing the level of military expenditures in national budget) unless it has been cleared by the organization. This is intended to avoid embarrassment to the organization in situations where the staff member's personal views would inevitably be attributed to the organization itself and possibly strain its relations with the political authorities in the country involved.

Perhaps another reason for the adoption of rather comprehensive rules on staff conduct by international organizations stems from the fact that these organizations and their officials enjoy certain privileges and immunities under their governing charters. At the IMF, these privileges and immunities are provided in the Articles of Agreement. In particular, officials are immune from judicial process with respect to acts performed in their official capacities. Although officials do not have immunity with respect to their personal conduct outside the workplace, the immunity of the organization

[2] *See* Rules N-3 through N-10 of the Rules and Regulations of the International Monetary Fund.

may have the unintended effect of insulating that conduct from the reach of the legal system. For example, if a staff member fails to pay a legal judgment for alimony or child support; the court may then order the IMF as the employer to remit a prescribed amount of the wages to the employee's spouse or other creditor (which the court could do from other employers in the US). However, the IMF – unlike private employers – is immune from the garnishment order, as it is immune from any form of judicial process. The result is that the staff member may appear to have evaded his private legal obligations by "hiding behind" the IMF's immunity. In order to prevent this result – which would undoubtedly lead to complaints that immunity was being abused – the IMF has a standard of conduct stating that the failure to meet private legal obligations may be grounds for disciplinary action. Moreover, it will voluntarily give effect to certain types of garnishment orders (in the family law context), notwithstanding its immunity. These types of measures are intended to allow the IMF to demonstrate to its membership and the public that there are standards of conduct to which its staff will be held, and that these standards are taken seriously and enforced.

Because the N-Rules themselves are written in very broad terms, IMF management has issued implementing regulations pertaining to various aspects of behavior in the workplace, such as harassment, discrimination, and the proper use of office e-mail and Internet access. In addition, a Code of Conduct for staff was issued in 1999. Although the Code is not a legal document per se, it is intended to provide a practical understanding of what is permissible or not in the eyes of the organization, by providing interpretations and specific illustrations of the more general pronouncements in the rules and regulations.

II. Enforcement of the Rules of Conduct

The imposition of disciplinary measures for violations of the rules of conduct takes place only after appropriate investigation of the matter and the opportunity of the staff member to respond to the allegations of misconduct and the basis therefor. Such investigations are normally (but not exclusively) undertaken by the IMF Ethics Officer. The Terms of Reference for the Ethics Officer call upon him to investigate allegations of misconduct by IMF employees and to report his findings to the official who is authorized to decide whether to impose disciplinary action on the individual in question. Another important aspect of the ethics function is to give advice to the staff at large and on an individual basis, on any matter concerning ethics, conflict of interest and the like. The Ethics Officer also provides training to IMF staff on ethics-related matters.

The allegations of misconduct that may trigger an inquiry can come from any source: the management of the IMF can refer a matter to the Ethics Officer; staff members may report that they believe some form of misconduct has occurred; or there may simply be a phone call from an outside party complaining about the behavior of an IMF employee. These may all trigger an inquiry, although the Ethics Officer will not follow up on an anonymous lead; these are considered too unreliable.

The Ethics Officer is to investigate any matter that is covered by the IMF's rules of conduct. This could include a wide variety of behavior: leaks of confidential information to the press; misuse of IMF benefits; sexual harassment, as defined in the IMF's comprehensive policy on harassment; improper use of e-mail or Internet on IMF computers. The Ethics Officer will also look into matters involving private behavior outside the office *if* this type of behavior violates the IMF's rules. The most common example of this involves alleged mistreatment of domestic employees who are brought to the United States under a special visa that is sponsored by the IMF. If staff members fail to comply with local labor laws regarding their personal servants, (*e.g.* paying less than minimum wage, not providing adequate time off), this is considered a violation of the rules of this special program. For this reason, such action can be – and has been – a basis for disciplinary action. The Ethics Officer has also received complaints from spouses or ex-spouses about a staff member's failure to pay alimony or child support. Again, although it involves a family matter, this is considered appropriately within the organization's interest, in order to avoid the perception that staff are "hiding behind" IMF immunities so as not to meet their private legal obligations.

The Terms of Reference for the Ethics Officer set out various procedural safeguards regarding how investigations are to be conducted. This is intended to protect the rights of staff who are being investigated. It is important to the credibility of the process that they have a full opportunity to give their side of the story and respond to the allegations against them, including the underlying evidence.

After the Ethics Officer completes his investigation and reports his findings, the next step in the internal disciplinary process is at the level of management, with respect to complaints against senior staff, and the Director of the Human Resources Department, for the rest of the staff. These officials are to consider the facts and, if warranted, charge the staff member with misconduct; after taking into account what the staff member has to say about the matter, they decide whether to impose disciplinary sanctions and what those penalties will be. This can run the range from a warning or written reprimand (least severe) to loss of employment (most severe). In between, there could be forfeiture of benefits, demotion, or reduction in pay, so long as the penalty is proportional to the seriousness of the misconduct.

III. Conflict of Interest

To an increasing extent, in both the public and private financial sectors, as well as other professions (including lawyers), there are internal rules on conflict of interest by their employees. This is to prevent the misuse of confidential information and other ways of taking improper advantage of one's position, e.g., the paralegal in the law firm who learns of an impending merger and tips off his family to buy stock; the advisor to a government whose spouse deals in bonds issued by that government; the reporter who learns of a new drug about to released in the market in the course of an interview and buys shares in the pharmaceutical company before the information becomes public.

Reflecting this trend, international organizations like the IMF have also adopted special measures to ensure that the private financial activities of their employees do not involve the use of non-public information learned in the course of their employment or otherwise pose a conflict of interest with their employment. These measures are taken for the reputation and credibility of the organization.

Certainly, international organizations are subject to close scrutiny when allegations of wrongdoing or conflicts of interest become public. In such cases, it is very important for the organization to be able to demonstrate that it has taken measures to avoid and, if needed, to resolve such conflicts.

At the IMF, there are three basic rules dealing with the issue of staff conflict of interest, which are spelled out in more detailed administrative orders:

Rule N-6 prohibits staff from disclosing or using for personal financial gain confidential IMF information, both during and after IMF employment.

Rule N-7 prohibits staff from engaging in any outside business activity or other public or private employment without the approval of IMF management.

Rule N-10 prohibits staff from accepting gifts or honors from outside parties, including member governments, for their services with the IMF.

The Code of Conduct gives some practical examples of how these rules will be applied. With respect to avoiding conflicts of interest, and how this affects private business and financial activities, the Code provides the following guidance:

1. Staff must avoid any situation involving a conflict or the appearance of a conflict between their *personal interests and the performance of their official duties*. For example, staff who carry out procurement activities are expected to tell their supervisors about any potential conflict of interest, so that the supervisor can decide whether the staff member must withdraw from the activity in question. This could happen, for example, if the IMF was considering whether to hire a company where the staff member's wife was employed; the staff member would obviously have to recuse himself from that decision and not attempt to influence the result.
2. Another potential conflict could arise in situations where a staff member is *negotiating for a new job* outside the IMF. If so, he must maintain an arms-length relationship with the prospective employer in all matters relating to the work of the IMF. For this reason, he would be expected to recuse himself from involvement in sensitive IMF work that could benefit, or be perceived to benefit, his prospective employer.
3. With respect to *outside business activities*, staff members are allowed to engage in such activities only with permission and only if the activity is undertaken outside of normal working hours and does not involve the use of IMF resources, like fax, phone, etc. With respect to whether permission will be granted, this depends on the nature of the activity. If it is in any way related to the work of the IMF (e.g., giving investment advice), unlikely to be approved; on the other hand, if unrelated to the IMF, such as doing carpentry or preparing tax returns, there is normally no objection on IMF's part.
4. The question of *personal investments* and what would constitute a conflict of interest is considerably more difficult, given the organization's role at the center of the international financial system. At the IMF, staff are generally free to conduct their personal financial affairs as they wish, with two exceptions. First, because of the IMF's role in exchange rate surveillance, all staff members are prohibited from engaging in short-term trading (i.e., combination of buying and selling within six months) in gold, foreign currencies and closely related financial instruments, for speculative purposes. (This would not prevent "one way transactions", where staff member sells foreign exchange in order to pay for expenses incurred abroad.) Second, staff are prohibited from disclosing, or using for personal financial gain, confidential information to which they have access at the IMF.

In terms of monitoring compliance with these conflict of interest rules, various public and private organizations require some form of disclosure of financial holdings to confirm the absence of any conflict of interest. The IMF has two requirements in this regard:

- First, all staff members, regardless of rank or specific work assignment, must annually file a statement with the IMF confirming that they have read and understood the rules with respect to financial holdings and transactions; that neither they nor their immediate family members have any undisclosed financial or business interests that might give rise to an actual or apparent conflict with their duties as a IMF staff member. This rule covers not only the staff member but his/her immediate family; this is quite typical, given the obvious loophole that would exist if the rules did not extend to the financial holdings of those with whom staff have a common financial interest.
- Second, all IMF staff at the managerial level must submit an annual statement listing their individual financial holdings in excess of a prescribed amount ($10,000), without having to disclose actual value of the asset (just the range).[3] Transactions in those holdings must also be disclosed. These financial assets include stocks, mutual funds, annuities, bonds, government securities and funds held in retirement plans. Assets that are not financial in nature, such as the personal residence or other real estate, need not be disclosed (although liabilities must be disclosed). The disclosure requirements cover financial holdings of spouses and dependents as well.

In terms of the mechanics of the financial disclosure process, the information is submitted on a prescribed form to a Compliance Officer, who reviews them for potential conflicts of interest, taking into account the employee's particular job and the information to which he/she may have access because of that position. The IMF has retained a major accounting firm to provide this service, and it is contractually required to maintain the confidentiality and privacy of information reviewed in the course of this process. If the Compliance Officer believes there may be a perceived or actual conflict of interest, the matter is to be discussed with the individual staff member with a view to resolving the matter informally and not having to bring it to the attention of management (unless there is evidence of a flagrant violation for which disciplinary sanctions would be appropriate, which has not occurred to date).

There would be a perceived conflict if a reasonable observer would conclude that the staff member was acting on the basis of confidential IMF information in making an investment; e.g., the staff member participates in a mission to reach agreement on a new economic program in a particular

[3] Other staff may be subject to this requirement if their positions are such that they have access to nonpublic, market-sensitive information.

country, and upon return purchases shares in a bank stock fund in that country. If there is a perceived conflict, various options are available to resolve the matter. First, there would typically be a discussion with the individual staff member with a view to resolving the matter informally; including:

(i) divestiture of the asset;
(ii) "freezing" of the asset, on the understanding that the staff member may seek permission from the Compliance Officer to liquidate the investment, for reasons unrelated to confidential information; or
(iii) reassignment or recusal on a particular matter. For example, if the staff member's spouse has gone to work for an emerging markets mutual fund, the staff member should not work on countries covered by that fund.

The role of the Compliance Office should be regarded as a protection for staff, as they may rely on the Compliance Officer's interpretation of the rules and his clearance of their investments if they are ever accused of having a conflict of interest. In terms of results, nearly 400 staff have been subject to this new disclosure requirement, and it has been implemented without much difficulty, and no major problems have been encountered. It must be acknowledged, however, that the system is self-policing; there is no way to ensure that someone is being truthful and complete in disclosing this information.

IV. Code of Conduct for Members of the Executive Board

After management issued a Code of Conduct for IMF staff, the Executive Board adopted its own Code of Conduct in 2000. It is perhaps the most comprehensive code of conduct for the governing board of a public international organization.[4]

The Board's Code is not identical to the staff code, and there are indeed a number of key differences. The reason for these differences is that the situation of Board members is not entirely comparable to that of the staff: they are not expected to be neutral on political issues or to refrain from expressing their views publicly. The special situation of Executive Directors is reflected in the preamble to the Board code:

> Executive Directors of the Fund are entrusted by the member countries that have selected them with responsibilities for ensuring that the Fund carries

[4] The World Bank and European Bank for Reconstruction and Development also have such codes for their executive boards.

> out the mandate prescribed in its Articles of Agreement. The office of Executive Director of the Fund requires personal and professional conduct that meets the highest standards.

However, members of the Executive Board are officials of the IMF; as such they have certain ethical responsibilities towards the organization, including maintaining the security of confidential information provided to, or generated by, the IMF, and avoiding conflicts of interest between their personal interests and the performance of their official duties. The Code of Conduct for the Board recognizes this special responsibility, in setting out the expectation that Executive Directors, in the performance of their duties, will carry out the mandate of the IMF to the best of their ability and judgment and maintain the highest standards of integrity. It further provides that Executive Directors, in their conduct outside the workplace, should observe local laws, so as not to be perceived as abusing the privileges and immunities conferred on the IMF and its officials.

The Code of Conduct for the Executive Board is largely self-policing; there is no mechanism for imposing disciplinary measures on Executive Directors or for removing them from the Board, as they are either elected or appointed by member countries. However, if there is a complaint about an Executive Director's conduct, there is a mechanism in place for such concerns to be considered by a special Ethics Committee of the Board. If the complaint is considered valid, the Committee may recommend that the Board censure the Director in question, and inform the member countries that have selected him/her about the matter.

The Board has also adopted a system of annual financial disclosure and review by an outside compliance officer, similar to that in place for the staff.

THREE

Accountability at the United Nations – in Need of a Genuine External Enforcement Body

François Loriot[1]

I. Introduction

From September 2004 to June 2005, the UN General Assembly and the UN Administration have adopted various measures proposing sweeping changes to the Organization's accountability system and establishing an external independent panel to "*re-design*" the internal justice system. These new policies will be debated in coming months and at the September 2005 Summit held on the occasion of the 60th General Assembly and Anniversary of the United Nations. The present article is a contribution to the ongoing discussions at the United Nations to improve its accountability and internal justice systems. It gives a review of past efforts to strengthen accountability and recovery of losses at the United Nations, pinpoints various obstacles hampering internal reforms at the UN and reviews some of the United Nations Administrative Tribunal jurisprudence on these issues.

II. Main Features of Recent UN Reforms and Proposals on Accountability Matters

A

In its resolution 59/283 of 13 April 2005[2] the UN General Assembly decides to transfer the responsibility over the internal justice decisions from the Department of Management to the Office of the Secretary-General

---

1 Barrister & President Bar Association for International Governmental Organizations. The author is a retired head of legal services at the United Nations, which included responsibilities in the internal justice system and in the efforts to redesign its accountability and internal justice policies.

2 Annex VIII.

(paragraph 17); it also invites staff to consider the establishment of a staff-funded legal aid insurance scheme which could provide advice and support to staff members (paragraph 26). It proposes to dismantle the Administrative Law Unit in distinct operational units separating appeals, from disciplinary matters and from other advisory services (paragraphs 29–30). It also amends Staff Rule 111.2(a) in order to have a copy of requests for administrative reviews sent to the heads of offices, departments or programmes concerned (paragraph 33). This resolution also calls for the independence of the Tribunal from the Office of Legal Affairs (OLA) and for a direct transfer of budget from OLA to UNAT (paragraphs 36–37), and requires that, as of 1 January 2006, appointments of its judges will be amongst legal professionals ("*with judicial experience in the field of administrative law or its equivalent* . . .", paragraph 40). The resolution stresses again the importance "*of the eventual harmonization of the statutes of UNAT and ILOAT*" (paragraph 45). In its paragraphs 47 to 52, the resolution mandates the Secretary-General to institute a panel of external independent experts "*to consider redesigning the administration of justice system*", and provides the terms of reference for this Panel which *inter alia* would include consideration of arbitration and of a two-layer system. The Panel will begin its work in February 2006 and submit a report by July 2006. The Secretary-General must provide his comments on this report for the General Assembly Fall session of 2006.

B

Staff Bulletin ST/SGB/2005/8 of 13 April 2005[3] redefines the structures of the Department of Management. It maintains therein the "*overall supervision of the internal system for the administration of justice*" (paragraph 3.5) and creates in that Department an *Office for Oversight and Internal Justice* (paragraph 8). This new Office somehow appears in contradiction with the above-mentioned 5th resolution, which is seeking a complete transfer of internal justice decisions to the Office of the Secretary-General (paragraph 17).

C

Staff Bulletin ST/IC/2005/19 of 24 March 2005[4] describes new whistle blowing modalities and procedures for staff wishing to report impropri-

[3] Annex IX.
[4] Annex X.

eties, abuses or other violations committed by work colleagues or supervisors. This circular prohibits any retribution against whistleblowers acting in "*good faith*" (paragraph 4) and announces that it is developing a system for their protection, currently being discussed with staff representatives.

D

Staff Bulletin ST/SGB/2005/1 of 1 January 2005[5] amends Staff Rules 110.4 to 110.7 creating special Joint Disciplinary Committee Panels in accountability and recovery cases. The composition of such panels would include only members at the same level as the staff whose financial responsibility is engaged, with the addition of an OLA legal officer as *ex officio* member. This new staff rule was complemented by an administrative instruction on the conduct of accountability and recovery cases and investigations.[6] However, the General Assembly resolution quoted above,[7] indicates in its paragraph 14, that this new measure has not yet been implemented and it requests a report on its implementation. On 20 March 2005, the UN Secretary-General, Mr. Kofi Annan, proposed in his report on UN reforms entitled "*In Larger Freedom: Towards Development, Security and Human Rights for All*"[8] the establishment of "*a Management Performance Board (MPB)*" *to ensure that senior officials are held accountable for their actions and the results their units achieve*" and also proposed other measures in order "*to further improve accountability and oversight*".

E

Staff Bulletin ST/SGB/2005/13 of 5 May 2005[9] on the new *Management Performance Board* replacing the *Accountability Board* (which was created by ST/SGB/2000/14), clarifies, strengthens and expands the functions, role and responsibilities of this new Board on accountability matters, including a "*review of the outcome of administration of justice proceedings . . . for accountability purposes*" (cf. XXVIII below).

---

[5] Replacing ST/SGB/2004/14 of 29 September 2004, for text see Annex XI.
[6] ST/AI/2004/3 of 29 September 2004, for text see Annex XII.
[7] Annex VIII.
[8] A/59/2005; http://www.un.org/largerfreedom/report-largerfreedom.pdf.
[9] Annex XIV.

III. Accountability Events in 2004–2005

The year 2004 has been coined *annus horibilis* by Mr. Kofi Annan, the Secretary-General of the United Nations. It was also a disappointing year for all those who believe in the United Nations' humanitarian missions and multilateral goals. The Organization has seen worst crises before. But never in its history has the credibility and relevancy of the UN been so heavily damaged by a series of corruption, mismanagement and sexual harassment scandals, reaching the highest levels of authority. The year 2004 began with a reminder of the 10th anniversary of UN's inaction in the Rwanda genocide, continued with sex abuses by Congo Peacekeepers, the Iraq Oil-for-Food-Programme (OFFP) scandals and ended with the December tsunami which engulfed countries in South East Asia, where the efficiency and capacity of the UN to deliver aid was again challenged. These events all underlined the weaknesses inherent to the UN system and the urgent need to design a new, more efficient and accountable multilateral machinery to face such situations. In 2004, an independent survey conducted throughout the United Nations system, had found that a large majority of its staff had no trust in senior UN officials. Likewise in 2004, UN staff unions complained that senior management did not even comply with its own *Nine Global Compact Principles* (GCP), raising their voices and concerns over the lack of transparency and accountability at the United Nations. The UN reacted with a 23 June 2004 statement that it would comply in its internal management with these *Global Compact Principles* (GCP) and, on that occasion, added two new GCP focusing on *Transparency* and the *Fight Against Corruption.* In 2005, the OFFP independent investigation revealed major procurement irregularities, gross negligence in contract administration and misconduct by top UN officials. These events challenge the Organization's credibility in accountability matters.

IV. Studies and Reports on Accountability at the UN

The United Nations has been prolific in its accountability literature. A score of reports, studies and circulars have been produced over the last 15 years on the issue of accountability, transparency, ethics, etc, at the United Nations. The list would be too long to quote, but reference to the most important ones is found in Appendix. The last 3 reports by the OFFP/IIC quoted in Appendix, dated 9 January, 3 February and 29 March 2005 are of great importance for the UN future. They reconfirm, from an outside and independent view, the major flaws and serious gaps in the UN accountability system, reaching the highest levels of the UN senior management at the USG and SG levels. The OFFP Independent Inquiry Committee has announced that

> as its investigation proceeds, the Committee will make recommendations concerning greater institutional transparency and accountability in making such important financial decisions

(page 18 of its *Interim Report*). The OFFP/ICC final report is due later in the year 2005 and is expected to contain valuable recommendations to improve the UN accountability systems.

V. Current Accountability Situation at the UN

Like any other human construction, the UN is an organization made up of human beings most of whom believe in its ideals and corporate values, but which also includes its own lot of abusers, crooks, felons and white-collar criminals. The only difference with civil societies is that law and accountability enforcement at the United Nations is almost nil, being applied mostly at the lower levels, and rarely at higher levels.

Using the sacrosanct argument of "*UN privileges and immunities*", its senior management has often defended impunity as a policy tool, rather than facing justice on gross negligence, mismanagement, corruption, embezzlement and other types of abuses.

Already in 1977, Plantey in his "*International Civil Service*" and in a 1982 article was alluding to the growing need for public morality and ethics in the governance of international organizations "*. . . in the absence of any international criminal law, the code of ethics governing the international civil service is based on these institutions' internal regulations and on the legal principles enshrined by the judicial authorities*".

Some 30 years later, little has been done to establish a genuine system of internal justice at the United Nations dealing with accountability issues. Even the UN Administrative Tribunal's numerous calls seeking the application of Staff Rule 112.3 and its calls for independent investigations have remained mostly unheeded by UN senior management.

VI. Impunity at the Senior UN Levels

At senior levels of the UN, up to the Secretary-General, the "*doctrine*" has been to consider the Secretary-General, his Deputy, his ASGs as well as USGs to be immune, to a large extent, from the application of accountability, Staff Rules, Financial Rules, etc.

This eventually permeates also the D.2 and D.1 levels, who work closely with the most senior UN officials. Although each and every one of these senior officials is a UN staff member, including the Secretary-General himself, they often consider themselves to be in a category above Staff Rules and Financial Rules. For this purpose they will even marshal the support and legal advice of legal officers at the Office of Legal Affairs (OLA) to argue that while "*the Secretary-General must follow Staff Rules in administering the UN staff* [. . .] *he is not bound to follow them personally because he is not a staff member*" (see OFFP/IIC *Second Interim Report*, letter by Mr. Rashkow of OLA of 24 March 2005, pp. 11–12).[10]

There is hardly any legal rationale behind such a statement, in international civil service, considering the UN Charter and the jurisprudence (ex: Judgement ILOAT No. 2232 of 16/7/2003 stating

> *the Director-General* [of OPCW] *like other staff members, is clearly deemed to have the status of an international civil servant. Consequently, the Director-General must be regarded as a staff member both for the purposes of the Organization's submission to the Tribunal's jurisdiction and Staff Rule 11.3.01(a).*

The legal views of OLA did not convince much the OFFP Independent Inquiry Committee. It found that the UN Secretary-General himself had failed to conduct a proper investigation on the conflict of interest involving his son's employer COTECNA (page 78 of *Second Interim OFFP/IIC Report*). The current accountability system at the UN appears like a pyramid, where responsibilities mostly begin and rest at lower levels where it is widely spread amongst lower ranking staff members. Afterwards, but only to a certain extent, it rises to mid-level managers, but rarely permeates the level of senior managers.

When an accountability issue becomes a threat to senior managers, the internal justice machinery can be activated against their subordinates, in order to freeze the whole accountability process at lower levels, an exercise which may last between 4 to 5 years at the United Nations, giving enough time for senior managers to turn around the situation, manipulate the evidence and get off the hook.

While the concepts of "accountability" and "transparency" have become part of the "new management" culture in many national public administrations, in order to reinforce the concept of civil servants' responsibility, the UN internal reports tend to use the concept of accountability as a tool to dilute responsibilities whenever it reaches the highest levels of officials. The 25 March 2005 proposal by Kofi Annan to establish a "*Management*

[10] http://www.iic-offp.org/documents/InterimReportMar2005.pdf.

Performance Board (MPB) to ensure that senior officials are held responsible for their actions . . ." is a move in the right direction, in order to replace the former *Accountability Board* which had yielded very few known outputs.

The new "*strengthened and expanded functions*" of the MPB have been promulgated only on 5 May 2005. It will be presided by the Deputy-Secretary-General (DSG), with 2 USG and an external expert "*in public sector management*" for a 2-year mandate. It is mandated to "*put in place a system of peer review to ensure adherence to acceptable standards of managerial conduct*" (art. 1.2) and "*review the outcome*" of internal justice cases, including Tribunal cases, for "*accountability purposes*" (art. 1.1c). Without more information on how this "*peer review*" will take place, on how its transparency will be assured and by whom, the role and functions of the MPB remains to be closely assessed in order to ensure that this new body will be the genuine authority to *enforce* UN accountability principles and policies at the highest levels of hierarchy.

VII. Institutional Amnesia on Accountability Issues

UN member-States often suffer from a short memory span on accountability matters, even on issues raised just a few years back, leading to serious shortcomings in the follow up of accountability issues. This situation is mainly caused by the constant rotation of delegates from member-States posted at the United Nations, whose learning-curve and short mandates of 3 or 4 years in New York are not conducive to and do not allow for much continuity on these issues.

The same applies to the Board of Auditors whose mandate is of short duration, rotated between member-States and with a new caseload of audit cases awaiting the new external auditors replacing their predecessors.

A typical example of such corporate memory shortcomings by member-States and by the UN Board of External Auditors are the contractual overpayments, corruption and bribery surrounding the UNDP's Reserve for Field Accomodation (RFA) contracts, in the early 90's, leading to estimated losses of over $25 million in the construction of housing and office units for the United Nations African operations. When these financial losses were disclosed to the UNDP Executive Board, in 1995–96, delegates of member-States expressed their outrage and deep concerns over the "*breakdown*" which had occurred in internal controls and accountability at UNDP, and they requested that strong actions be taken to identify the responsible officials, to recover the financial losses and to prosecute staff members and third parties involved (DP/1996/39 of 15/100/96 para. 63).

In 1996–97, extensive reviews and investigations took place identifying the senior officials at UNDP and some of its mid-level managers involved in the decision-making which led to fraudulent RFA transactions, bribes and corruption.

Up to five audit and investigation teams reviewed the RFA procurement actions and found responsibilities pointing up to the level of an Assistant Secretary-General and his deputies. This Assistant-Secretary-General's oversight and supervisory authority over the RFA management and construction projects were found seriously negligent and a contributing factor in the $25 million losses. The UNDP Accountability information circular on the case of this case indicates that, following a review by a peer body, the ASG was indeed reprimanded and his ASG contract was not renewed by UNDP, as a result of his improprieties and failures in these construction projects. But just a few days later the same ASG was immediately re-hired in another ASG position.

Meanwhile, Mr. G., the ASG's subordinate whose performance had been highly-rated by the same ASG (despite many violations of the UN Financial and procurement rules) was summarily dismissed for gross negligence, from which he appealed to the Tribunal. Later on, a grand jury indicted Mr. G. for fraud and bribery in his RFA management, and he was charged before a New York Criminal Court (Mr. G. died before a verdict was reached in the New York Criminal Court and before the UN Administrative Tribunal had rendered its judgement on his case).

VIII. Scapegoats in the UN Accountability System

In November 2002, ten years later, on this whole RFA scandal involving many senior officials, *only one case* of a lower general service staff (working under the supervision of the ASG and of Mr. G.) reached the hearing and judgement stages of the Tribunal (see UNAT No. 1034, *Levy*). Mr. Levy had been found guilty of and dismissed by UNDP for falsifying the records of RFA losses and of its overpayments and complained that he had become a "*scapegoat*", while none of the other UNDP officials involved in the supervision or review of his work had been prosecuted nor sanctioned. Mr. Levy raised a vicarious argument on the presumed legality of the instructions he had received from his supervisors to skew the RFA figures, as well as the hostile work atmosphere prevailing at UNDP which was preventing him from expressing his reservations or from reporting his supervisors' improprieties. The Disciplinary Committee which heard this case recognized that the responsibility of Mr. Levy for the losses was minor, considering his secondary role, but found that this whole fraudulent scheme had been "*masterminded*" and was supervised by "*other officials senior and superior to him . . .*" at UNDP:

> 30. The Committee took note of the Standards of Conduct in the International Civil Service, and in particular articles 15 and 16 thereof. It recognized that [the Applicant]'s failure to record his reservations about the propriety of the financial transactions which he questioned or his failure to ask his supervisor for written instructions concerning them, violates these standards. It also recognized, however, that should staff members in such situations record their views or ask for written instructions, they would do so at their hazard; the climate in the Organization is not hospitable to such behavior and a staff member who would overtly challenge a supervisor in this manner would suffer the consequences. In this regard, the Standards of Conduct call for a level of independence, professionalism and courage that is, unfortunately, at present, more apt to be punished than rewarded.

The Tribunal weighed these arguments in its final judgement in the *Levy* case, which was rendered five years after Mr. Levy's summary dismissal:

> Based on the findings of the JDC, the Tribunal holds that the Applicant was negligent in maintaining grossly inaccurate and misleading records, and that he improperly followed orders by failing to note his reservations in "Notes to the File". Although the Applicant claims that he is being disproportionately disciplined based on his rank in the chain of command, his failure to ask his supervisor for written instructions concerning the improprieties, together with his admissions, constitute serious misconduct and violations of UNDP policies". (UNAT No. 1034)

The Tribunal dismissed Mr. Levy's arguments that a hostile work atmosphere at UNDP surrounding the RFA activities had prevented him from seeking proper instructions from his supervisors who were pressuring him to falsify the records of RFA overpayments. With this Tribunal judgement, the whole RFA $25 million losses have now been put to rest, with no accountability follow up against the senior officials who had been involved in Mr. Levy's work.

IX. A UNAT Judgement on UN Scapegoats: the Bangoura Case

On 5 January 1997, an article in the Washington Post claimed that Mr. Bangoura, a UNDCP staff fighting drug traffic operations in Africa, had committed sexual harassment towards a female colleague while serving in Africa and had also embezzled UN funds. On 9 January 1997, *only 4 days later*, the Office of the Secretary-General issued a press statement announcing that such misconduct would not be tolerated during his tenure as Secretary-General and that the staff member would be severed from service.

Except for a very flimsy and biased internal report, which had never been debated with Mr. Bangoura, there was no evidence whatsoever from the outset which could hold Mr. Bangoura guilty of these accusations. Nevertheless M. Bangoura lost his job, became a refugee, remained unemployed for more than 5 years and had to defend himself from outside the United Nations.

In April 1997, Mr. Bangoura filed an appeal before the Joint Appeals Board (JAB).

On 3 July 1998, the JAB recognized that the Office of the Secretary-General breached all the rules of due process, as well as that of presumption of innocence in Bangoura's case, by using publicly an "*information about the Appellant which he knew or ought to have known to be false*" [. . .] "*an improper use of discretion, was arbitrary and a denial of due process for the Appellant*". On 17 February 1999, more than *seven months later*, the Secretary-General finally took a decision on this JAB report, by rejecting its recommendation for a public apology and for a $20,000 compensation for defamation. The Secretary-General's decision on that JAB Report insisted "*that on substance however, there was ample justification for this decision*". On 28 February 1999, Bangoura filed an appeal before the UN Administrative Tribunal. It took almost *5 years* after his 1997 dismissal for a judgement to be issued on this case, mostly due to repetitive requests by the UN Legal Counsel for extensions and delays in the production of his pleas and arguments. On 21 November 2001, the Tribunal found that no disciplinary proceedings had ever been instituted against Mr. Bangoura, that he never had any opportunity to defend himself and that "*he was summarily judged by the press*" (XVI). The Tribunal endorsed the JAB findings that there was a major breach of due process in this case by the Administration and a violation of the rule of presumption of innocence. The Tribunal concluded to an "*abuse of power*" on the part of the United Nations and chastised the Office of the Secretary-General for "*disseminat[ing] information which has not been verified and that moreover is not later corroborated about a staff member whose reputation is permanently affected as a result . . .*" (XXI). Instead of the $20,000 compensation recommended by the JAB, the Tribunal awarded $150,000 in compensation for the damages suffered by Mr. Bangoura, a meager sum considering his sufferings and the *loss of employment during more than 5 years.* The Tribunal is legally constrained by a 2-year net base salary award limitation which is part of its Statute.

X. Recurring Defamation by the Office of the Secretary-General

Not much lessons appear to be learned from the Tribunal's judgements, and from its past awards for compensation, such as in the *Bangoura* case. Unfortunately, the low level of the compensation by the Tribunal often becomes an enticement for senior management to continue the same abuses. As recently as 17 March 2005, the Secretary-General again issued a press release announcing that he had summarily dismissed and suspended a dozen of UN staff members on charges of sexual abuses in the Congo. However, this announcement was again based on flimsy preliminary reports, without any prior judicial review or due process, and without credible evidence made available to the parties or to the public. This announcement was seen as another face-saving and politically-motivated device after the public outcry which had followed the Secretary-General's initial defense of the head of HCR sexual misconduct, before the latter finally decided to resign. Likewise, in early 2005, following the OFFP interim reports, and although they had not yet been found guilty before any accountability or disciplinary committee nor external courts, the Office of the Secretary-General announced publicly that it had suspended three staff members involved in the OFFP programme, causing them irreparable damages and slander to their reputation. Will the new accountability rules and the Management Performance Board's authority become applicable to the Office of the Secretary-General, and to those responsible for such defamation? In the absence of an independent external body to monitor and enforce accountability in these situations, one can expect discretionary authority to be used again to provide protection, impunity and immunity to those working in the Office of the Secretary-General, in order to use defamation whenever compelling public pressures or political opportunities call for a face-saving press release on accountability issues. Under present conditions, the long-arm of the Tribunal accompanied by its small monetary awards, do not constitute a strong deterrent against defamation originating from the Office of the Secretary-General.

XI. Insufficient Accountability Follow-Up by Member-States and Board of Auditors

With the above UNAT *Levy* judgement (No. 1034) confirming, that beside Mr. Levy, other senior UNDP officials also shared responsibilities in the $25 million losses, one would have expected the UN authorities and member-States to actively pursue the matter, and hold accountable his supervisors and the other officials who had the duty, at higher levels, to supervise and check Mr. Levy's work. Ten years after the facts and three years after this UNAT judgement has been issued, no follow up action has ever been taken by member-States (and even less by the UN Administration), and the whole RFA matter and its $25 million in losses appear to be forgotten . . . except for Mr. Levy "*holding the bag*" alone for his supervisors' improprieties and gross negligence. Except for the recovery of a few thousand dollars, the bulk of the $25 million in overpayments in the RFA construction projects has never been recovered from staff members, senior officials, contractors, architects and other persons responsible for these losses. Member-States sitting on the UNDP Executive Board or the new Board of External Auditors have little follow-up system and do not appear to have learned any lessons from the accountability collapse and financial losses in the RFA cases, despite the fact that taxpayers' money is involved. Only in 2004, through the compelling pressure from the press, the public and some governments, did the Secretary-General agree to an *external* and *independent* review of the losses and frauds surrounding the Iraq Oil-for-Food Programme. Other, similar corruption and fraudulent situations in the UN which warrant external and independent investigations will continue to elude the press, the public and member-States, as long as the accountability and enforcement systems remain as weak as they are now.

XII. Secrecy and Complacency Surrounding OIOS Reports and Investigations

Created in 1994, OIOS was compelled until recently by the Secretary-General to publish only heavily censured extracts of its audit reports and none of its investigations reports. Its most sensitive investigations were never reported to the Member-States of the UN General Assembly, and even less to their taxpayers. In 1999, Mr. Karl T. Paschke, the first USG in charge of OIOS, upon completing his 5-year tour of duty submitted a final report stating "*. . . further improvement within the United Nations is still necessary in many ways. Internal controls are not strong enough yet; accountability continues to be blurred and misunderstood; delegations of authority must be effectively executed and human resources management is in need of further reform . . .*".[11] Mr. Paschke's report concludes with examples of some audit recommendations where corrective actions have never been completed. On 9 January 2005, in the same line of conduct, the Volcker Commission disclosed a series of internal audit reports on the United Nations Oil-for-Food programme (OFFP)

[11] A/54/393 of 23/9/1999, page 8.

which, between 1999 to 2003, had remained without proper follow up by UN authorities, including by the Secretary-General and the Deputy-Secretary-General: "*The [OIOS] recommendations database shows that 22 critical recommendations were not implemented (page 7)*" and the Report suggests that a lack of internal controls at the UN may have encouraged the "*surcharge scheme*" which had plagued the OFFP management and led to billions of dollars in overpayments, bribes, corruption, etc. On 3 February 2005, for the first time in its history and under pressure from member-States, the Secretary-General has finally agreed to disclose and make available to those interested member-States the investigation reports produced by the Office of Investigation and Oversight Services (OIOS). But OIOS remains for now a service subordinated to the Secretary-General's Office (OSG), which can screen, filter, stall and overturn its audit and investigation recommendations, as it did in the Iraq Oil-for-Food Programme. It is widely expected that the Volcker mission, in its final report due in mid-2005, will recommend severing this subordination between OIOS and the OSG. On 20 March 2005, pre-empting the OFFP/ICC recommendations, the Secretary-General in his latest reform proposals has asked the General Assembly to "*commission a comprehensive review of OIOS with a view to strengthening its independence and authority, as well as its expertise and capacity*". As a result, in March 2005, an Oversight Committee was created, composed of five members with two members from outside. Taxpayers funding the United Nations should expect a genuine independent external enforcement body on accountability issues.

XIII. Failures of the *UN Accountability Board*

Despite a very clear Staff Rule 112.3 on the responsibility of UN officials for financial losses, the Secretary-General has never implemented most of UNAT's recommendations against its own senior officials (ex: judgements of the Tribunal Nos. 1052, 1008, 914, 887, etc. recommending sanctions against responsible UN senior officials). In 2000, great expectations were created by the constitution of the *Accountability Board.* But after 5 years of existence, it has yielded little or no results in accountability matters at the UN. This Board was constituted, *inter alia*, to study how UNAT judgments recommending the activation of Staff Rule 112.3 could be executed against responsible senior UN officials.[12] After 5 years of discussions, this Accountability Panel has yielded no tangible results in the enforcement of

[12] *Cf* ST/SGB/2014 of 23 October 2000.

accountability against senior UN officials, and the Secretary-General has recommended that it be disbanded, while the General Assembly asked that it be maintained with reinforced powers. In September 2004, the Secretary-General decided to vest new powers and authority into the Joint Disciplinary Committee, in order to address accountability and recovery issues involving senior UN officials[13] and, on 20 March 2005, announced the establishment of what is now called the new "*Management Performance Board*" in order to "*ensure that senior officials are held accountable for their actions* . . ." (see item V above and XXVII below).

XIV. Ethics and Standards of Conduct at the UN

During the 90's, extensive efforts were undertaken to update the 1954 Standards of Conduct into a new UN Code of Conduct in line with modern accountability and transparency practices. A first proposal was submitted on 17 October 1997 as a "*UN Code of Conduct*" to the General Assembly, but failed to get its approval (A/52/488 + Add.1). This first proposal had nothing in the nature of a codification but was rather a compendium of past practices combined with recent UNAT jurisprudence. It went as far as imposing on family members of staff members a duty to report their assets and investments, despite the absence of legal links between them and the UN. This draft Code was scrapped and a new version submitted in 1998 and approved by GA resolution 52/252 of 8 September 1998 under the title *Status, Basic Rights and Duties of United Nations Staff Members.* In this new version, article 1.2 (n) provides that only those staff members at the levels of ASG and above are required to make a financial disclosure in respect of themselves and their dependents on any "*transfers of assets and property*" . . . "*that might constitute a conflict of interest* . . .". This new issuance is considered as a complement to the 1954 *UN Standards of Conduct* and constitutes a major improvement on accountability issues, but remains without a proper enforcement machinery which would include a fair and efficient internal justice machinery at the United Nations. While the UN Joint Disciplinary Committee (JDC) has been used over the years to prosecute staff members mostly at the P.5 level and lower, for financial improprieties and losses, no senior UN official was ever prosecuted before a JDC panel. Internal justice at the UN has maintained a double standard for lower level and for senior officials, with impunity applied to the latter

[13] *Cf* ST/AI 2004/3.

group in most cases. *Public reporting* of disciplinary and accountability cases involving lower level staff are published annually in circulars at UNDP, at the UN Secretariat, and elsewhere.[14] But the outcome of cases involving the most senior officials are never reported (unless public pressure compels the Secretary-General to disclosure, such as in the cases of a USG targeted by the OFFP/ICC report or of the High Commissioner of HRC or a UNDCP Director-General who resigned from their functions).

XV. Integrity of Senior Management at the United Nations

Unfortunately for its work atmosphere, double-standards are endemic in the accountability and in the internal justice systems at the UN, and have created a major confidence crisis between the Organization's 18,000 staff members and its senior officials, as observed in the June 2004 "*Integrity Report*" produced by Deloitte Consultants and commissioned by OIOS. This survey indicates that the majority of staff have no confidence in senior management. Similar global staff surveys conducted annually in the 140 offices of UNDP have come to the same conclusion in recent years. On 4 June 2004, the Secretary-General had to issue a defensive letter on the UN survey in order to qualify its contents, as well as the "*perceptions by staff members*". "*Nevertheless,* writes Mr. Kofi Annan, *staff believe that not enough action is taken to investigate and address instances of unethical behaviour, and those who expose such breaches may put themselves at risk of reprisal. Staff also perceive that the disciplinary process is applied unevenly and that the outcome of the process is generally not known*". Mr. Annan concluded his letter on a positive note stating "*We will inform all staff about the means available to them for reporting on suspected misconduct. We will also develop measures to reinforce formal protection for whistle-blowers, while ensuring that they are not used to cloak false accusations*". Again, on 3 January 2005, Mr. Annan wrote another letter to staff members promising "*stronger protection for whistle-blowers*" and "*internal justice procedures which are more transparent, more effective and fully in line with modern management practices*". At the date of completion of this article, more than one year later, the "*the means and measures*" promised in order to protect whistle-blowers and to improve the internal justice system at the UN, which instead will be the subject of a review Panel constituted of independent experts.[15]

---

14 See, for example, UN/ST/IC/2004/28, UNDP/ADM/2001/18, UNDP/ADM/2002/33, etc.

15 Pls. supply.

XVI. Contempt Towards the UN Administrative Tribunal Judgements

Another example of inaction by the UN on accountability matters: on 30 September 2003, the UN Administrative Tribunal requested in its judgment No. 1123 that UN authorities investigate procurement and construction irregularities in its Nepal/UNFPA offices, where reports of losses, bribes, corruption, cover up by UN senior officials and other improprieties had led to overpayments and major losses. The prosecutor investigating the matter had been arbitrarily and suddenly removed from this case by UNDP and UNFPA, in the middle of his investigation, which then grinded to a halt:

> Para. XIII: The Tribunal was also alarmed that, allegedly, efforts were made by the Administration to hinder the investigation of issues related . . . to irregularities and mismanagement that took place in the Nepal office. The Tribunal's apprehension arises from the alleged improper removal of a legal advisor involved in, and concerned with, the investigation. (. . .) The Tribunal feels that such allegations deserve further investigation by the appropriate UN authorities.

The legal advisor removed from that case wrote in January 2004 to the Secretary-General asking that the investigation sought by the Tribunal take place. Other parties also wrote to the Secretary-General seeking such investigation. In a 28 October 2004 statement sent to the UN Administrative Tribunal, in the Alok case the UN Legal Counsel replied, that the investigation requested by the Tribunal would *not* take place. In a recent judgment of 31 January 2005 (No. 1217), the Administrative Tribunal complained again against the UN authorities' failure to investigate the removal of the legal advisor in charge of the Nepal corruption and overpayment cases:

> The Tribunal recalls that it had occasion earlier, in its judgement No 1123, Alok (2003), to express its concerns about what was happening at UNDP in relation to the treatment of [the legal advisor removed from his duties]. . . .

With the enemy of time, the loss of evidence and the unavailability of witnesses any meaningful investigation of this corruption case becomes elusive. A Tribunal judgement on accountability is once more stifled by an Administration reluctant to hold accountable senior UN officials responsible for financial losses.

XVII. The Tribunal's Limitations on Internal Accountability and Justice Systems

The very restrictive authority given by member-States to the Tribunal contributes to protect the impunity of senior officials. Under normal conditions, one would expect the Tribunal to be able to take a more proactive stance on any major issue related to the organization and administration of justice at the United Nations. But a recent judgement of 31 January 2005 (No. 1217) indicates that its authority is constrained on such issues. In that case, the Administrative Tribunal was asked to pass judgement on two important issues related to the independence of the internal justice system at the UN, including the role and protection of prosecutors investigating criminal cases. One question was related to the UNDP management's unilateral *re-engineering* and changes in the internal accountability and justice system at UNDP. The litigation arose in September 1999 when the UNDP Chief of its Legal Section asked the UNDP Administrator for an investigation on the arbitrary closure of many accountability and recovery cases without any prior review or prosecution against the culprits, and in which the Organization had suffered losses in the millions of dollars. Besides vendors and contractors, many senior officials were involved in these bribes, corruption, improprieties and overpayments. On 7 October 1999, the UNDP Administrator replied to the Chief, Legal Section promising him an *independent investigation*, and asking him for more information on these bribery and corruption cases, and on other abuses. In December 1999, after detailed information was forwarded to the Administrator by the Chief, Legal Section, the UNDP Administrator took two (2) decisions: a) *abolition of the post of the Chief, Legal Section* (who had sought the investigation), b) *re-engineering of that internal justice post merging it with procurement matters*. On the issue of *re-engineering* of the UNDP internal justice system:

> V. The Tribunal notes, first of all, that many criticisms were raised during the course of the reorganization process. Although it does not appear that the Consultative Group on Staff Matters was formally consulted and asked to comment on the proposed reform, the UNDP Staff Council expressed its views and said that it was very concerned about the establishment of the new structure; it indicated, as reported in a memorandum dated 28 April 2000, that the new office could give rise to a number of conflicts of interest, namely:
>
> - the possible conflict of interest arising from merging the regular procurement functions with legal functions;
> - the possible conflict of interest of having any kind of audit functions situated in OLPS; and, finally,
> - the perceived conflict of interest of the function reporting to the Director, [Bureau of Management], who also has management responsibility and accountability for the Human Resources management function in the organization.

> Moreover, in a letter dated 14 July 2000, the Council said that "[a]lthough the Staff Council agreed not to question structural decisions and to concentrate on implementation, we cannot do so in this case because structure is key to an independent internal justice system". . . .
>
> "It is true, as the Assistant Administrator and Director, Bureau of Management, in the above-cited letter dated 28 April 2000, addressed to the Administrator acknowledged: "I do not dismiss that there could be situations of conflict of interest between the procurement advisory function and the legal function".

The Tribunal notes that the statutory bodies of Staff Regulation VIII have not been consulted in this reform of the internal justice system at UNDP, and that only one of its Staff Unions was able to express its strong objections on the proposed reforms, but did not consider this lack of mandatory consultation on the internal justice system as a major procedural violation. This is understandable for a Tribunal whose jurisdiction is essentially limited to *individual* staff grievances and prohibited from substituting itself to or judging the Administration, in its managerial decisions where *discretionary powers* still prevail. The Tribunal will rarely interfere with any internal reorganization, even in a case such as this one where it may affect the whole internal justice system:

> IV. With regard to the restructuring, the Tribunal recalls that it has consistently held that the reorganization of administrative services falls within the discretionary powers of the Administration . . . The Tribunal's findings in Raj are particularly pertinent here.
>
> V.
>
> II. The Tribunal has previously held that decisions of this nature fall within the discretionary powers of the Administration and that it is not within the Tribunal's competence to examine whether a given office should be organized in any particular way or whether better results would be obtained if a reorganization took or failed to take place (Judgement No. 117, Van der Valk [1968]).

Of course, the Tribunal will verify, as it always does, that discretionary powers have not been exercised arbitrarily, as it also indicated in Raj:

> III. According to the Tribunal's consistent jurisprudence, the only possibility for a staff member to challenge a decision of the Administration on these matters is to prove that such a decision was vitiated by prejudice or some other improper motive.
>
> IV. The mere fact that a reorganization may hinder the prospects or in any way affect the career of a staff member does not necessarily point to the existence of discrimination or improper motives in the Administration and thus does not in itself give grounds for any claim against the decision taken.

Unless the Tribunal's Statutes, competence and jurisdiction are modified and extended to control reforms affecting the internal justice system, this judgement No. 1217 opens the door in the future for more unilateral changes in the UN justice system by the Administration which can derail any effort to institute a genuine accountability and internal justice system at the United Nations. Since this jurisprudence recognize no mandatory role to the Staff Unions nor to the Tribunal to criticize or comment on "*whether a given office should be organized in any particular way or whether better results would be obtained if a reorganization took or failed to take place*", senior UN officials can continue to impose an internal justice system which offers them impunity, while denying fairness to staff members. Any reform of the internal justice system, including accountability enforcement, requires that such *discretionary power* of the UN administration over accountability and internal justice be abolished, and revert to member-States' control or to some external monitoring bodies.

XVIII. A "Surprising" UNDP Reform of its Internal Justice System

The Tribunal expressed its "*surprise*" at the UNDP "*reorganization*" which had merged internal justice responsibilities with procurement decisions:

> Although it may seem surprising, viewed from the outside that the same office should be in charge of concluding procurement contracts and of taking the legal measures necessitated by irregularities in such contracts . . .

After its "surprise", the Tribunal stopped short of commenting on the substance of such a reorganization of the internal justice system at UNDP was again compelled to accept a reform of the internal justice and accountability systems at face-value, without much screening or control of the "*larger picture*" "*viewed from the outside*". The Tribunal was compelled to restrict its findings and limit its judgement on how such a reform of the justice system may have deprived one individual staff member of his rights or violated his conditions of work. Instead of judging the whole reform *per se*, the Tribunal had to impose on the Appellant a *subjective* burden of proof demonstrating through this reform of the justice system the existence of discrimination or improper motives against an individual staff member, as if this reform was only of interest or concern for one staff member. With no class action allowed before the Tribunal, such burden of proof imposed on one individual staff member, rather than on the Administration itself to prove the validity of this internal justice reform, reinforces the very restrictive Statute and limited jurisdiction of the Tribunal, limiting its competence *ratione materiae* only to staff members' grievances and to their individual conditions of work. Member-States should consider revising the Tribunal's Statutes in order to enable it to judge such reforms not only in the light of *individual subjective* considerations raised by a staff members, but also on *objective* factors such as the basic principles applicable to all civilized judicial systems, such as recognized by the United Nations' own Basic Principles on Judicial Independence, on the Role of Lawyers and Prosecutors, etc., (which are applicable to all member-States' judicial systems). With the Tribunal's decision not to interfere in this reform of the accountability and internal justice systems, the final responsibility and accountability for this restructuring currently rests solely on senior UN officials, one of the two opposing parties in all Tribunal cases, whose record of integrity and impartiality are often questioned (as shown by the recent scandals and Tribunal judgements). A genuine external and independent enforcement and monitoring body should oversee the administration of justice at the UN, rather than be left to the Administration which is already a party as Defendant in all internal justice cases, and whose Legal Counsel represents and often defends unacceptable abuses, improper conduct and improprieties by senior UN officials.

XIX. Integrity and protection of prosecutors at the UN

In this same judgement No. 1217, the Tribunal was invited to address the issue of protecting the role of legal advisors and prosecutors at the United Nations, who are charged with prosecuting corruption, bribery and other criminal cases:

> Some of [the Applicant's] requests – for example, that the Secretary-General should establish "a protection mechanism to ensure the reliability, professionalism, integrity and independence of lawyers working within the administration of justice at the United Nations" – are completely outside the competence of the Tribunal and thus will not be addressed.

This lack of "*ratione materia competence*" by the Tribunal to develop a jurisprudence on such important issues as the autonomy of prosecutors in the discharge of their duties and on the implementation of the *UN Basic Principles on the Role of Lawyers and Prosecutors*, is most unfortunate, as it deprives the Organization, its managers and its legal advisors of clear professional and ethical guidelines in the conduct of accountability and disciplinary cases. The Secretary-General, June 2004, recognized that the UN *Human Rights* declarations, statements and principles applied also to the United Nations, and that the UN, in its internal management, never would "*wilfully*" breach the Basic Principles of the Global Compact (which include the *UN Basic Principles on the Role of Lawyers and Prosecutors*). The June 2004 commitment by the Secretary-General to integrate the 1999 *Global Compact Principles* and all its related international covenants in the UN internal management is closely linked with accountability and internal justice. Member-States should ensure that actions are taken to implement the Global Compact in the UN internal management.

XX. A $100,000 Sentence against UNDP for Bias, Violations and Discrimination in its Appointment of the Director in Charge of Accountability and of the Internal Justice System

While the Tribunal maintained its traditional approach regarding "*internal reorganization*" of justice and accountability services at the United Nations (and at UNDP in particular), its judgment No. 1217 took a stricter approach on the Administration's violation of its own appointment procedures in the case concerning the appointment of the Director in charge of accountability and internal justice matters at UNDP, where the Administrator decided to eliminate arbitrarily the director of its Legal Section and appoint his own favorite candidate:

> VI. With regard to the procedure for selecting the new Director, **the fact that the reorganization as such is not censured by the Tribunal does not necessarily mean that its implementation, which resulted in the elimination of the Applicant, might not have been effected in a manner that violated the Applicant's rights**. With respect to the procedure followed in choosing the new Director, it is the Tribunal's consistent jurisprudence that it cannot substitute its assessment for that of the Secretary-General in relation to the evaluation of a candidate . . . **However, the Tribunal has always reserved the right to verify that the Administration's discretionary power of appointment was not exercised in an arbitrary manner** and, in particular, that the established procedures were followed (see Judgements No. 1056, Katz (2002) and No. 1122, Lopes Braga (2003)).[16]

The Tribunal then reviewed and weighed the procedures followed by the UNDP Administrator leading to the appointment of the new Director in charge of internal justice and accountability matters:

> The selection panel for the new post of Director of OLPS met on 11 July 2000 and interviewed the two short-listed candidates: the Applicant, who was at the D-1 level and was Chief of the Legal Section, **responsible in that capacity for the internal justice system at UNDP**, and Mr. S., who was at the P-5 level and was Chief of the Policy and Control Unit, Inter-Agency Procurement Services Office. On 7 August 2000, the panel's rec-

[16] Emphasis added.

> ommendation was submitted to the Executive Team, consisting of senior managers of UNDP and chaired by the Administrator.[17]

And the Tribunal concludes on the selection and appointment procedures:

> XXI. This serious procedural irregularity, as the Applicant sees it, was just one aspect of a *broader pattern of biased treatment* of the Applicant by the Administration. The file is full of examples cited by the Applicant as demonstrating, in his view, highly discriminatory treatment against him. The Tribunal recalls that it had occasion earlier, in its Judgement No. 1123, Alok (2003), paragraph XIII, to express its concerns about what was happening at UNDP in relation to the treatment of the Applicant . . .
>
> XXV. For these reasons, the Tribunal:
> Finds that the recruitment of the Director of OLPS was carried out in **violation of applicable procedures** and in addition was vitiated by **discriminatory** factors . . .[18]

This strong condemnation by the Tribunal on the UNDP Administrator's violations of procedures and discrimination, in order to fill a key post dedicated to the enforcement of accountability and to the internal justice system, is a Member-States should consider the creation of an external enforcement and monitoring body to oversee the appointment processes in the administration of justice at the United Nations.

XXI. New Legal Approaches on Accountability and Financial Recoveries at the UN

On 29 September 2004, under the pressure of the Oil-for-Food scandal, the Secretary-General issued a new circular on *Financial Responsibility of Staff Members for Gross Negligence*[19] which, for the first time at the United Nations, spells out a formal machinery to prosecute financial losses under the authority of article 112.3 of Staff Rules. The circular empowers the existing Joint Disciplinary Committee with the authority to hear such financial recovery cases. A similar experiment had taken place at UNDP in 1997, where circular ADM/97/17 on "*Accountability and Disciplinary Measures and Procedures*" had empowered the UNDP Disciplinary Committee to hear accountability and financial responsibility/recovery cases stemming from Staff Rule 112.3. However, in the past at UNDP, its Disciplinary Committee mem-

[17] *Idem.*
[18] *Idem.*
[19] ST/AI/2004/3.

bers have squarely declined to exercise the joint responsibility of judging disciplinary together with financial responsibility cases, as can be seen, for example, in the *Levy* (UNAT No. 1034), *Alok* (UNAT No. 1123), *Gowandan*, etc. cases. In the recent *Alok* case, the UNDP/UNFPA Disciplinary Committee clearly refused to pass judgement on Mr. Alok's financial responsibility, and asked the administration to undertake such a review in the first place. Despite such setbacks and negative experiences, without consulting staff representatives, the UN Secretariat hastily drafted and promulgated in September 2004 circular ST/AI/2004/3 amending the rules applicable to its Joint Disciplinary Committee (JDC), together with an information circular explaining the new accountability and recovery processes. We will review its potential to become an efficient and genuine machinery to enforce accountability and recovery matters at the UN Secretariat.

XXII. The JDC Limited Jurisdiction on Recoveries

Under this new circular ST/AI/2004/3, not all financial losses come under the JDC's jurisdiction. In the first place, losses suffered by the Organization resulting "*from inadvertent error, oversight or simple negligence, or inability to foresee the negative consequences of a chosen course of action*" will not be prosecuted but addressed within the annual performance appraisal review system (PAS). Hence, only "*gross negligence*" will be prosecuted before the JDC, which is defined "*1.3 . . . negligence of a very high degree involving an extreme and willful or reckless failure to act as a reasonable person in applying or in failing to apply the regulations and rules of the Organization . . .*". "*1.4 . . . disciplinary action and recovery action for financial losses shall be consolidated whenever grounds exist to initiate both actions*". This definition of "gross negligence" stems from the *Eren, Robertson, et al* judgement (No. 744) of the Tribunal related to the Skylink scandal, where it stated:

> There might be instances when failures in performance are of such extreme dimension as to constitute misconduct for which disciplinary measures would be reasonable. In the circumstances here, the Tribunal does not find that the performance matters mentioned by the JDC are of this nature, absent the wrongful intent originally charged. . . .

As a result of this *Eren* judgement, the JDC is not expected to be seized of any sub-standard performance cases causing losses for the Organization, unless it reaches "*such extreme dimension*" and becomes a "*gross negligence*" case. Another exception to the JDC jurisdiction in the ST/AI/2004/3 circular are *losses to UN property* caused by gross negligence, which will continue to be judged by the UN "*Property Survey Board*" (PSB) in accordance with UN

Financial Rule 105.21. Consequently, losses on a UN vehicle resulting from a staff member's drunken or reckless driving would end up before a PSB, rather than the JDC. The PSB can order recovery of financial losses, but no disciplinary sanctions against the drunken driver. Consequently, in such cases, any disciplinary measure or charge of drunken or reckless driving against the culprit would have to be submitted separately to a JDC, where the staff member would find himself in double jeopardy. It would be in the interest of the Organization and of staff members to harmonize and resolve these conflicts of jurisdiction.

XXIII. Enforcement of UNAT Judgements by the JDC

The question arises whether the new jurisdiction given to the JDC by ST/AI 2004/3 will include cases where the Tribunal in its judgments requests the Secretary-General to implement Staff Rule 112.3 against the responsible staff member(s). In recent years, many Tribunal judgements requested the Secretary-General to implement Staff Rule 112.3 against staff members involved or responsible for "*maladministration, détournement of procedures and other abuses*" which had led to huge financial compensation and awards by the Tribunal (see above para. XIII). However, no subsequent recovery action against senior officials were ever pursued by the Secretary-General on these orders from the Tribunal, under the pretext that due process was required in any recovery procedure, which would require a *de novo* hearing. In practice, when 5 or 6 years had lapsed after the improprieties have been committed, when most witnesses have disappeared, when the complainants have sometime retired or died, when the paper-track and documentary evidence have disappeared, it is doubtful that the culprits can ever be prosecuted before a JDC, with due process for all the parties. For example, in the *Alok* judgement (No. 1123) quoted above, the initial incidents arose in 1998–99 in Nepal. Since then, most staff members concerned by these incidents have retired or been separated from service. The main victim, Mr. Alok, has retired to India and is under medical treatment. The local witnesses on the bribery and corruption may have moved or died. The lawyer representing Mr. Alok has retired in Asia. The legal advisor and prosecutor handling these cases at UNDP has been removed and has retired to his home country. The 30 September 2003 judgement by UNAT seeking the conduct of an investigation has never received any follow up by the Secretary-General. In those conditions, it is difficult to see how the Joint Disciplinary Committee could exercise its new jurisdiction under ST/AI 2004/3. It is clear, by now, that all those senior officials who may have been involved in the financial losses which have occurred in the *Alok* case will not face justice, and no recovery will take place against any of them. If the current excessive delays of 5–7 years prevailing in the UN internal justice system before a final judgement in a Tribunal case, it is doubtful that the new ST/AI/2004/3 circular will become more efficient in prosecuting those staff members responsible of gross negligence and financial losses, after so many years, even when a Tribunal judgement recommends taking action. To really have an impact and some bite, this new ST/AI circular should allow for a preliminary investigation and preemptive action to be undertaken immediately when such potential financial losses for the UN are identified by OIOS or at the Audit level, and no later then when an Application is filed at the Tribunal.

XXIV. Conduct of Accountability and Recovery Investigations

The new ST/AI/2004/3 circular also provides in its Section 3 that a preliminary investigation on allegations of gross negligence will be undertaken either under the authority of the head of department where the staff is employed, or by the UN Controller or by OIOS. In cases, where the head of a department is himself charged with gross negligence leading to financial losses, the investigation will be undertaken by the UN Controller (unless OIOS decides to take over). This diversity of investigations is conducive to serious inconsistencies in the internal justice system. These preliminary investigations must be concluded and "*completed within 6 months unless extraordinary circumstances arise . . .*". The circular also provides for the suspension from duty of the staff member, whenever circumstances warrant such action. Furthermore, to avoid an abuse so often seen at the United Nations during previous financial scandals, a staff member will not be allowed to separate nor retire before or during such investigation and disciplinary proceedings. If the staff still decides to separate, the Controller can withhold "*final separation payments until the proceedings have been concluded (section 3.6)*". In 2004, it will be noted that when that circular had been issued, some of the most senior officials (ASGs and USGs) blamed or designated by the Iraq Oil-for-Food Enquiry had retired or were allowed to retire and to get their pensions and entitlements before their accountability and responsibility could be investigated.

XXV. Discrimination Between Staff Members of Different Levels

Most likely unintentional, the new ST/AI/2004/3 provisions nevertheless underline some major flaws and current weaknesses in the United Nations internal administration of justice. In anticipation that some of its senior officials will be prosecuted for gross negligence recovery cases, the new circular provides that JDC panels hearing such cases must be constituted "*by members at least the same as the level of the staff member*" being prosecuted. This measure has the effect of weakening the value of other disciplinary cases where a mixture of staff members at different levels (D1–P-GS) is applied in the hearing of disciplinary cases. Under this new provision, only UN senior officials at the levels of D-2, ASG or USG would sit on JDC Panels to judge colleagues of the same level. Lower level staff members would be excluded. The whole collegial spirit, the *equality of treatment* between staff members and the peer traditions in the UN administration of justice is destroyed by this new system where participation by lower level staff members is excluded. Furthermore, proceedings taking place between work colleagues of "*the same level*" will inevitably raise suspicions, knowing how in a small milieu such as the United Nations, senior officials fraternize in the same clubs, activities and meetings. In a similar situation in 1992 in the *Claxton* case (UNAT Nos. 560 & 798), the UN Secretary-General attempted to set up a Panel made up of USGs only, in order to review allegations of sexual harassment filed by a female staff against a USG. This proposal was heavily criticized at the time and was finally abandoned, the matter being ultimately investigated by an ILOAT judge (after which the USG resigned). Likewise, whenever JDC Panels are made up exclusively of USGs, or of ASGs or of D2s, one can expect the whole credibility of such panels to be questioned and challenged whenever any major issue of gross negligence or financial losses is prosecuted before such Panels under this new ST/AI/2004/3 circular.

XXVI. A Fifth Wheel in the Conduct of JDC Recovery Cases

The ST/AI/2004/3 circular innovates in the internal justice system, by the introduction of a new player: an *ex officio representative from the Office of Legal Affairs acting in "an advisory capacity" to the JDC Panel.* This measure is difficult to understand within the context of the UN administration of justice. The JDC already uses a Secretary and assistant-secretaries who have legal backgrounds and expertise and are familiar with disciplinary proceedings and due process. In addition, disciplinary cases at the United Nations are already prosecuted by lawyers working in the Administrative Law Unit of OHRM. The addition of a fifth member, a legal officer from OLA, to participate in the JDC Panel *in an advisory capacity* either seems to indicate that the two other legal officers already representing the Administration in disciplinary proceedings are unable to do their work and must receive the support of one more lawyer, or that JDC Panel members are not competent enough to hear such cases and make a judgement by themselves. As a matter of due process, challenges can be expected on the role and participation of one more legal officer in the deliberations of a JDC panel, unless the accused staff member and/or his counsel is also allowed to be present, debate and challenge any *advice* given by the OLA legal officer during these proceedings. If no such due process is made available on the OLA legal officer's *advice*, it may appear as a covert measure to unduly influence the JDC Panel members, and may eventually be challenged before the UN Administrative Tribunal. This idea of an *ex officio* representative from OLA should be abandoned, considering that OLA represents the Administration in these same cases which will eventually be appealed before the Tribunal. The conflict of interest is too obvious, or the functions of OLA should be changed.

XXVII. An Impractical Recovery Tool for the Iraq OFFP Accountability Cases

The new ST/AI/2004/3 issued by the Secretary-General was meant, amongst other cases, to respond to the OFFP disciplinary and recovery cases. But it may prove most elusive and impractical. The UN Office of Legal Affairs is in a major conflict of interest in the OFFP scandals and few (or none) of its legal officers could impartially sit on any JDC Panel as an *ex officio* advisor to offer legal opinions on the professional conduct of two of their most prominent colleagues. On the one hand, the Under Secretary-General of the Office of Legal Affairs (Mr. Hans Corell) was himself a key member of the OFFP Steering Committee which was found by the OFFP/ICC to have ignored UN procurement rules, UN Financial Rules and failed in its oversight of the OFFP. And, another senior legal officer formerly with OLA and who chaired the UN Contracts Committee could also be charged with improperly approving many irregular procurement contracts or for ignoring violations committed in the award and administration of contracts. According to the OFFP/IIC, the lack of oversight and monitoring and the procurement violations in the award of contracts, led to briberies, corruption and to huge financial losses for the OFFP. With 2 of the most senior legal officials of the United Nations deeply involved in questionable procurement actions, the *surprise* expressed by the Tribunal in case No. 1217, on the merger of procurement and internal justice matters, takes all its meaning (see para XVIII above).

XXVIII. The New *Management Performance Board* (MPB)

The Secretary-General issued on 5 May 2005 a circular on the establishment of this new internal justice machinery, which supposedly will target the conduct and performance of senior UN officials, and is empowered to create "*a system of peer review to ensure adherence to acceptable standards of managerial conduct*" (art. 1.1c of ST/SGB/2005/13). At first glance, the concept of a jurisdiction of exception reserved exclusively for senior UN officials will confirm the current practice of double standards at the United Nations in accountability and internal justice matters. This new machinery will most likely raise the same objections mentioned above in our paragraphs XXIII–XXV. Furthermore, without an external enforcement and monitoring system to control and verify the work of the new MPB, including the Secretary-General's decisions on future MPB recommendations, the credibility of this new scheme will remain highly questionable.

XXIX. The Challenge of Matching Collegiality, Delegations of Authority and Accountability at the United Nations

Collegiality in decision-making is a basic tenet of the United Nations management. As seen in the OFFP/ICC Inquiry reports, all the USGs who were members of the OFFP Steering Committee acted in a collegial fashion, with none of them accepting individually to take the blame for any of the OFFP decisions. This approach is the opposite of what accountability means, and of the jurisprudence in the *Levy* and in other disciplinary and Tribunal cases where *individual* staff members are held accountable. The United Nations operates with hundreds of such steering committees in its operations, where decisions are often taken in a collegial fashion, through the participation of many work colleagues in the deliberations. If the pretext of collegiality prevails, no accountability at senior levels will ever be possible. As seen in the *Levy, Alok* and other cases, delineating the respective responsibilities between supervisees and supervisors at the UN remains one of the most daunting challenge, which has derailed most of the previous efforts to devise an efficient accountability and internal justice system. It is not rare that staff members will have two, three or more supervisors to whom to report, creating a confusion in the line of authority. The job descriptions are often inexistent or not updated to the reality of the posts. Classification of posts and salaries are often decided in an arbitrary fashion. Accountability, as mentioned in Mr. Paschke's final Report "*continues to be blurred and misunderstood*" in the United Nations environment (above para. XII). Delegations of authority at the UN are also inefficient and have too often become a one-way street where responsibilities are ultimately discharged on lower staff. In such a context, any litigation surrounding accountability and recovery issues inevitably falls into byzantine debates on the respective responsibilities within the UN hierarchy, where the upper-hand always belong to senior officials who currently control the conduct and handling of internal justice cases.

XXX. Towards a Genuine Accountability System at the UN: a Few Solutions

A. Enforcement Authority at the UN on Accountability Matters

Past experiences, such as the OFFP, RFA and other scandals indicate that little or no credible internal enforcement of accountability policies is feasible through the UN senior management itself, which holds a position tantamount to being a judge and party in most cases. History shows that the Secretary-General, with all his other political responsibilities, has little time or interests for internal controls which, in the past 20 years have been delegated and diluted in the UN hierarchy. Only under great pressure, when the credibility of the whole internal justice machinery is low, such as in the OFFP and Claxton situations, will the Secretary-General resort to external investigators. Such use of external expertise to enforce and monitor accountability within the UN should be institutionalized on a permanent basis. The new MPB and ST/AI 2004/3 extending the JDC jurisdiction in accountability are insufficient measures to re-establish efficient internal controls and confidence. They will do little to alleviate the criticism against the United Nations' incapacity to deal objectively with its own accountability problems. In view of the United Nations failures to establish a sound and efficient accountability and internal justice system, Member-States and taxpayers throughout the world should seek the constitution of an interagency independent external enforcement body which would oversee accountability and responsibility issues involving senior officials of these organizations. In addition, this external enforcement and monitoring body could review cases submitted by whistle-blowers and by harassment victims who are now currently left without recourse and in a legal limbo at the United Nations. The status of OIOS could also be modified in order to play a proactive role in this external enforcement and monitoring agency, provided that other substantial changes take place also in its staffing, resources and corporate culture. This enforcement agency could become the corporate memory which is now missing at the member-States level, and could ensure a transparent follow-up on all cases of corruption, financial losses, bribery, etc.

B. Professionalism in the Adjudication of Cases at the JAB and JDC Levels

In the last 20 years, the JAB and JDC fact-finding systems at the United Nations have become deficient, unreliable and inconsistent. In their current format, the JAB and JDC panels can bring little contribution to the UN accountability and recovery efforts, even with the changes proposed in ST/AI/2003/4. The recent amendment to staff rule 110.7(e) adding an OLA *ex officio* advisor in accountability and recovery cases is a sign that the Administration has little confidence in the current fact-finding system. The 1995 consensus reached between the Administration and the Staff Unions aiming to professionalize and to improve the accountability and internal justice system at the UN should be revived. This 1995 reform, introducing professional Arbitration Boards at the UN was initially stalled for budgetary reasons and as a result of some disagreements on the appointment of the chairpersons to the Arbitration Board. The Administration has recently agreed that Management and Staff representatives will "*select jointly*" the list of presiding officers at the JAB (ST/SGB/2003/1 para. F). Consequently, there is no more reason to further delay the Arbitration Board reform, nor to maintain the current pre-litigation system which needs to be seriously overhauled. In the absence of Staff-Management consultative meetings in recent years, the General Assembly should intervene between the Administration and the Staff Associations in order to facilitate a solution for the appointment of chairpersons, in order to re-introduce this reform which would provide a fair and credible system of justice and accountability at the UN. With the General Assembly Resolution 59/283 to constitute a "*panel of external independent experts to consider redesigning the administration of justice system*" (see Annex VIII) lessons and experiences can be learned from a similar consultation which took place in 1994–1995 and led to a consensus between all parties.

C. Judicial Costs in the UN Internal Justice System and OLA's Role

In 2003, the Administration has issued an amendment to Staff Rules allowing staff members to be represented by members of the Bar, practicing outside the United Nations, in cases submitted before the JAB or JDC. External counsels were already allowed before the Tribunal, which occasionally awards symbolic amounts for legal costs to the winning staff member. The participation of recognized jurists at the JAB and JDC levels to represent staff members was considered a major victory for due process and an improvement for the UN internal justice system, considering that very few professional jurists are available and taking justice cases, within the UN staff ranks. But a few months after adopting this amendment, the

Staff Rule was again amended stating that the attorney's fees would only *be at the staff member's own expense*, regardless of the outcome of the case. This approach is a major injustice and equivalent to a spoliation of the staff member's basic rights and assets. It also discriminates between categories of staff, when the Administration pays its lawyers top fees and salaries to defend its senior officials who have committed improprieties, but denies the same privilege to staff members whose lawyers win their cases. This policy is also a major deterrent in the sound administration of justice, as it discourages staff from defending their legitimate rights, and it encourages the Administration to pay its own lawyers to pursue frivolous and undefendable cases, a situation which already in the 1980s was heavily criticized. In the judicial systems of most member-States, costs are always awarded against the party loosing a case, subject to judicial discretion and review. The current system at the UN encourages what a former UN Legal Counsel called *defending the most undefendable cases*, up to the Tribunal, thus wasting precious time and resources of the Organization and of its staff members. In order to maintain a genuine accountability and internal justice system, legal costs should be awarded to the staff counsel winning a case. The legal fees could at least be the equivalent of the time, salary or fees the Administration has paid its own counsel to defend and loose the case. Recovery of these legal costs should then take place in accordance with Staff Rule 112.3, against the UN officials responsible for loosing the case.

D. Eliminating Delays and Violations of the Rules of Procedure by the Administration

The UN Administration has a long history and a track-record of systematically violating statutory time-limits at the Tribunal and at the Joint Appeals Board, and in other internal justice cases. Filing of the Respondent's Responses are also regularly delayed by 6 to 12 months, and sometime even more. Final decisions by the Secretary-General on Joint Appeals Board and Joint Disciplinary Committee reports and recommendations are delayed by over a year in many cases. Article 16 of resolution A/59/283 (Annex VIII) provides that strict time-limits will become *mandatory* within the appeals process, possibly as of 1 January 2006 ("*once adequate capacity is in place*"). However, no enforcement measures are in place to implement this measure. Statutory penalty should be instituted in compensation for any excessive delay which is not mutually agreed between the Parties. Another option, once the Administration has exceeded the statutory time-limits to present its Response, would be to allow the staff member to change of venue and submit his or her case directly to the Tribunal.

E. No Limits on the Tribunal's Judicial Awards

There will never be any genuine accountability system at the UN, as long as the current impunity system is maintained, whereby the worst abuses against the dignity, the health, the life and the reputation of victims yields only a few thousand dollars for local staff members, and not much more than $100,000 to $200,000 for international staff members. The current low compensation system constitutes a victory and a reward for the abusers and for the violators, rather than for the victims. It greatly contributes to the deteriorating work atmosphere at the United Nations and to the loss of confidence towards its senior officials, as observed in all the staff surveys of recent years. The limits on the Tribunal awards for compensation should therefore be abolished.

F. Stopping Defamatory Press Releases by the OSG

The OSG should stop or rethink its practice of press releases, when the internal course of justice has not been completed in accountability and disciplinary cases. Otherwise, these press releases not only harm the reputation of staff members whose case have not yet been heard, but also harm the prospect of a fair and impartial trial.

G. Protection of Prosecutors Against Obstruction

The Secretary-General should make good on his promise to implement the Global Compact Principles, including all the related internal Covenants, Agreements, Treaties, Basic Principles on Judicial Independence and on the Role of Prosecutors. In case of abuses or obstruction in the discharge of their duties, UN prosecutors should be allowed to appeal directly to their national Bar Association or Law Societies, or to the Tribunal or to an external enforcement body to whom UN prosecutors should report and be accountable. Lawyers working at OLA should be free to refuse to take cases which, in their conscience and professional ethics, they deem to be legally unconscionable. Financial Rules and Regulations at the UN should be amended in order to allow and facilitate the settlement of cases rather than impede such settlements as is the case now.

H. Conflicts of Interest and Ethical Issues

Conflicts of interest are pervasive and everywhere in the internal justice and accountability systems at the UN and they raise the most serious ethical issues for any dedicated professional who wishes to exercise his or her legal professional skills with integrity. The establishment of a new "*Management Performance Board*" on 5 May 2005 already suffers from the same perception that senior officials at the UN are subject to their own special system of justice, where conflicts of interests between USGs and the Secretary-General are omnipresent. Likewise, despite Resolution 59/283 (Annex VIII), it appears that the Secretary-General has now decided to restructure the Department of Management in order to establish and maintain therein an Office for Oversight and Internal Justice (see ST/SGB/2005/8–section 8). Member-States should insist that such an Office should not be under the same USG/DM who oversees the activities of OHRM, including investigations, disciplinary actions, appeals, etc. As a matter of transparency and accountability, the Secretary-General should be responsible for his internal justice decisions. As was done for many other Departments at the United Nations, it is also great time that the functions and practices of the Office of Legal Affairs (OLA) be revisited and improved. For the same reasons that the General Assembly in its resolution 59/283 has asked OHRM to dismantle ALU and to operate separately in different units its conflicting legal functions, it is inadmissible that OLA continues to offer legal advice to the Administration on various contentious issues, and at the same time participates in the prosecution of accountability and disciplinary cases and defends before the Tribunal the improprieties and abuses committed by some senior UN officials. These contradictory functions place OLA's legal officers in a very difficult position in terms of professional ethics and of conflicts of interest. With the SG decision taken in June 2004 to implement the 1999 Global Compact Principles in the UN internal management, OLA should take the initiative to implement in its practices and policies the *UN Basic Principles applicable to Judicial Independence, to Lawyers and to Prosecutors*, in order to strengthen its professionalism and credibility in legal matters.

XXXI. Conclusion

The debate now beginning on the reform of the United Nations is aiming to reinforce an institution in which the whole humanity believes. The United Nations deserves a better accountability and internal justice system, in order to reestablish confidence in its humanitarian and development missions. It must be insulated against abuses, corruption and improprieties committed by its officials, whatever their ranks may be. Given the serious shortcomings revealed in the findings of the Volcker Inquiry and in other instances of misconduct, it is clear that a more robust approach is required to control, oversee and monitor such situations. Events of recent years have shown the dangers for the Organization of operating in a cocoon where impunity is pervasive and transparency obfuscated by immunities and privileges. The recent creation of an *Oversight Committee* for the UN Secretariat where 2 members out of 5 would come from outside is a step in the right direction. Rebuilding trust and confidence will become possible, both inside and outside of the United Nations, only by resorting more systematically or truly independent external boards and inquiries, by increasing the role and authority of the Administrative Tribunal and of similar independent bodies, by empowering them to enforce accountability policies and to control the internal justice system.

Appendix: List of Select Studies, Circulars and Reports on Accountability at the United Nations

- A/49/219 of 4 August 1994 "*Review of the Administrative and Financial Functioning of the United Nations* (Toward a new system of performance appraisal in the United Nations Secretariat: Requirements for a successful implementation)".
- A/C.5/49/1 of 5 August 1994: "*Establishment of a transparent and effective system of accountability and responsibility*" Report of the Secretary-General.
- ADM 97/17 of 13 May 1997: *Accountability, recovery and disciplinary procedures at UNDP.*
- A/53/414 of 13 Oct 1998 "*Human resources management reform*" Report of the Secretary-General.
- A/54/1 Supplement No. 1 1999, 54th session 1 *Report of the SG on the work of the Organization.*
- ST/SGB/1998/19 of 10 December 1998: *Status, Basic Rights and Duties of United Nations Staff Members.*
- A/55/253 of 1 Aug. 2000: "*Human Resources Management Reform*" Report of the Secretary-General.
- A/55/270 of 3 Aug. 2000: "*Accountability and Responsibility*" Report of the Secretary-General.
- ST/SGB/2000/14 of 23 Oct. 2000 "*Accountability Panel*" Secretary-General's bulletin.
- A/55/499 of 19 Oct. 2000 "*Human resources management reform, accountability and responsibility, personnel practices and policies and management irregularities*" ACABQ report.
- A/55/857 Add.1 18 April 2001 "*Report of the JIU on the delegation of authority for management of human and financial resource in the United Nations secretariat*" Note by the SG. See Recommendation 9 on OHRM monitoring (paras. 25 and 26) and Rec. 10 on Accountability (para. 27 a,b,c, paras. 28–32).
- A/56/82 20 June 2001. "*Review of efficiency of the administrative and financial functioning of the United Nations*" Report of the Secretary-General.
- A/56/846 and A/57/469 ACABQ reports on Human Resources.
- A/57/293 « *Human Resources Management Reform* » of 8 August 2002. Report of the SG.
- 27 February 2004 "*The Right Road . . . on the Global Compact and the Practice of Administration in the United Nations*" report by Karen S. Burstein to the USG/DM.
- 4 June 2004 Report of the SG on the "*United Nations Organizational Integrity Survey*" (conducted by Deloitte Consulting).
- 14 July 2004 "*Managing for Results in the UN System*" (by the Joint Inspection Unit), parts 1, 2 and 3.
- 9 January 2005 "*Independent Inquiry Committee into the United Nations Oil-for-Food Programme: Internal Audit Reports Briefing Paper*".
- 3 February 2005: "*Iraq Oil-For-Food-Programme: an Interim Report*" by the Independent Inquiry Committee (presided by Paul A. Volcker).
- 29 March 2005: "*OFFP/IIC Second Interim Report*".

FOUR

Due Process: The Rights Of World Bank Staff In Misconduct Investigations

Howard Dean[1]

I. Introduction

This paper describes the due process rights of staff members of the World Bank Group (the "Bank")[2] against whom allegations of misconduct are raised. This subject will be addressed, first, by explaining the Bank's Conflict Resolution System, and second, by outlining the stages of a misconduct case handled by the Bank's Department of Institutional Integrity (INT), the unit designated by the Bank to investigate allegations of staff misconduct.[3]

II. Understanding the Bank's Conflict Resolution System

The Bank and its staff benefit from the protection of certain privileges and immunities bestowed by the Bank's Articles of Agreement and international conventions.[4] The Bank's immunities have consistently been recognized by courts as precluding unilateral interference by a member country or its courts with the internal operations of the Bank, including the employment relationship between the organization and its staff.[5] The Bank is also pro-

---

[1] Senior Counsel, World Bank Legal Vice Presidency; former Counsel, World Bank Administrative Tribunal. The views expressed here are personal views that should not be taken to represent the official views of the World Bank.

[2] The World Bank Group is composed of five organizations: the International Bank for Reconstruction and Development (IBRD), the International Development Association (IDA), the International Finance Corporation (IFC), the Multilateral Investment Guarantee Agency (MIGA), and the International Centre for Settlement of Investment Disputes (ICSID).

[3] INT conducts all investigations, except where INT requests a staff member's manager, or where the President or the Vice President, Human Resources for the Bank designates a person outside of INT to conduct the investigation. For cases involving IFC staff, the President or the Vice President, Human Resources for the Bank will consult with the Vice President, Human Resources for IFC, before designating a person outside of INT to conduct the investigation. There have been very few situations in which INT has not conducted the investigation. Therefore, INT will be referred throughout this paper as the investigating body.

[4] Articles of Agreement, Article VII.

[5] *See, e.g., Mendaro v. World Bank*, 717 F.2d 610, 618 (D.C. Cir 1983); *Morgan v. International*

tected from the compulsory disclosure of information and evidence through subpoenas or court orders.[6] Similarly, Bank staff are immune from legal process with respect to the acts performed by them in their official capacity except when the Bank waives this immunity.

Since the Bank's internal operations are to be free from interference by member countries, the Bank has established over the years facilities and procedures for the resolution of employment disputes. The current organization of these facilities and procedures make up what is known as the Conflict Resolution System.

The Conflict Resolution System presently comprises five distinct components: the Office of the Ombudsman, the Mediation Office, the Office of Ethics and Business Conduct, the Appeals Committee and the World Bank Administrative Tribunal (the "Tribunal").[7] The Office of the Ombudsman helps staff find ways to address concerns they are reluctant, or uncertain how, to raise through regular channels. The Mediation Office offers a voluntary process that facilitates dialog between those with a problem or conflict. The Office of Ethics and Business Conduct advises and trains staff and managers about actions that might constitute misconduct and on the process for handling allegations of misconduct. The Appeals Committee makes recommendations to senior management on cases submitted by staff challenging decisions affecting the terms or conditions of their employment – such as decisions on misconduct. The Tribunal is the forum to which staff may go if they are dissatisfied with the outcome of their cases before the Appeals Committee.[8]

Bank for Reconstruction and Dev., 752 F. Supp. 492, 494–95 (D.D.C. 1990); *Chiriboga v. International Bank for Reconstruction and Dev.*, 616 F. Supp. 963, 967 (D.D.C. 1985).

[6] Articles of Agreement, Article VII. *See also, e.g., Atkinson v. Inter-American Development Bank*, 156 F.3d 1335 (D.C. Cir.), wherein the Court held that international organizations are immune from garnishment orders.

[7] The Bank's Conflict Resolution System (CRS) was created in March 1999. It was established following the recommendations of a Grievance Process Review Committee that was appointed by Bank senior management in 1998 to review the Bank's then-existing system for resolving staff member disputes. That system was a collection of mechanisms introduced at different times as ad hoc responses to emerging concerns. The Appeals Committee was the first formal mechanism established in the Bank (in the late 1970s) to resolve employment disputes. The Tribunal was established in 1980, and the Office of the Ombudsman was created in 1981. While an office handling ethics matters has existed in the Bank for many years, the current Ethics Office was established following the Grievance Process Review. The creation of the Mediation Office was also an outcome of the Grievance Process Review. The key concept of the CRS is to provide a multi-entry, independent and flexible system to address work-related conflicts in the World Bank Group. The different units of the CRS interact as a cohesive system to better manage conflict, to strengthen outreach efforts, and to improve monitoring of the Bank's handling of staff grievances.

[8] The Tribunal also has jurisdiction to hear appeals from staff on decisions of the Pension Benefits Administration Committee and the Workers' Compensation Administrative Review Panel.

A. The Appeals Committee

The Appeals Committee is a peer review process. It allows staff to challenge administrative decisions that allegedly alter or are in breach of their terms of employment, or formal disciplinary actions based on misconduct.

The Committee consists of a pool of Bank staff. At least ten Committee members are appointed each by:

(i) the Vice President of Human Resources in consultation with the Staff Association (these members are Director level or above);
(ii) the Vice President of Human Resources; and
(iii) the Staff Association. Cases submitted to the Appeals Committee are heard by a Panel of three Committee members (one staff member from each of the three above categories).

Panels are selected randomly by the Appeals Committee Secretariat, taking into consideration the availability of members and any potential conflicts of interest. The Chair of each Panel is selected from the pool of staff members appointed by the Vice President of Human Resources in consultation with the Staff Association.

In Appeals Committee cases, a "Respondent's Representative" represents the Bank before the Appeals Committee. A lawyer from the Legal Vice Presidency assists the Respondent's Representative in the case. Such assistance includes preparing the written pleadings for submission and preparing the Respondent's Representative and the witnesses for the oral hearing.

The Respondent's Representative is typically the manager who made the decision that is being challenged. In those cases involving a staff member challenging a decision based on the outcome of a misconduct investigation, the Respondent's Representative is usually the Human Resources Vice President or the Vice President's designee, as the Vice President is in almost all cases the senior manager responsible under the Staff Rules for deciding whether misconduct occurred and what disciplinary measure, if any, to impose.[9] The decision is based on the factual findings and

[9] Where the investigation has been conducted by INT or by a person designated by the President or the Vice President, Human Resources for the Bank, the determination whether misconduct has occurred and what disciplinary measures, if any, to impose will be made: (i) by the Vice President, Human Resources for the Bank; or (ii) where there is conflict of interest for the Vice President, Human Resources for the Bank, a Managing Director, or the President. Where a person designated by the President has conducted an investigation, the determination whether misconduct occurred and what disciplinary measures to impose will be made by the President, or by a person designated by the President for that purpose. For cases involving IFC staff, the Vice President, Human Resources for IFC will be consulted before a decision is made regarding misconduct.

conclusions of an investigation report prepared by INT, the Bank's investigations unit. INT is discussed in greater detail below.

The Appeals Committee's scope of review in all cases is "whether the [contested] decision constitutes an abuse of discretion, in that it was arbitrary, discriminatory or carried out in violation of the applicable Bank Group procedures." The Appeals Committee prepares its own report and submits it, along with recommendations as to the disposition to the case, to the senior manager designated under the Staff Rules to decide whether to accept or reject the recommendations. In misconduct cases, it is usually the Managing Director, Operations, who decides whether to accept or reject the Appeals Committee's recommendations since, as noted above, in misconduct cases it is usually the decision of the Human Resources Vice President that is under review by the Appeals Committee.

B. The World Bank Administrative Tribunal

Staff members dissatisfied with the outcome of their cases before the Appeals Committee may file an "application" with the Tribunal within prescribed time limits.[10] The Tribunal is composed of seven members, all of whom are nationals of different member countries of the Bank. Tribunal members must, pursuant to its Statute, be persons of "high moral character" and must "possess the qualifications required for appointment to high judicial office or be juriconsults of recognized competence in fields such as employment relations, international civil service and international organization administration." The Tribunal members are appointed by the Executive Directors of the Bank from a list of candidates drawn up by the President of the Bank after appropriate consultation. Their term of appointment is five years and may be renewed once.

It has been the practice of the Tribunal, which convenes two to three times per year as needed, to hear cases in panels of three or four mem-

---

Where the investigation has been conducted by a manager of a staff member, the manager will determine whether misconduct has occurred and, if so, may censure the staff member orally or in writing. If a manager believes the discipline should be something other than oral or written censure, the manager will make a recommendation to the Vice President, Human Resources for the Bank, regarding a decision on the finding of misconduct and the discipline to be imposed. For the purposes of this paper, and in order to avoid confusion, the person who decides whether misconduct occurred and what disciplinary measures, if any, to impose, will be referred to as "the decision-maker."

[10] Recourse to the Appeals Committee is a condition precedent to filing an application with the Tribunal save in exceptional circumstances, determined by the Tribunal, or if the applicant and the Bank have agreed that the applicant can bypass the Appeals Committee process.

bers. An examination of the Tribunal's judgments, which specify the composition of the Tribunal in each case, indicates that the full Tribunal usually only sits for factually or legally complicated cases, cases that present novel issues and cases that could have a broad impact in the Bank. Approximately one half of all misconduct cases heard by the Tribunal have been decided by the full Tribunal.

Unlike cases heard before the Appeals Committee, where oral hearings take place almost as a matter of course, the Tribunal decides the great majority of its cases based on the written pleadings submitted. This phenomenon can perhaps be explained by the fact that the written pleadings usually always include the transcript of the oral hearing before the Appeals Committee, and that both the number and size of the pleadings submitted to the Tribunal tend to be greater than those submitted to the Appeals Committee. It may be noted that oral hearings before the Tribunal have never been held in a misconduct case.

Cases before the Tribunal are reviewed on a *de novo* basis. In non-misconduct cases, this review generally consists of determining whether the contested decision was an abuse of discretion, i.e., whether it was arbitrary, discriminatory, improperly motivated or carried in violation of a fair and reasonable procedure.

The standard applied by the Tribunal in misconduct cases is, however, much broader. This standard, which was first articulated by the Tribunal in *Carew*, WBAT, Decision No. 142 [1995], para. 32, expressly allows the Tribunal to go beyond deciding whether the contested decision was an abuse of discretion. Thus, in misconduct cases, the Tribunal

> examines (i) the existence of the facts, (ii) whether they legally amount to misconduct, (iii) whether the sanction imposed is provided in the law of the Bank, (iv) whether the sanction is not significantly disproportionate to the offense, and (v) whether the requirements of due process have been observed.

The Tribunal, in applying this standard, has focused a considerable amount of attention on the last criterion, i.e., whether the requirements of due process have been observed. The Tribunal's jurisprudence on the question of due process has played an important role in the shaping of investigative standards and procedures in INT which, as noted earlier, is the department responsible for investigating allegations of staff misconduct.

III. The Stages of a Misconduct Case

INT's investigative standards and procedures, in addition to being shaped by the Tribunal's jurisprudence, are based on internationally recognized protocols and standards; World Bank Group mandates, policies, and due process requirements; the experiences of experts in the field of professional investigations; Appeals Committee reports; procedures benchmarked against multinational, international and national institutions/organizations; and rigorous departmental quality control and oversight. The standards and procedures are memorialized in the Staff Rules as well as in investigative manuals prepared for use by INT staff.

The standards and procedures address five stages in a misconduct case:

(1) the preliminary inquiry;
(2) the notice to the affected staff member;
(3) the fact-finding process;
(4) the final report; and
(5) the decision on the final report.

These five stages present issues for discussion concerning the due process rights of staff members against whom allegations of misconduct have been raised. A sixth stage, which will also be discussed, arises when an INT investigation concludes that the laws of a member country may have been violated, and the Bank decides to refer the results of the investigation to the concerned member country.

A. The Preliminary Inquiry

When INT receives an allegation of staff misconduct, a preliminary inquiry is initiated to determine if the allegation is credible and if the allegation, even if proved, constitutes misconduct. The allegation may be reported by an individual who wishes to remain anonymous or to have his or her name kept confidential. Confidentiality is not absolute: individuals asking for confidentiality are informed that the source of the allegation will not be revealed to anyone outside of the investigative team unless the individual consents to disclosure, or the Bank is requested by a competent judicial authority within a member country (and the Bank agrees to comply with the request), or it is determined that the individual knowingly made a false allegation of misconduct.

The Tribunal's jurisprudence on the source of allegations and the manner in which allegations are received has evolved from being initially conservative to being, more recently, more liberal. In *Koudogbo*, WBAT Decision No. 246 [2001], para. 43, the Tribunal held that the "[t]he initiation of investigations, preliminary or otherwise, on the basis of rumors and allegations by questionable sources, clearly does not comport with the basic elements of due process." (Para. 43.) The *Koudogbo* case followed an earlier case decided the same year (*Cissé*, WBAT Decision No. 242 [2001], para. 29) in which the Tribunal criticized the initiation of a preliminary inquiry based on anonymous allegations, holding that the anonymity of the allegations "detracted from the reliability of the information." More recently, however, in *Kwakwa*, WBAT Decision No. 300 [2003], para. 28, the Tribunal held that there was no merit to the applicant's argument that the Bank's decision to investigate him was the result of accusations made by persons who were biased against him and were untrustworthy:

> [T]ips are unlikely to come from pillars of the community who have benevolent feelings toward the accused. Indeed, tipsters may be wholly disreputable. The issue was whether the ensuing investigation was fair, and whether the burden of proof was met.

It is noteworthy that the *Koudogbo* and *Cissé* cases were cases in which the Tribunal found that most (*Koudogbo*) or all (*Cissé*) of the allegations of misconduct were unsubstantiated, and that there were numerous procedural flaws in the conduct of the investigations.[11] In *Kwakwa*, however, the Tribunal dismissed the Applicant's application on the merits, strongly endorsing all of the findings of misconduct and the applicant's termination of employment.[12]

One final point on preliminary inquiries is that Bank staff against whom allegations are raised are rarely interviewed during the preliminary inquiry stage. The purpose of the inquiry is to assess the allegation discreetly to determine its credibility and whether there is sufficient evidence to notify the staff member in writing of the allegations and of the initiation of an investigation.

In those preliminary inquiries that do not lend themselves to a discreet review due to the nature of the allegation, INT is in the tenuous position of seeking to elicit information from the staff member while at the same time respecting the staff member's rights. INT addresses this situation by providing notice to the staff member of the preliminary inquiry, which explains the nature of the allegation, the purpose of the preliminary inquiry, and the process followed in preliminary inquiries and investigations. Further, the staff member is informed that any statement made, or document provided, by him or her during the course of the preliminary inquiry will

---

[11] The allegations in the *Koudogbo* and *Cissé* cases were investigated prior to the creation of INT in March 2001. The Ethics Office, as it was then configured, handled misconduct investigations before March 2001.

[12] In a subsequent case *D*, WBAT Decision No. 304 [2003], one of the applicant's central claims on due process was INT's initiation of a preliminary inquiry on the basis of what the applicant characterized as "loose talk . . . at a cocktail party." The Tribunal, although characterizing the allegation that prompted the inquiry as being "triple hearsay," reached no conclusion as to the appropriateness of initiating the inquiry.

become part of the record and could be used in making a determination as to whether it appears that the staff member may have committed misconduct.

B. *The Notice of Misconduct*

Under Staff Rule 8.01, if the information gathered by INT during the course of a preliminary inquiry provides a "sufficient basis to merit an investigation," INT must inform the staff member in writing of the allegations, of the staff member's rights and obligations and of the process that will be followed during the investigation. The allegations must be framed with sufficient specificity and clarity to allow the staff member the opportunity to satisfy one of his principal rights – the right to respond fully to the allegations. The seminal Tribunal decision on this issue is *King*, WBAT Decision No. 131 [1993], para. 35, wherein the Tribunal held:

> It needs to be appreciated that [the notification] requirement necessarily implies not some general notification but one which informs the staff member that as a result of the investigation some specific alleged conduct of the staff member may be punished. In other words, the notification must in substance be an accusation or a charge. Moreover, it must be expressed in such terms that the accused staff member is made aware from the outset of the scope of the possible default alleged against him. The notification must be reasonably exact in the specification of the wrong alleged. If it is not so expressed, and is not set out in sufficient detail, then the staff member cannot know of what he is being accused, may remain unaware of considerations material to the allegation as it affects him and can thus be left unable to make a properly directed or considered response. Such a situation would evidently be inconsistent with the basic rule of due process that an accused person should be confronted with a specific charge and be given an opportunity to reply to it.

Other rights of staff under investigation, which are articulated in the written notice from INT, consist of:

(i) the right to be accompanied at investigation interviews by another staff member who is not connected to the matter under investigation;
(ii) the right to a presumption of innocence; and
(iii) the right to comment on the report and evidence before it is submitted to the decision-maker for a determination as to whether misconduct occurred and what disciplinary measures, if any, should be imposed.

Additional due process rights, which one would normally observe in the context of a judicial proceeding – such as the right to counsel at investigation interviews, and the right to depose, confront or cross-examine persons who have been asked to contribute to the investigation – are not extant in a misconduct investigation.[13] This is a reflection of the administrative, not adjudicatory, nature of misconduct investigations. (*See, e.g.*, *Rendall-Speranza*, WBAT Decision No. 197 [1998]; and *Kwakwa*, WBAT Decision No. 300 [2003].)

An important issue concerning notice is whether and in which circumstances written notice should be provided *prior* to the point at which notice *must* be provided under Staff Rule 8.01, i.e., when, following a preliminary inquiry, there is a "sufficient basis to merit an investigation." In *D*, WBAT Decision No. 304, the Tribunal noted that INT had set out factors in its investigation manual to be weighed in assessing whether early notification is warranted or should be held in abeyance until the sufficiency standard is met. Under the manual, early notification is warranted where one or more witnesses have already been interviewed and as a result there is a risk of the spread of rumors or gossip concerning the allegations. On the other hand early notification is not warranted where:

(i) there is a reasonable risk that material witnesses may be intimidated by the subject, or
(ii) there is a reasonable risk that physical or documentary evidence may be tampered with or destroyed by the subject.

The Tribunal paid particular attention to the latter two factors, as they were used by INT as a basis for not providing early notification to the applicant in the *D* case. The Tribunal held that the two factors are reasonable and should be taken into account, but that INT should err on the side of providing a staff member who is the subject of a preliminary inquiry formal notification of the alleged misconduct at "the earliest reasonable moment." (Para. 65.) It was the Tribunal's view that early notice – something short of a formal notification of misconduct – "can provide an opportunity to the subject to respond to the charges, to explain his suspect behavior, to inform the investigators, and so better to focus and expedite (and perhaps conclude) the preliminary inquiry." (*Id.*) The Tribunal noted that in the applicant's case, had he been informed at an earlier stage in the process of the evidence, even though such evidence was inculpatory, "he might very well have been able to shorten or eliminate much of the time devoted by the investigators to the interviewing of witnesses . . ., much to the benefit of the Bank, of INT, of the interviewees, and of the Applicant." (*Id.*)

[13] Staff may, however, retain counsel.

C. The Fact Finding Process

The principal role of the INT investigator during the course of an investigation is to establish all the facts (whether they substantiate or refute the allegation of misconduct) and to obtain, evaluate and analyze information and evidence (both inculpatory and exculpatory). INT presents its findings in a report that is submitted to the decision-maker for a decision as to whether misconduct occurred and what disciplinary measures, if any, to impose. As noted earlier, the staff member under investigation has an opportunity to comment on the report before it is submitted to the decision-maker.

INT is, during the fact finding stage, limited in its investigative capacity. It has no subpoena power and, therefore, when seeking information outside the Bank must rely on the cooperation of the outside parties. Further, INT cannot compel accused staff members to cooperate – although such staff have a duty to cooperate and a failure to do so could itself result in a finding of misconduct. Witnesses who are Bank staff also have a duty to cooperate with INT absent a showing by the staff member of reasons, determined by the person conducting the investigation, to be sufficient to justify failure to cooperate.

An important investigative tool available to INT is a review of the electronic records of staff under investigation in appropriate circumstances. Pursuant to Bank policies, INT may monitor and examine the contents of a staff member's computer files and electronic mail databases where it has shown that "there is a reasonable basis to suspect a violation of Bank policy, a criminal act, or other misconduct." Such monitoring and examining must be pre-approved by the senior manager responsible for the investigation, a Managing Director, and the Vice President and General Counsel.

Any review by INT of the electronic records of staff is typically carried out during the preliminary inquiry stage of the process without notifying the staff member alleged to have engaged in misconduct. The rationale for not notifying the staff member of the review is four fold:

(i) to determine whether further investigation is warranted prior to conducting interviews that would reveal to colleagues and others that a staff member is under investigation;
(ii) to gather evidence, inculpatory and exculpatory;
(iii) to identify potential witnesses; and
(iv) to obtain evidence against which the credibility of witnesses can be assessed during the course of interviews.

The Bank's policy on the review of the electronic records of staff garnered some attention by the Tribunal in *D*, WBAT Decision No. 304 [2003]. There, the Tribunal expressed the view that the standard INT must satisfy in order to the review the electronic records of staff (i.e., reasonable basis to suspect misconduct):

> carefully balance[s] the Bank's interest in electronic files as employer and property owner with the staff members' interest in a reasonable measure of privacy. (Para. 58.)

However, while endorsing the standard the Tribunal also defined it in a way that raises the bar for INT to review the electronic records of staff under suspicion for misconduct. In this respect, the Tribunal held that:

> [e]xcept in situations in which an accusation is of a most grave and exigent nature,

a reasonable basis to suspect

> will ordinarily require some objective corroboration. (*Id.* at para. 59.)

This definition minimizes the subjective element of suspicion and, therefore, goes one step further in avoiding unnecessary intrusions into staff privacy.

One final point of interest concerning the due process rights of staff during the fact finding process involves the placement of staff on paid administrative leave pending completion of an investigation.[14] Under Staff Rule 8.01, the Vice President, Human Resources, or a Managing Director, may place a staff member on administrative leave pending completion of an investigation. Administrative leave can last up to six months, and can be extended when the Vice President, Human Resources determines that additional time is needed to complete an investigation. Staff placed on administrative leave must be notified in writing of the decision, the reason for the decision, and the duration of the administrative leave.

The Tribunal has not taken issue with the Bank's discretion to place staff on administrative leave. However, the Tribunal has set out standards that should be applied in the decision-making process. Thus in *D*, WBAT Decision No. 304 [2003], the Tribunal held that a decision to place an accused staff member on administrative leave pending the completion of a misconduct investigation must be made in good faith and be reasonable. The decision, added the Tribunal, cannot be based on an effort to afford the staff member more time to devote to his defense or to avoid work disruptions that would likely result from future INT interviews of the staff

[14] Administrative leave is absence from duty with pay for staff members excused from duty for a number of reasons, including pending completion of a misconduct investigation.

member. However, it would be reasonable to remove from a position of financial responsibility a staff member accused of serious financial wrongdoing. Lastly, the Tribunal emphasized that if staff are to be escorted off Bank premises when placed on administrative leave, it should be done in as inconspicuous manner as possible so as to avoid rumors and possible reputational harm to the staff member.

D. The Final Report, and the Decision on the Final Report

As earlier discussed, INT submits its final report, which includes the evidence and statements and comments of the staff member, to the decision-maker for a determination as to whether misconduct occurred and what disciplinary measures, if any, should be imposed. The decision-maker is required to consider the findings of fact and conclusions in the final report, but may also consider the recommendations from any other official the decision-maker consults for advice. It may be noted that in *D*, WBAT Decision No. 304 [2003], para. 71, the Tribunal rejected the applicant's argument that INT exceeds its powers in presenting its conclusions in the final report.

The decision-maker, in assessing the final report and any recommendations from other officials, must be cognizant of three important standards set out by the Tribunal. First, the staff member must be given the benefit of the doubt when the relevant Staff Rule on misconduct is ambiguous and where there are significant disciplinary consequences. (*Cissé*, WBAT Decision No. 242 [2001], para. 31.) Second, "[t]he burden of proof of misconduct is on the Respondent." (*Dambita*, WBAT Decision No. 243 [2001], para. 21.) And third, in cases in which the decision-maker decides that termination of employment is the appropriate disciplinary measure, "there must be substantial evidence to support the finding of facts which amount to misconduct." (*Arefeen*, WBAT Decision No. 244 [2001], para. 42.)

Strict observance of the above standards is particularly important where a staff member is alleged to have engaged in misconduct for which termination of employment is mandatory under the Staff Rules, because the stakes are higher. Under Staff Rule 8.01, termination is mandatory if it is found that a staff member misused Bank Group funds or other public funds for his or her personal gain or the personal gain of another in connection with Bank Group activities or employment, abused his or her position in the Bank Group for the personal gain of him/herself or another, or is convicted of a felonious criminal offense.

In those cases in which termination is not mandatory the decision-maker must, in assessing the appropriate disciplinary measure, take into account such factors as the seriousness of the matter, any extenuating circumstances, the situation of the staff member, the interests of the Bank Group, and the frequency of conduct for which disciplinary measures may be imposed. A review of the Tribunal's jurisprudence indicates that the Tribunal places significant weight on the situation of the staff member, with particular emphasis on the quality and longevity of the staff member's service, the existence of prior disciplinary measures in earlier cases and the frequency of the current misconduct. (*See D*, WBAT Decision No. 304 [2003]; *Kwakwa*, WBAT Decision No. 300 [2003]; *Smith*, WBAT Decision No. 158 [1997]; *Carew*, WBAT Decision No. 142 [1995]; and *Planthara*, WBAT Decision No. 143 [1995].)

Finally, once the decision-maker has made a decision, the staff member must be notified of the disciplinary measures that will be taken, the reasons for their imposition, and the right to appeal by the person who determined what the measures will be. Except where the measure is oral censure, the notification must be in writing. The staff member must also be notified of the provision under the Staff Rules that served as the basis for the misconduct decision. (*See Koudogbo*, WBAT Decision No. 246 [2001], para. 53.)

E. Referrals to Member Countries

A possible final stage in a misconduct case is the situation in which the Bank decides to refer the results of an investigation to a member country if the Bank believes that the laws of the member country may have been violated. This situation raises issues concerning the rights of current and former staff members in respect of the disclosure outside the Bank of INT investigative records in misconduct cases.

Staff Rule 2.01 lists the "staff records and personnel information" that may be released to persons outside the Bank Group without the staff member's authorization. The Bank is proscribed from releasing "other personnel information," i.e., information not included on the list of "staff records and personnel information," to outside parties, including member countries and their representatives, without the staff member's authorization, except in cases of emergency situations or upon the advice from the Legal Vice Presidency of the Bank to release information for legal proceedings or law enforcement efforts. However, in such cases, the staff member must be notified "as soon as reasonably possible of what information is released and to whom."

The Tribunal, in *C*, WBAT Decision No. 272 [2002], held that the same notification requirement applying to "other personnel information" in the Staff Rules should also be applied to the release of INT reports to member countries, thereby assuring that the due process rights of Bank staff are strictly observed. However, the Tribunal interpreted the notification standard "as soon as reasonably possible" as "justifying withholding information or delaying notification to the staff member" in exigent circumstances, such as "a danger that the accused might attempt to destroy evidence, flee the jurisdiction, or harass and intimidate witnesses." (Para. 24.)

Thus, as a general matter, staff must be advised of the fact and content of a referral. However, the notification may be delayed where the member country has identified to the Bank the existence of exigent circumstances justifying such delay, and the Bank agrees.

IV. Conclusion

The processes and procedures used in the Bank's grievance system, and applied by the Bank in its handling of misconduct cases, are designed to protect the rights of all staff members. As this paper has shown, the processes and procedures are modified from time to time to take into consideration evolving standards and norms. Such modifications are an indication that the documents in which the processes and procedures and memorialized are "living documents" that strive for perfection but which invariably will continue to be changed periodically.

FIVE

Challenges in Applying Codes of Ethics in A Small Professional Community: The Example of The WTO Rules of Conduct For the Understanding on Rules and Procedures Governing the Settlement of Disputes

Yves Renouf[1]

I. Introduction

Rules of ethics are new neither for lawyers, nor for international civil servants. Rules of conduct have existed in the legal profession in general for a very long time. They are more developed in some countries and legal traditions than in others. Standards of conduct have been incorporated in staff rules and regulations of many international organizations for the past 50 years. However, the development of instruments such as supranational dispute resolution mechanisms have generated renewed interest in ethical norms.

Throughout the Uruguay Round of international trade negotiations conducted under the aegis of the General Agreement on Tariffs and Trade ("GATT"), which led to the establishment of the World Trade Organization ("WTO"), some States pushed for a stronger dispute settlement system, believed to be essential to the implementation of the new rules and disciplines which had been negotiated. However, that stronger system also had to be "reliable", and some Member States expressed the view that, in order to be credible and serve its purpose, such a powerful system had to provide sufficient guarantees of independence and objectivity. Hence the need for rules of conduct.

However, there was a risk that, given the structure of WTO dispute settlement and its dependence on the limited number of specialists in the field to adjudicate cases, rules that would make it too easy to challenge the impartiality of those in charge of resolving disputes could paralyse the system. This article aims at giving a brief overview of the provisions adopted by the WTO, which represent to date some of the most advanced set of rules of conduct applicable to an international system of dispute resolution.

---

[1] Yves Renouf is counsellor in the Legal Affairs Division of the WTO Secretariat, Geneva. The views expressed in this note are exclusively personal and may not be attributed to the WTO, any of its Members or its Secretariat.

It also intends to outline how a balance was struck by the negotiators between, on the one hand, the need to ensure the objectivity and the independence of those in charge of operating the dispute settlement system and, on the other hand, the necessity to ensure that the application of rules of ethics do not lead to the unnecessary exclusion of skilled specialists and to the paralysis of a system which relies on a small number of experts for its functioning.

The history of the negotiation of the Rules of Conduct for the Understanding on Rules and Procedures Governing the Settlement of Disputes (hereafter the "Rules of Conduct")[2] and the principles underlying this text have already been addressed in a much more exhaustive work than this one.[3] The purpose of this note is therefore to briefly examine the Rules of Conduct from the perspective of their application to international officials with overlapping responsibilities within and outside resolution of disputes and to a small community of specialists called upon to play the role of adjudicators. In order to understand the technical context in which the WTO rules of conduct on dispute settlement operate, the following section (Section II) briefly describes the WTO dispute settlement mechanism and, more particularly, the status and roles of those in charge of operating this mechanism to which the Rules of Conduct are supposed to apply. Section III outlines some of the issues relating specifically to the development of rules of ethics in relation to a dispute settlement system like that of the WTO. Section IV describes the Rules of Conduct themselves and how they address those issues.

II. The WTO and its Dispute Settlement System

A. Scope and Functions of the World Trade Organization

The World Trade Organization, set up by the Marrakesh Agreement Establishing the World Trade Organization (1994),[4] entered into force in 1995 and replaced the GATT. WTO membership is composed of almost

---

[2] Document WT/DSB/RC/1, 11 December 1996, reproduced in Annex VII.

[3] On the historical background, the negotiation and the content of the WTO Rules of Conduct for the Understanding on Rules and Procedures Governing the Settlement of Disputes, see Gabrielle Marceau: *Rules on Ethics for the New World Trade Organization Dispute settlement Mechanism: The Rules of Conduct for the Understanding on Rules and Procedures Governing the Settlement of Disputes*, Journal of World Trade, Vol. 32, No. 3, June 1998.

[4] Agreement Establishing the World Trade Organization, signed in Marrakesh on 15 April 1994. (hereafter the "WTO Agreement"). See http://www.wto.org.

150 States and customs territories. The WTO Agreement not only contains institutional provisions (those providing for the creation and functioning of the WTO as an international organization), but also an extensive body of substantive rules and disciplines in the form of specific agreements regulating almost all sectors of international trade (trade in goods, services and trade-related aspects of intellectual property).

The WTO essentially has three functions: (a) it provides for a permanent negotiation forum for its Members; (b) it applies on a daily basis the substantive rules and disciplines contained in the WTO Agreement; and (c) – last but not least – it operates an advanced system of resolution of disputes between WTO Members in relation to the rights and obligations of the latter under the WTO provisions.[5]

B. Resolution of Disputes between WTO Members

The WTO dispute settlement system combines many features of international and domestic dispute settlement and judicial systems, in addition to peculiarities inherited from the GATT dispute resolution mechanism. The provisions of the WTO Agreement dealing with dispute settlement are found essentially in the *Understanding on Rules and Procedures Governing the Settlement of Disputes*, also known as the "DSU", which stands for "Dispute Settlement Understanding", its most common name.[6]

In a nutshell, a WTO Member wishing to have recourse to the WTO dispute settlement system must refer that matter to the Dispute Settlement Body ("DSB"), a political organ composed of all WTO Members which supervises the operation of the dispute settlement system. The DSB formally issues recommendations and rulings which are binding on the parties to the dispute. However, the DSB itself does not actually review the matters in dispute. This task is assigned by the DSB to *panels* and, on appeal, to the *Appellate Body*.

Panels are generally composed of three experts (the *panelists*). Panels are not permanent; each panel is established *ad hoc* by the DSB to review a given case. As a result, panelists are only appointed to work on one case. Even then, their contract with the WTO is not one of employment but one of service provider (called a *special service agreement*) and applies only to the periods when they come to the WTO headquarters in Geneva to meet

[5] Pursuant to Article XII of the WTO Agreement, "any States or separate customs territory possessing full autonomy in the conduct of its external commercial relations and of the other matters provided for in the WTO Agreement may become Member of the WTO.

[6] WTO Agreement, Annex 2 (the text of the DSU is reproduced in Annex VII).

with the parties or discuss the case among themselves. Special service agreements also provide for the compensation of preparatory work at home. Government officials serving in panels do not receive any compensation for their work. Other panelists from the public or private sector receive a largely symbolic compensation, which can be compared neither with the salaries or fees they may obtain in their main professional activities, nor with the fees that may be charged in some other types of dispute resolution mechanisms, such as private international arbitration. As a result of this minimal contractual link and limited compensationn, panelists are not expected to suspend their other professional activities during their term of appointment.

As a matter of fact, one of the advantages of the panel system is the possibility to appoint panelists from different origins in terms of nationality and expertise.[7] Panelists are recruited among delegates of WTO Members posted in Geneva, officials from central administrations in capitals, academics and private sector specialists. Even then, the number of persons who may be called to serve in a panel remains relatively limited to the extent that a qualification in international trade and on the matter subject to the dispute is required. Moreover, people with the necessary background for a given case are often not more than a handful. This constraint is accentuated by the fact that nationals of the parties to the dispute and of other Members having reserved their right to intervene in the proceedings (third parties) are normally barred from serving on panels.[8]

Like domestic disputes, WTO disputes sometimes involve technical or scientific aspects and panels are entitled to call upon experts to assist then by providing factual opinions.[9] In the course of proceedings, experts are generally given full access to the submissions of the parties. Their contributions can often be essential in factually intensive cases, since panels may rely heavily on their views when drafting their findings.

Finally, panels are assisted in their review of cases by officials of the WTO Secretariat, which provide administrative and legal support to them. Each panel is generally assisted by a Secretary and a Legal Officer. Assisting panels is time consuming, but it is not the only duty of Secretariat officials, as will be explained below. The actual involvement of the WTO Secretariat in the resolution of a dispute varies from one panel to the next, and this uncertainty sometimes gives to the outside observer a feeling of lack of

---

[7] See Article 8.1 of the DSU. Panelists are proposed by the WTO Secretariat, but they must normally be accepted by the parties to the dispute, unless a party requests the Director-General of the WTO to appoint them (Article 8.7 of the DSU).

[8] Article 8.3 of the DSU.

[9] Article 13 of the DSU.

transparency regarding the role played by the Secretariat. The situation is clearer as far as the supporting staff of the Appellate Body is concerned, since its only task is to assist the Appellate Body which, in addition, is composed of permanent members.

Panels issue reports on the dispute submitted to then. Those reports contain legal reasoning and conclusions which may be appealed before the Appellate Body.

Unlike panels, the Appellate Body is a permanent entity, composed of seven individuals with experience in international trade law appointed for four years.[10] If a panel report is appealed, a division of three members of the Appellate Body will review the issues of law raised by the parties, but not issues of fact. Appellate Body members are not staff members of the WTO. However, they have a special contract ensuring that they are permanently available to review a case on appeal, since the Appellate Body operates under strict time constraints. At the outcome of its review, the Appellate Body issues a report addressing the legal issues appealed.

Panel and Appellate Body reports have to be adopted by the DSB. Unlike other multilateral and probably most regional dispute settlement systems, in which parties have to accept the award, the WTO Agreement provides for the quasi-automatic adoption of panel and Appellate Body reports by the DSB. Indeed, WTO panel and Appellate Body reports are adopted unless there is consensus within the DSB against their adoption, something quite unlikely. In other words, as is the case for judgements in a domestic litigation, a WTO Member cannot prevent the adoption of the panel and/or Appellate Body report by the DSB. This quasi-automatic adoption of panel and Appellate Body reports is one of the most striking features of the WTO dispute settlement system.

III. Problems Related to the Development of Rules of Conduct for the WTO Dispute Settlement System

It can be said that the difficulties in applying a code of ethics in the field of WTO dispute settlement have essentially to do with (i) the universal – as opposed to regional – nature of the Organization; (ii) the multiple responsibilities of the WTO Secretariat and (iii) the limited number of experts able to serve in a WTO dispute settlement procedure.

First, as an international organization with almost 150 Members, the WTO includes a wide diversity of cultures, including legal cultures.

[10] Their mandate is renewable.

Apparently, not all Members immediately saw the need for a code of ethics for dispute resolution when the DSU entered into effect. This may partly account for the duration of the negotiation of the Rules of Conduct.[11]

Moreover, the DSU itself already contained provisions dealing with the independence and impartiality of panelists and Appellate Body Members.[12] For their part, the provisions applicable to the WTO staff also reflected the obligation to act impartially and independently.[13] In that context, a code of ethics specific to dispute settlement may have seemed redundant, mostly since standards of conduct already applied to the daily work of WTO officials, irrespective of their sectors of activity.[14]

Another concern of some Members was that the introduction of rules of ethics may push the Secretariat to avoid situations likely to generate conflicts of interest by advising Members on legal issues susceptible of leading to a formal dispute. Such an evolution would have primarily penalised developing Members who rely on the assistance of the Secretariat for legal opinions on any aspects of the functioning of the WTO.

It was also felt by some that an extensive recourse to Rules of Conduct, primarily by defendants in disputes, and an extensive interpretation of the requirements contained in those Rules, could paralyse the dispute resolution process, thus nullifying the potential efficiency gain that was supposed to result for the binding nature of the new WTO dispute settlement mechanism.

Secondly, the WTO dispute settlement system is operated with a certain mix of "lifetime" employment and occasional co-operation. As mentioned above, panelists are "hired" by the WTO on an *ad hoc* basis. On the contrary, the WTO Secretariat, which provides technical and legal

---

[11] In some legal cultures, impartiality is supposed to be achieved through the status of the persons involved in the resolution of disputes (judges, clerks and other judicial staff). Professional training, statutory independence ("inamovibilité") and a specific career path are supposed to deal with most risks of conflicts of interest. In other cultures, which have for a long time favoured an approach where the function of judging is not a career but a career step, where judges are sometimes elected and where professional mobility is prevalent, the same "institutional" protections against potential conflicts of interest may not exist. Actually, codes of ethics are essential to preserve a professional mobility rendered necessary by the temporary nature of the functions.

[12] Article 11 of the DSU provides that panels must make an objective assessment of the matter before them. Article 8.1 requires that panelists be independent and serve in their individual capacity. Article 8.9 provides that Members must not give instructions to panelists or seek to influence them. Article 18.1 prohibits *ex parte* communications. Public statements on the case are also prohibited, deliberations are confidential (Article 18.2). Similar obligations apply to Appellate Body Members (see Article 17, paras. 3, 10, and 11.

[13] See Articles VI:4 of the WTO Agreement and Article 27.2 of the DSU. WTO Staff ules and Regulations also reflect these obligations.

[14] Standards of Conducts applicable to WTO officials, Annex A to the WTO Staff Rules. These Standards of Conduct are adapted in part from the ICSAB Reports on Standards of Conduct in the International Civil Service.

assistance to panels and the Appellate Body, could be compared with a career-based judiciary. Indeed, turnover of staff members with regular contracts remains relatively low at the WTO. The difference in status of the various categories of participants may call for rules adapted to each case.

However, assisting in dispute settlement proceedings is only one of the functions of the WTO Secretariat staff. Staff members must also be able to inform and assist Members in the other sectors of activity of the WTO mentioned in the introduction.[15] Even in the field of dispute settlement, the Secretariat is expected, pursuant to Article 27 of the DSU, to provide at least four types of services:

(i) Assist panels;
(ii) Assist Members in respect of dispute settlement in general, at their request;
(iii) Provide additional legal advice and assistance in respect of dispute settlement to developing country Members in a manner ensuring the continued impartiality of the Secretariat;
(iv) Conduct special capacity-building training courses for interested Members regarding dispute settlement rules and practice.

As already mentioned, panels are normally assisted by a Secretary, appointed in the division normally responsible for the handling of the issue raised.[16] Legal advice is provided by a Legal Officer, generally from the Legal Affairs Division.[17] The Legal Affairs Division was originally created to assist panels in dispute settlement. Its responsibilities have expanded to almost reach those attributed to any legal service in other international organizations, including providing legal assistance in the negotiations of the very texts which will have to be interpreted by a panel in case of dispute.

The involvement of the staff assisting panels in other activities than dispute resolution may be questioned. It is not common practice, in a legal system based on the separation of powers, for staff assisting judges to also assist the legislative branch and it has sometimes been suggested either that the Legal Affairs Division should concentrate on assisting exclusively panels, or that officials assisting panels be exempted from assisting Members in

[15] The Appellate Body Secretariat is, in this respect, in a particular position, since its exclusive role is normally to assist the Appellate Body.
[16] For instance, the Agriculture Division will provide the secretary to the panel in a dispute relating to phytosanitary measures.
[17] In case of disputes relating to anti-dumping, subsidies, safeguard measures, state trading or trade in civil aircraft, this responsibility is assigned to lawyers from another division of the Secretariat: the Rule Division.

negotiations or in daily requests for legal advice. Some proposals made in the context of the current negotiations on the reform of the WTO dispute settlement system and suggesting the appointment of a permanent body of panelists could *de facto* go in that direction. Permanent panelists would have more authority than the present day panelists, and legal officers may gradually become legal assistants to those panelists, in the same way as legal clerks or *référendaires* are related to judges in other international jurisdictions.

One should, however, differentiate between the various activities in which a WTO staff member may be involved. Assisting in negotiations, to the extent that it is a service rendered to the Membership in general and not to Members individually is normally an activity that should not raise any question of conflicts of interest. The staff member may acquire an insider knowledge of the negotiation of a text which a judge would normally not have, and he may be tempted to favour the "intent" of the negotiators over the ordinary meaning of the text, but that is not a situation of conflicts of interest. Actually, such knowledge may be useful in certain circumstances where the negotiated text is particularly unclear.[18]

Direct assistance to Members either prior to a dispute or during a dispute is, on the contrary, a source of conflicts of interest, to the extent that the staff member concerned may have had access to information which he/she would not possess otherwise. It is normal, under such circumstances, to provide for the exclusion of the staff member concerned from related panel proceedings. As we have seen, assistance to parties during a dispute is formally provided by Article 27.2 of the DSU and assigned to identified staff members. The establishment of an Advisory Centre on WTO Law,[19] which provides legal assistance to developing countries, has most probably reduced the pressure on the Secretariat to provide extensive assistance to developing WTO Members before and during disputes. Therefore, the issue relates mostly to the treatment of informal consultations with Members which, if the matter is subsequently subject to a dispute, could lead to the disqualification of the staff member concerned to serve as legal officer or secretary to the panel which will be established to review that matter.

The problem then becomes, in an organization with limited staff resources, to combine the extensive functions of the Secretariat, including the Secretariat's duty to inform and assist Members, with the obligation to

[18] While panelists and the Appellate Body generally seek to interpret legal texts starting from their ordinary meaning, a knowledge of the negotiating history may be useful to the extent that the concept of "dispute settlement" also implies, to a certain degree, finding a solution which will be applicable in practice. In that context, suggesting a solution that takes into account the intent of the negotiators may sometimes be helpful.

[19] On the operation of the Advisory Centre on WTO Law, see http://www.acwl.ch.

ensure the objectivity of dispute settlement. In that context, a reaction consisting of refusing to informally advise a Member or limiting the advice to general considerations because this may subsequently lead to a conflict of interests is normally not acceptable. However, there are, in practice, few other possibilities to ensure that staff members will be available to perform their functions as legal officers.

Thirdly, the specificity of WTO law is such that the number of individuals with sufficient relevant experience is still not large. As an illustration of this, from 1 January 1995 (date of entry into force of the WTO Agreement) to 30 September 2004, 315 disputes were initiated. As of 30 September 2004, 159 of these disputes had led to the establishment of 129 distinct panels, 177 individuals have served as panelists. Since panels are composed of three persons, this means that several individuals have served in more than one panel procedure. One should also note that the indicative list of persons proposed by Members as potential panelists, from which panel members may be selected, contains no more than 300 names, most of which are specialised in only one aspect of international trade.

As already mentioned, since panelists are only paid for the actual number of days during which they work on a case, they cannot afford to quit their other professional activities (and are actually not expected to do so). Moreover, it should be recalled that the involvement of panelists in a case often goes beyond the panel stage. The DSU provides that the original panel should be requested to serve as "compliance panel"[20] and as arbitrator on the level of countermeasures[21] to be taken by the winning parties if no compliance takes place. As a result, a panelist may remain involved in a case for a period of sometimes up to three years, with serious consequences on its discretion to engage in matters relating to the dispute.

In a context of increased demand for panelists due to the multiplication of cases in the WTO, conflicts of interest become a serious threat to recruitment. The number of experts available to serve in panels is of course growing, due to the expanding interest in international trade and the growing number of government officials, academics and private sector professionals specialising in this sector. However, the world of international trade experts remains relatively small and increasing demand for their expertise from other sources than the WTO (advice to States in litigations or in drafting trade legislations) multiplies circumstances of potential conflicts of interest. Moreover, some presumptions of conflict of interest are built in the DSU, such as being a national of one of the parties or third parties.

---

[20] Article 21.5 of the DSU.

[21] Article 22.6 and 22.7 of the DSU.

Nationals of the main users of dispute settlement such as the United States or the European Communities, in which many experts in international trade originate, are *de facto* excluded from serving in most panels, thus further limiting the choice of candidates.

IV. How the WTO Rules of Conduct Strike a Balance between Preservation of the Objectivity and Independence of the Dispute Settlement Process and the Risk of Extensive Recourse to the Rules of Conduct

A. Introductory Remarks

The result of the negotiations of a WTO Code of Conduct for dispute settlement has been a text which formally seems to meet its objective of preserving the independence and impartiality of the system, while attempting to avoid its paralysis through extensive interpretation of and unfettered recourses to its provisions. This achievement is illustrated by the main features of the text highlighted in this section.

The Rules of Conduct are not part of the WTO Agreement. They take the form of a decision of the Dispute Settlement Body, one of the bodies set up by the WTO Agreement to carry out activities assigned to the Organization by the WTO Agreement.[22] As many decisions of the WTO, the Rules of Conduct were subject to a review within two years of their adoption.[23]

B. The Objective of the Rules of Conduct: An Independent and Objective Dispute Settlement Mechanism

The Rules' Preamble essentially repeats the reasons behind the proposal for rules of conduct in the field of dispute settlement. It refers to the stronger and more legal system that was put in place by the Marrakesh Agreement establishing the WTO and to its more effective and reliable

[22] Paragraph II.1 of the Rules of Conduct provides in this respect that "These Rules shall in no way modify the rights and obligations of Members under the DSU nor the rules and procedures therein". The inclusion of this sentence does not only reveal the concern of some Members that the application of the Rules of Conduct could undermine the text of the DSU, it also seems to underline the lack of clarity in the legal relation between the treaty and subsequent texts adopted by Members in WTO bodies.

[23] Para. IX:1 provided that a decision would have to be taken as to whether to continue, modify or terminate these Rules. Members agreed within the DSB to carry on with the application of the Rules of Conduct, but no formal decision was adopted.

dispute settlement system. It also recalls the purpose of the new Rules of Conduct: just as the Preamble presumes that a more "judicial" system will be more effective in the resolution of disputes, it also presumes that this system needs rules of conduct to maintain its integrity, impartiality and the confidentiality of proceedings.

Section II contains the governing principle of the Rules of Conduct and provides that each person covered by those Rules must be independent and impartial, must avoid direct and indirect conflicts of interest and respect the confidentiality of proceedings of bodies involved in dispute resolution so as to preserve the integrity and impartiality of the mechanism.[24]

C. Scope of Application

The Rules of Conduct are applicable to all the actors of the WTO dispute settlement system, except the parties and third parties to disputes.

Section IV (Scope) lists the categories of persons to which the Rules of Conduct apply, each being subject to specific rules in relation to its status:

- Panelists;
- Appellate Body Members;
- Arbitrators under Articles 21.3(c); 22.6 and 22.7, 26.1(c) and 25 of the DSU and XXI.3 and XXII.3 of the GATS;
- Secretariat staff assisting panels or arbitrators (pursuant to Article 27.1 of the DSU); and
- Appellate Body support staff called to provide administrative or legal support to the Appellate Body pursuant to Article 17.7 of the DSU.

Section V deals specifically with the Textile Monitoring Body (TMB), which is no longer in operation since 1 January 2005, due to the termination of the Textiles and Clothing Agreement, one of the agreements on trade in goods annexed to the WTO Agreement.

D. A System Based Primarily on Self-Disclosure

Section III concerns the observance of the governing principle. Such observance requires in the first place that the persons falling within the scope of application of the Rules of Conduct (the "covered persons") adhere strictly to the provisions of the DSU and take due care of avoiding any

[24] Moreover, the covered person must not delegate his/her responsibility to any other person. For instance, a university professor consulted as expert is not supposed to request one of his/her research assistant to prepare his/her opinion.

direct or indirect conflicts of interest in respect of the subject matter of the proceedings.

However, the most important element of this Section is the requirement to disclose the existence or the development of any interest, relationship or matter that a covered person could reasonably be expected to know and that is likely to affect, or give rise to justifiable doubts, as to that person's independence or impartiality.

While the circumstances where disclosure will be required are quite numerous if one refers to Annex 2 of the Rules of Conduct, it is important to note that the covered persons must consider only matters raised in, and necessary to fulfil their responsibilities within, the dispute settlement proceeding in which they are involved.

Finally, the covered person must not accept responsibilities or benefits that would in any way interfere with, or *could give rise to justifiable doubts* as to the proper performance of that person's dispute settlement duties. For instance, a private lawyer serving as panelist must refrain from working for any of the parties, even on an unrelated subject, since even this might give rise to justifiable doubts.

Section VI governs the self-disclosure requirements applicable to covered persons. The Rules of Conduct require that all covered persons be made aware of their obligations under the Rules. They also require self-disclosure of information that such persons could reasonably be expected to know and which is likely to give rise to justifiable doubts as to their independence or impartiality. This information includes that described in the illustrative list contained in Annex 2 to the Rules of Conduct.[25]

Section IV nevertheless addresses possible abusive requests by parties by requiring only the disclosure of information likely to give rise to *justifiable* doubt. It also excludes the disclosure of matters of insignificant relevance to the dispute at issue. It recalls the need to respect the personal privacy of the covered persons. Finally, Section IV states that the disclosure requirement must not be so administratively burdensome as to make it impracticable for otherwise qualified persons to participate in the dispute settlement process as panelist, member of the Appellate Body or in any other role.

Section IV provides for specific disclosure requirements applicable to each of the four main categories of covered persons:

(i) Panelists, arbitrators or experts are requested to complete the form contained in Annex 3 to the Rules of Conduct. If the completed form

---

[25] See Annex VII.

contains any specific information, it will be disclosed to the Chair of the DSB for consideration by the parties to the dispute.

(ii) Members of the Appellate Body must also complete the form in Annex 3 before they can participate in the review of any given appeal. The disclosure form is reviewed by the Appellate Body as a whole, which decides whether that particular Member can hear the appeal.

(iii) Staff members of the Appellate Body Secretariat must disclose any relevant matter to the Appellate Body, whereas other staff members of the Secretariat considered to assist in a dispute must make their disclosure to the Director-General. The requirement goes beyond what is requested from panelists, arbitrators or experts, since it extends to earlier formal consideration of the specific measure at issue in a dispute under any provision of the WTO Agreement, including through formal legal advice to Members under Article 27.2 of the DSU, as well as any involvement with the dispute as an official of a WTO Member government or in any other professional capacity before having joined the Secretariat. Another interesting element is the inclusion of a clause in the WTO Staff Regulations.[26]

The obligation to disclose applies throughout the procedure, as soon as the covered person becomes aware of a matter that should be disclosed in application of the Rules of Conduct.

E. Protection of Confidentiality in Dispute Settlement Proceedings

Section VII addresses confidentiality in the proceeedings. To a large extent, it repeats the obligations (confidentiality of deliberations and proceedings and of information identified as confidential, prohibition of *ex parte* communications during the proceedings) which are already found in Articles 14, 17 and 18 of the DSU. Section VII also prohibits the use of any information acquired during dispute settlement proceeding in order to gain personal advantage or advantage for others. In this respect, it extends obligations already applicable to staff members pursuant to the WTO Staff Rules and Regulations to participants in the resolution of disputes who are not WTO officials.

In addition, neither the Chair of the DSB, nor the Secretariat, the parties to the dispute or any individual involved in dispute settlement may

[26] Paras. 34 and 35 of the Standards of Conduct, Annex A to the WTO Staff Regulations, which correspond to parts of the Rules of Conduct applying to WTO staff members.

disclose the information revealed through the disclosure process, even after the completion of the proceedings.

F. "Material Violations"

Section VIII is one of the most important clauses of the Rules of Conduct, to the extent that it deals with the procedures applicable to disclosure after the initiation of a dispute settlement procedure and to possible material violations of the Rules by a covered person. Probably mindful of the disruptive potential of a mechanism allowing reporting of conflicts of interest at any time after the initiation of a panel or Appellate Body procedure, the drafters seem to have tried to strictly define the conditions of application of this clause.

Section VIII:1 provides for an obligation for any party to a dispute (i.e. WTO Members) to report evidence of material violation of the obligations of independence, impartiality or the avoidance of direct or indirect conflicts of interest by any covered person which may impair the integrity, impartiality or confidentiality of the dispute settlement mechanism.

However, the Rules of Conduct impose a number of conditions apparently designed to prevent abuses. Such reporting must be made in writing. More importantly, it must be made at the earliest possible time. Any failure to do so must be explained by the reporting party and will be taken into account when assessing the violation.[27] Submission of evidence must also be made on a confidential basis to the Chair of the DSB, the Director-General or the Appellate Body, as applicable in accordance with the procedures on disclosure by covered persons. Other WTO Members who come into possession of such evidence may provide it to the parties to the dispute, but there does not seem to be any obligation to do so.

A failure to disclose, by a covered person, a relevant interest, relationship or matter, is not as such a sufficient ground to disqualify that person from continuing to participate in the proceedings. The reporting party must also submit evidence of a *material violation* of the obligations applicable to the covered person in application of the Rules of Conduct.[28] What make a violation "material" is, however, not mentioned.

Once the evidence has been submitted, the matter must be reviewed within 15 working days. This time period has to be considered in the light of the relatively short time periods applicable under the DSU to the review of cases (six to nine months before a panel, maximum three months before

---

[27] Para. VIII:3.
[28] Para. VIII:2.

the Appellate Body).[29] This time period is also to be considered in the light of the fact that, in application of the principle of presumption of innocence, the person concerned shall continue to participate in the proceedings until it is decided that he/she has committed a material violation of the Rules of Conduct.[30]

The procedures applicable to the review of evidence of material violation differ according to the covered person. However, in all instances, the procedure is designed to ensure that the covered person is given an opportunity to make his/her views known and that an objective decision is reached.

When panelists, arbitrators or experts are concerned, the evidence of material violation must be provided to the Chair of the DSB, who will forward such evidence to the covered person concerned. The Chair will first conduct consultations with the covered person with the aim to resolve the issue. If the matter is not solved, the evidence and any additional information provided by the person concerned will then be communicated to the parties.

In all instances, the Chair of the DSU will consult with the Director-General of the WTO and chairpersons of the relevant WTO Council(s)[31] and shall provide a reasonable opportunity for the parties and the person concerned to be heard. Once this has been done, the Chair of the DSB shall decide whether a material violation of the Rules of Conduct has taken place, unless the person concerned resigns, or the parties to the dispute agree that a material violation of the Rules of Conduct has taken place, in which case it is expected that the Chair will confirm the disqualification of the person concerned, "consistent with maintaining the integrity of the dispute settlement mechanism".[32]

When the covered person who is the subject of evidence of material violation is a WTO staff member, the evidence is provided only to the Director-General who must immediately inform the staff member concerned

---

[29] See also para. VIII:19.

[30] Para. VIII:9.

[31] The three main sectors of trade covered by the WTO Agreement (trade in goods, services, trade-related aspects of intellectual property rights) are each supervised by a Council composed of representatives of all WTO Members, in addition to the General Council, which acts as the governing body of the Organization. Disputes between WTO Members may relate to provisions of agreements on trade in goods, trade in Services or to trade-related aspects of intellectual property rights. Hence the involvement of the chairpersons of the councils in case of conflicts of interest.

[32] This approach is in line with the currently prevailing view that entities involved in the conduct of WTO dispute settlement proceedings should defer to the views of the parties when the latter agree.

and the other party/ies to the dispute, as well as the panel. The Rules of Conduct respect the authority of the Director-General as head of the Secretariat, since it is for the Director-General to decide whether to initiate or not any appropriate disciplinary action[33] and the parties and the panel are only informed of the final decision.[34] As already mentioned, the specific situation of the involvement of staff members in dispute resolution is reflected in the WTO Staff Regulations.

In cases involving Appellate Body members or staff members of the Appellate Body Secretariat, the procedure is once again different, since the party in possession of evidence of material violation of the Rules of Conduct must first provide the evidence to the other party to the dispute and only thereafter to the Appellate Body. However, as in the other situations, the principle remains that the person concerned must be given access to the evidence and a reasonable opportunity to be heard. It is then for the Appellate Body to take any appropriate action, including when the person concerned is one of its supporting staff, which would seem to suggest that, under such circumstances, the staff members of the Appellate Body Secretariat escape the authority of the Director-General. This would also seem to suggest that staff members of the Appellate Body Secretariat may not be subject to disciplinary actions in case of material violation of the Rules of Conduct, unlike their colleagues of other divisions of the Secretariat, except if the Appellate Body requests the initiation of such action by the Director-General. Indeed, the Appellate Body as such has no power to sanction its staff under the WTO Staff Rules and Regulations.

The submission of evidence of material violation of the Rules of Conduct may lead to the following results: either it is decided that the covered person has not committed any material violation or, in the case of a panelist, arbitrator, expert, or even a staff member of the WTO, the person resigns. The appointment of the person may be revoked, or he/she may be excused from serving on the case. In such cases, existing procedures for appointment of panelists, arbitrators or experts will be applied to designate a new person.

---

[33] Para. VIII:12.

[34] This situation has to be contrasted with that of the Appellate Body in cases involving staff members of the Appellate Body Secretariat who, even though they are staff members of the WTO subject to the authority of the Director-General, are on a number of matters including conflicts of interest, under the exclusive authority of the Appellate Body.

V. Conclusion

In conclusion, some lessons may be drawn from the WTO experience:

First, in a mechanism involving different categories of persons such as staff members, on the one hand, and outside persons under service contracts, on the other hand, specific requirements and procedures have to be applied to each category of persons in order to make the system workable and efficient. Indeed, this allows each case to be treated as discretely and promptly as possible, having regard to the individual situation of the person concerned.

Second, the system must be designed in such a way that it can protect both staff members and the parties to the dispute. Because staff members are regularly involved in disputes as part of their duties, they should not become regular victims of tactical actions of parties to a dispute.

Third, the system must be sufficiently flexible to avoid that formal mechanisms be triggered in all cases. In this respect, the procedures for material violation provided in the Rules of Conduct have, to our knowledge, never been fully applied. Generally, the matter is solved by the resignation of the panelist concerned or, in the case of a WTO official, the staff member is excused by the Director-General from serving on the proceedings concerned. As a matter of fact, of the 105 panels and 58 Appellate Body proceedings which had been completed as of 30 September 2004, there have been very few instances where the parties have formally challenged individuals involved in the panel or Appellate Body proceedings. This is an indication that the litigants to date have generally not found it necessary to invoke the Rules of Conduct because any potential conflict had apparently been resolved before the proceedings got underway. In this regard, there have been a number of instances where Secretariat staff or Appellate Body members have recused themselves in compliance with the Rules of Conduct. In other words, the Rules of Conduct seem to date to have been operating successfully without any need to trigger the formal exclusion mechanisms contained therein. Further support of this is that never, after a decision has been rendered, has a panel or the Appellate Body been challenged on grounds of lack of independence or impartiality, or due to conflict of interests.

Fourth, governing bodies of organizations must also be careful that provisions designed to protect the integrity of a mechanism be not diverted from their purpose and used to prevent the mechanism from operating effectively. In the case of the WTO, this has apparently be achieved by imposing strict conditions to recourses to the Rules of Conduct.

Finally, the rules must strike the right balance between the need to ensure impartiality and the need to ensure that suitable persons are not prevented from contributing in the procedure subject to the rules.

SIX

Revision in the OECD of Title II of the Staff Regulations "Basic Principles, Rights and Duties"

Sylvie Vanston[1]

I. Introduction

The recent (October 2002) revision of the Staff Regulations and Rules applicable to Officials of the OECD focused on the incorporation, on the basis of an ethics policy, of normative provisions regarding the rights and obligations of officials. It concerned the whole of Title II to the Staff Regulations (Regulations 2 to 5) previously entitled "Duties, Obligations and Privileges", which became "Basic Principles, Rights and Obligations".

The purpose of this revision was to meet the following objectives:

1 Review the rights and obligations of officials in order to simplify understanding of the fundamental legal principles involved;
2 Specify the scope of basic rights as well as the obligations of OECD officials;
3 Define a policy on ethics for the Organisation, particularly by introducing into the Staff Rules new provisions about such items as the acceptance of benefits from an outside source, personal use of the OECD's resources, prevention of resources, carrying out of public activity, objective expression of the professional opinions of the officials, respect for privacy, use of privileges and immunities as well as combating sexual and personal harassment;
4 Specify the disciplinary sanctions in case of failure to respect these essential principles.

The revision specifically intended to amend texts as follows:

1 Put greater emphasis on the basic principle of independence as a general principle of international civil service law, as well as on the obligations of integrity, loyalty, tact and discretion; the relevant regulations (2, 3 and 4) were redrafted in order to incorporate elements of an ethics policy;

[1] Organisation for Economic Co-operation and Development.

2 Regroup the fundamental rights of officials in a single Regulation (Regulation 5, entitled "Basic individual rights and rights of association) which includes the principle of non-discrimination, the right to be treated with courtesy, dignity and respect, the right to privacy, the right of association and finally the right to express professional opinions;
3 Regroup normative provisions regarding immunities and privileges under a sub-heading entitled "Protection of officials in the performance of their duties" (Regulation 5bis) while giving them a greater emphasis, in the light of the Supplementary Protocol N° 1 to the OECD Convention on the legal capacity, privileges and immunities of the Organisation;
4 Clarify the responsibility of officials with regard to the reputation of the Organisation as well as the possibility for the OECD to sanction any non-compliance of officials with the basic principles and obligations mentioned above, by making, for example, deductions from any sums due to the officials (under Regulation 21, "Discipline and civil liability);

As a consequence of the above revision, article 1c) of Annex III to the Staff Regulations ("Resolution of the Council on the statute and operation of the Administrative Tribunal") was amended by extending the range of grounds under which persons who are not OECD staff members can claim that they were subject to discrimination when applying for a job with the Organisation. This range, previously limited to "race, creed or sex", was extended to "racial or ethnic origin, nationality, opinions or beliefs, gender, sexual orientation, health or disabilities" of the applicant.

In addition, as a part of the policy on ethics, a decision of the Secretary-General concerning the policy to prevent and combat sexual and personal harassment was annexed to the Staff Regulations (*cf.* Annex XIV).

Rules relating to intellectual property rights, which pertained to the previous Title II, were to be moved in the provisions regarding the terms of appointment. However, pending a Council decision on the latter, they are currently presented in an annex. These rules are the following:

> *1. All rights, including copyright and patent rights, in any work produced by an official as part of his official duties are vested in or assigned to the Organisation, unless such rights are waived by the Secretary-General in favour of the official concerned.*
> *2. Requests for authorisation to publish or make use of any work, as specified in paragraph 1, above, should be made to the Secretary-General by the official concerned through his supervisor. The latter shall inform the Head of Human Resources Management.*

II. The Debate

It can be noted that some proposals made by individual countries, such as the introduction of "grammatical" gender neutrality in the Staff Regulations or the creation of a position of ethics officer, were not retained. The first concern was felt to be covered by a general provision to the effect that "in the Staff Regulations, Rules and Instructions, references to officials apply equally to men and women except when it is clear from the context that they are intended to apply only to men or only to women." As for the creation of a position of ethics officer, it was felt not to be necessary, the Organisation generally dealing with breaches of the relevant provisions within its current structure.

In the course of consultations with staff representatives, the Staff Association expressed reservations regarding this exercise, as in its view there is no place in staff rules and regulations for moral and ethical considerations. It also felt that the text was unnecessarily heavy and deplored that it placed more emphasis on the obligations of officials than on their rights.

TITLE II

Basic Principles, Rights and Duties

INDEPENDENCE AND INTERNATIONAL CHARACTER

REGULATION 2

a) The duties of officials of the Organisation are international in character. Officials are subject to the authority of the Secretary-General, and are responsible to him for the discharge of their duties.

b) Officials shall carry out their duties and regulate their conduct always bearing in mind the interests of the Organisation and the international character of their duties.

c) Officials shall neither seek nor accept from any Member country of the Organisation or any source external to the Organisation any instructions. Unless authorised to do so, they shall neither seek nor accept, any:

i) gratuity or benefit in connection with their official duties or by reason of their status as an official of the Organisation;
ii) honorary distinction; or
iii) remuneration.

Last update: Oct 2002

Instructions

Acceptance of remuneration and other benefits from external sources

102/1
Officials are authorised to receive:
a) retirement pay or pensions;
b) honoraria for public appearances or publications which are either turned over to the Organisation to fund activities of the official's directorate or donated to a recognised charity;
c) normal and customary hospitality and protocol gifts; and
d) honorary distinctions awarded for work accomplished before the official's appointment or for work unconnected with official duties, provided the Head of Human Resource Management was notified and did not raise any objection within fifteen days.

102/1.1
Officials shall report to the Head of Human Resource Management any protocol gift of over 100 Euros in value. When in doubt as to whether or not a gift exceeds 100 Euros in value, the official shall also report it to the Head of Human Resource Management.

102/1.2
A gift which the Organisation determines is not normal and customary shall be the property of the Organisation. The official concerned may be permitted to purchase the gift for its full value.

102/1.3
Any request for authorisation falling within the scope of Regulation 2 c) beyond those set out in Instruction 102/1 shall be made in writing to the Head of Human Resource Management (1).

Settlement of individual disputes

102/2
In view of the independence and international character of officials' duties, they shall settle any individual disputes they may have with the Organisation exclusively through the internal channels provided for in the Staff Regulations.
Last update: Oct 2002

1. Remuneration from a Member Government may be authorised exceptionally pursuant to Regulation 15 b).

INTEGRITY AND LOYALTY

REGULATION 3

a) Officials shall:

i) carry out their duties in accordance with the highest standards of integrity and loyalty;
ii) conduct themselves with objectivity and impartiality and avoid any conflict of interest, or appearance of conflict of interest, in the performance of their duties;
iii) carefully manage the resources of the Organisation for which they are responsible;
iv) not use the Organisation's resources for their own personal benefit or for the benefit of third parties;
v) report any fraud, corruption or misuse of the Organisation's resources;
vi) not use their position within the Organisation, its name or logo or any information acquired in the course of their official duties to obtain undue benefits for themselves or third parties, or for any other inappropriate purpose.

b) Officials shall not be subject to any form of retaliation or prejudice as a result of disclosure in accordance with Regulation 3 a) v) and any related instructions.

Last update: Oct 2002

Instructions

Personal use of the Organisation's resources

103/1
The Organisation's equipment, supplies and systems are furnished for performance of their official functions. Nevertheless, officials may, if the need arises, make an occasional telephone call, e-mail communication, or visit to an internet site for personal reasons while at the office. Officials are expected to use common sense and judgement in doing so, to pay for long-distance or other toll communications, and to comply with any rules or guidelines which the Executive Director may issue.

Avoiding conflicts of interest

103/2
Officials are to disqualify themselves from advising or acting in the course of their duties with respect to a matter in which they or someone with whom they have a close relationship has a

special personal interest. This includes, for example, procurement of goods or services from an enterprise in which they have a financial interest (other than a small investment in shares or securities of a widely held company); or the recruitment, performance evaluation, or promotion of family members. In exceptional circumstances, the official's supervisor (director, head of service, or above) may waive this requirement where it is in the interest of the Organisation and where, in the case of the purchase of goods and services, the order has been subject to competitive tendering.

103/2.1
If in doubt regarding these matters, officials should inform their supervisor.

Reporting any fraud, corruption or misuse of the Organisation's resources

103/3
In the event an official becomes aware of fraud, corruption or misuse of the Organisation's resources, he must bring it to the attention of the Secretary-General either directly or through a director or head of service, the Auditor-General or the Executive Director.

103/3.1
If an official considers that a significant problem communicated in this fashion has not been properly addressed, he must bring it to the attention of the Board of Auditors and may bring it to the attention of the Council through the Permanent Representative holding the position of Dean.

103/3.2
Officials should not bring frivolous or malicious charges.

Last updated: Oct 2002

TACT AND DISCRETION

REGULATION 4

Officials shall:

a) carry out their official duties and conduct themselves with the tact and discretion that the international character of their duties and the interests of the Organisation require;

b) refrain from any act which may harm the reputation of the Organisation or its officials;

c) refrain from seeking or holding public office, unless authorised by the Secretary-General;

d) refrain from publicly doing, stating or publishing anything incompatible with their duties or obligations or liable to involve the responsibility of the Organisation;

e) make public statements concerning the Organisation or its activities only with permission from the Organisation;

f) protect the confidentiality of sensitive, unpublished information that has come to their attention in the course of their official duties;

g) continue to be bound by the obligation referred to in f) above after leaving the Organisation.

Last update: Oct 2002

Instructions

Public activities

104/1

Public activities of a political nature other than seeking or holding public office, though not covered by Regulation 4c), shall nevertheless be subject to other provisions of the Staff Regulations, in particular, Regulations 2a), 3a) ii) and vi), 4 a) and b). Common sense and good judgement are required. For example, an official shall refrain from playing an active or prominent role in a non-governmental organisation which may seek to influence public policy debates within the Organisation. Similarly, an official shall refrain from playing a prominent role in partisan politics in a Member country which may impair his working relationship with representatives of the country concerned.

104/1.1

In line with the Organisation's policy of transparency and public accountability and subject to normal precautions, including non-partisanship and reserve concerning the positions taken by individual Member countries, officials may comment in public about activities of the Organisation in respect of which they have some responsibility. Directors and heads of service have responsibility for ensuring that the content of such comments is compatible with the Organisation's policies and interests, and officials shall seek guidance from them when appropriate. Directors and heads of service may delegate this task to heads of division.

Last update: Oct 2002

BASIC INDIVIDUAL RIGHTS AND RIGHTS OF ASSOCIATION

REGULATION 5

a) Officials shall not be subject to any discrimination on the grounds of racial or ethnic origin, nationality, opinions or beliefs, gender, sexual orientation, health or disabilities (1).

b) Officials are entitled to be treated with courtesy, dignity and respect (2).

c) Officials are entitled to respect for their privacy.

d) Professionally, officials have the right to express dissenting opinions in an appropriate fashion within the Organisation.

e) Officials are entitled to exercise the right to organise, and are in particular free to form trade unions and staff bodies within the Organisation and to join and become officials of such bodies.

f) All officials shall respect these rights in the course of their official duties and in their behaviour with other officials.

Last update: Oct 2002

(1) The Organisation may nevertheless grant expatriation benefits, take measures designed to ensure gender balance or the equitable distribution of posts among nationals of Members of the Organisation, or require that officials possess the degree of physical fitness needed for their post.

(2) The Organisation's policy and guidelines on combating harassment, a particularly serious violation of the right to courtesy, dignity and respect, are set out in Annex XX of the Staff Regulations.

Instructions

Expression of professional opinion

105/1
An official whose professional opinion is contrary to a policy or decision of his immediate superiors or of another part of the Organisation may express that dissent in a reasoned and discreet manner within the Secretariat, including to responsible senior officials.

105/1.1
The right to express a dissenting professional opinion shall not release the official from the obligation to implement a lawful policy or decision, once adopted. If, having expressed his disagree-

ment in accordance with Instruction 105/1, the official still has serious reservations, he may ask to be given written instructions.

Privacy

105/2

Officials having access to confidential personal information concerning other officials may utilise it only for duly authorised official purposes and must handle it with care.

105/2.1

Respect for privacy does not preclude the Organisation from acting with regard to an official whose conduct outside the Organisation or the scope of the official's functions impairs his ability to perform those functions satisfactorily or which is incompatible with the status of an international civil servant. This includes actions which could damage the Organisation's reputation or be perceived as an abuse of the privileges and immunities of the Organisation and its staff.

105/2.2

The electronic accounts made available to officials are intended for the performance of official duties and not for storage of confidential personal information. The Organisation may access the content of such accounts with the consent of the account holder or with the authorisation of or in accordance with guidelines established by the Executive Director.

Last update: Oct 2002

PROTECTION OF OFFICIALS IN THE PERFORMANCE OF THEIR DUTIES

REGULATION 5bis

a) Officials shall be entitled to the Organisation's protection in the performance of their duties. They shall continue to enjoy such protection after they have left the Organisation.

b) Officials enjoy certain privileges, immunities and facilities which are granted in the interests of the Organisation and not for the personal benefit of the individuals concerned. In particular, they shall not excuse officials from the performance of their private obligations or from the strict observance of law.

Last update: Oct 2002

Instructions

Requests for assistance

105bis/1
Any request for protection pursuant to Staff Regulation 5 bis)a) by an official threatened or attacked because of actions or status as an official of the Organisation shall be submitted to the Head of Human Resource Management. Protection may, for example, take the form of a contribution to the expenses occasioned by the legal defence of the official's interests or other help in this context.

Privileges and immunities

105bis/2
The right to decide whether immunities shall be claimed or waived is with the Organisation. An official wishing to invoke immunity shall address a request to the Secretary-General through the Head of Human Resource Management. If it was not possible to request a prior decision, an official claiming immunity shall immediately inform the Head of Human Resource Management.

105bis/2.1
Any other difficulty arising in connection with privileges and immunities should immediately be reported to the Head of Human Resource Management.

105bis/2.2
Officials should not seek or accept means-tested benefits to which, taking into account their income from the Organisation, they are not entitled.

Last update: Oct 2002

ANNEX I

Standards of Conduct for the International Civil Service

Introduction

For the past half century the international civil service has been guided by the *Standards of Conduct in the International Civil Service* prepared in 1954 by the International Civil Service Advisory Board. Although these standards have stood the test of time, an earlier era resonates in some of the content and tone. The onset of a new millennium provided the impetus for the revision of these standards to take into account global changes and to reflect, in more modern, gender-neutral language, developments and concepts that either did not exist or were of lesser importance in 1954. A renewed interest in the subject on the part of national civil services and the private sector in responding to new ethical challenges was a further stimulus to a new text.

The *Standards of Conduct for the International Civil Service* contained in this brochure were revised and updated by the International Civil Service Commission in consultation with participating organizations and the representatives of the staff over a three-year period. Upon their completion in 2001, they were welcomed by the United Nations General Assembly in its resolution 56/244. The ICSC *Framework for Human Resources Management*, approved by the General Assembly in 2000, illustrates the overarching nature of *the Standards of Conduct*, noting that they are linked to all elements of the *Framework*, and states that "although organizations' internal cultures may vary, they face similar ethical challenges. Standards for ethical conduct promote common values and define the behaviour and performance expected of international civil servants".

This new text aims at providing for the international civil service standards that, like those of 1954, become an indispensable part of the culture and heritage of the organizations and are of similarly enduring quality.

Mohsen Bel Hadj Amor
Chairman
International Civil Service Commission
January 2002

Standards of conduct for the international civil service

1. The United Nations and the specialized agencies embody the highest aspirations of the peoples of the world. Their aim is to save succeeding generations from the scourge of war and to enable every man, woman and child to live in dignity and freedom.

2. The international civil service bears responsibility for translating these ideals into reality. It relies on the great traditions of public administration that have grown up in member States: competence, integrity, impartiality, independence and discretion. But over and above this, international civil servants have a special calling: to serve the ideals of peace, of respect for fundamental rights, of economic and social progress, and of international cooperation. It is therefore incumbent on international civil servants to adhere to the highest standards of conduct; for, ultimately, it is the international civil service that will enable the United Nations system to bring about a just and peaceful world.

Guiding principles

3. The values that are enshrined in the United Nations organizations must also be those that guide international civil servants in all their actions: fundamental human rights, social justice, the dignity and worth of the human person and respect for the equal rights of men and women and of nations great and small.

4. International civil servants should share the vision of their organizations. It is loyalty to this vision that ensures the integrity and international outlook of international civil servants; it guarantees that they will place the interests of their organization above their own and use its resources in a responsible manner.

5. The concept of integrity enshrined in the Charter of the United Nations embraces all aspects of behaviour of an international civil servant, including such qualities as honesty, truthfulness, impartiality and incorruptibility. These qualities are as basic as those of competence and efficiency, also enshrined in the Charter.

6. Tolerance and understanding are basic human values. They are essential for international civil servants, who must respect all persons equally, without any distinction whatsoever. This respect fosters a climate and a working environment sensitive to the needs of all. To achieve this in a multicultural setting calls for a positive affirmation going well beyond passive acceptance.

7. International loyalty means loyalty to the whole United Nations system and not only to the organization for which one works; international civil servants have an obligation to understand and exemplify this wider loyalty. The need for a cooperative and understanding attitude towards international civil servants of other United Nations organizations is obviously most important where international civil servants of several organizations are serving in the same country or region.

8. If the impartiality of the international civil service is to be maintained, international civil servants must remain independent of any authority outside their organization; their conduct must reflect that independence. In keeping with their oath of office, they should not seek nor should they accept instructions from any Government, person or entity external to the organization. It cannot be too strongly stressed that international civil servants are not, in any sense, representatives of Governments or other entities, nor are they proponents of their policies. This applies equally to those on secondment from Governments and to those whose services have been made available from elsewhere. International civil servants should be constantly aware that through their allegiance to the Charter and the corresponding instruments of each organization, member States and their representatives are committed to respect this independent status.

9. Impartiality implies tolerance and restraint, particularly in dealing with political or religious convictions. While their personal views remain inviolate, international civil servants do not have the freedom of private persons to take sides or to express their convictions publicly on controversial matters, either individually or as members of a group. This can mean that, in certain situations, personal views should only be expressed with tact and discretion.

10. This does not mean that international civil servants have to give up their personal political views or national perspectives. It does mean, however, that they must at all times maintain a broad international outlook and an understanding of the international community as a whole.

11. The independence of the international civil service does not conflict with, or obscure, the fact that it is the member States that collectively make up (in some cases with other constituents) the organization. Conduct that furthers good relations with individual member States and that contributes to their trust and confidence in the secretariat strengthens the organization and promotes its interest.

12. International civil servants who are responsible for projects in particular countries or regions may be called upon to exercise special care in maintaining their independence. At times they might receive instructions from the host country but this should not compromise their independence. If at any time they consider that such instructions threaten their independence, they must consult their supervisors.

13. An international outlook stems from an understanding of and loyalty to the objectives and purposes of the international organization itself as set forth in its legal instruments. It implies, inter alia, respect for the right of others to hold different points of view and follow different cultural patterns. It requires a willingness to work without bias with persons of all nationalities, religions and cultures; it calls for constant sensitivity to how proposals, events and statements may look to others. It requires punctilious avoidance of any expressions that could be interpreted as biased or intolerant. Working methods can be different in different cultures. International civil servants should not be wedded to the attitudes, working methods or work habits of their own country or region.

14. Freedom from discrimination is a basic human right. International civil servants are expected to respect the dignity, worth and equality of all people without any distinction whatsoever. Assumptions based on stereotypes must be assiduously avoided. One of the main tenets of the Charter is the equality of men and women, and organizations should therefore do their utmost to promote gender equality.

Working relations

15. Managers and supervisors are in positions of leadership and it is their responsibility to ensure a harmonious workplace based on mutual respect; they should be open to all views and opinions and make sure that the merits of staff are properly recognized. They need to provide support to them; this is particularly important when they are subject to criticism arising from the carrying out of their duties. Managers are also responsible for guiding and motivating their staff and promoting their development.

16. It is natural for managers to be seen as role models and they have therefore a special obligation to uphold the highest standards of conduct. It would be quite improper for them to solicit favours, gifts or loans from their staff; they must act impartially, without intimidation and favouritism. In matters relating to the appointment or career of others, no international civil servant should try to influence colleagues for personal reasons.

17. It is naturally incumbent on managers and supervisors to communicate effectively with their staff and share information with them. International civil servants have a reciprocal responsibility to provide all pertinent facts and information to their supervisors and to abide by and defend any decisions taken, even when these do not accord with their personal views.

18. International civil servants have to follow the instructions they receive in connection with their official functions and if they have doubts as to whether an instruction is consistent with the Charter or any other constitutional instrument, decisions of the governing bodies or administrative rules and regulations, they should first consult their supervisors. If they cannot agree, the international civil servant may ask for written instructions. These may be challenged through the proper institutional mechanisms, but any challenge should not delay carrying out the instruction. International civil servants may also record their views in official files. They should not follow verbal or written instructions that are manifestly inconsistent with their official functions or that threaten their safety or that of others.

19. It must be the duty of international civil servants to report any breach of the organization's rules and regulations to a higher level official, whose responsibility it is to take appropriate action. An international civil servant who makes such a report in good faith has the right to be protected against reprisals or sanctions.

Harassment

20. Harassment in any shape or form is an affront to human dignity and international civil servants must avoid it. They should not engage in any form of

harassment and must be above any suspicion of it. International civil servants have the right to an environment free of harassment. It is the responsibility of organizations to explain their interpretation of the term and to establish rules and provide guidance on what constitutes harassment and how it will be dealt with.

Conflict of interest

21. It can happen that international civil servants are confronted with a question entailing a conflict of interest; such questions can be very sensitive and need to be treated with care. Conflict of interest includes circumstances in which international civil servants, directly or indirectly, would appear to benefit improperly, or allow a third party to benefit improperly, from their association in the management or the holding of a financial interest in an enterprise that engages in any business or transaction with the organization.

22. There can be no question but that international civil servants should avoid assisting private bodies or persons in their dealings with their organization where this might lead to actual or perceived preferential treatment. This is particularly important in procurement matters or when negotiating prospective employment. At times, international civil servants may be required to disclose certain personal assets if this is necessary to enable their organizations to make sure that there is no conflict. They should also voluntarily disclose in advance possible conflicts of interest that arise in the course of carrying out their duties. They should perform their official duties and conduct their private affairs in a manner that preserves and enhances public confidence in their own integrity and that of their organization.

Role of the secretariat

23. International organizations are constituted by member States, and their secretariats have the responsibility for providing services to them. The main function of the secretariat is to assist legislative bodies in their work and to carry out their decisions. The executive head is responsible for directing and controlling the work of the secretariat. Accordingly, when submitting proposals or advocating positions before a legislative body or committee, international civil servants are presenting the position of the executive head, not that of an individual or unit.

24. In providing services to a legislative or representative body, it goes without saying that international civil servants should serve only the interests of the organization. It would not be appropriate for international civil servants to prepare for government or other international civil service representatives any speeches, arguments or proposals on questions under discussion. It could, however, be quite appropriate to provide factual information, technical advice or assistance with such tasks as the preparation of draft resolutions.

25. It is entirely improper for international civil servants to lobby or seek support from government representatives or members of legislative organs to obtain advancement either for themselves or for others or to block or reverse unfavourable decisions regarding their status. By adhering to the Charter and the constitutions of the organizations of the United Nations system, Governments have undertaken to

safeguard the independence of the international civil service; it is therefore understood that government representatives and members of legislative bodies will neither accede to such requests nor intervene in such matters. The proper method for an international civil servant to address such matters is through administrative channels; each organization is responsible for providing these.

Staff management relations

26. Relations between management and staff should be guided by mutual respect. Elected staff representatives have a cardinal role to play in the consideration of conditions of employment and work, as well as in all matters of staff welfare. Freedom of association is a fundamental human right and international civil servants have the right to form and join associations, unions or other groupings to promote and defend their interests. Continuing dialogue between staff and management is indispensable. Management should facilitate this dialogue.

27. Elected staff representatives enjoy rights that derive from their status; this may include the opportunity to address legislative organs of their organization. These rights should be exercised in a manner that is consistent with the Charter, the Universal Declaration of Human Rights and the international covenants on human rights and does not undermine the independence and integrity of the international civil service. In using the broad freedom of expression they enjoy, staff representatives must exercise a sense of responsibility and avoid undue criticism of the organization.

28. Staff representatives must be protected against discriminatory or prejudicial treatment based on their status or activities as staff representatives, both during their term of office and after it has ended.

Relations with member States and legislative bodies

29. It is the clear duty of all international civil servants to maintain the best possible relations with Governments and avoid any action which might impair this; they should certainly not interfere in the policies or affairs of Governments. It is unacceptable for them, either individually or collectively, to criticize or try to discredit a Government. At the same time, it is understood that international civil servants may speak freely in support of their organizations' policies. Any activity, direct or indirect, to undermine or overthrow a Government constitutes serious misconduct.

30. International civil servants are not representatives of their countries, nor do they have authority to act as liaison agents between international organizations and their Governments. The executive head may, however, request an international civil servant to undertake such duties, a unique role for which international loyalty and integrity are essential. For their part, neither Governments nor organizations should place international civil servants in a position where their international and national loyalties may conflict.

Relations with the public

31. For an international organization to function successfully, it must have the support of the public. All international civil servants therefore have a continuing responsibility to promote a better understanding of the objectives and work of their organizations. This requires them to be well informed of the achievements not only of their own organizations but of the United Nations system as a whole. The opportunity to provide information to the public can arise at any time.

32. There is a risk that on occasion international civil servants may be subject to criticism from outside their organizations; in keeping with their responsibility as international civil servants, they should respond with tact and restraint. They have the right to be defended by their organizations against criticism for actions taken in fulfilment of their duties and they should be confident that this will be done.

33. It would not be proper for international civil servants to air personal grievances or criticize their organizations in public. International civil servants should endeavour at all times to promote a positive image of the international civil service, in conformity with their oath of loyalty.

Relations with the media

34. Openness and transparency in relations with the media are effective means of communicating the organizations' messages, and the organizations should have guidelines and procedures for this purpose. Within that context, the following principles should apply: international civil servants should regard themselves as speaking in the name of their organizations and avoid personal references and views; in no circumstances should they use the media to further their own interests, to air their own grievances, to reveal unauthorized information or to attempt to influence policy decisions facing their organizations.

Use and protection of information

35. The disclosure of confidential information may seriously jeopardize the efficiency and credibility of an organization. International civil servants are responsible for exercising discretion in all matters of official business. They must not divulge confidential information without authorization. Nor should international civil servants use information that has not been made public and is known to them by virtue of their official position to private advantage. These are obligations that do not cease upon separation from service. It is necessary for organizations to maintain guidelines for the use and protection of confidential information, and it is equally necessary for such guidelines to keep pace with developments in communications technology. It is understood that these provisions do not affect established practices governing the exchange of information between the secretariats and member States, which ensure the fullest participation of member States in the life and work of the organizations.

Respect for different customs and culture

36. The world is home to a myriad of different peoples, languages, cultures, customs and traditions. It is self-evident that a genuine respect for them all is fundamental for an international civil servant. Any behaviour that is not acceptable in a particular cultural context must be avoided. However, if a tradition is directly contrary to any human rights instrument adopted by the United Nations system, the international civil servant must be guided by it. International civil servants should avoid an ostentatious lifestyle and any display of an inflated sense of personal importance.

Security and safety

37. While an executive head must remain free to assign staff in accordance with the exigencies of the service, it is the responsibility of organizations to make sure that the health, well-being and lives of their staff, without any discrimination whatsoever, will not be subject to undue risk. The organizations should take measures to protect their safety and that of their family members. On the other hand, it goes without saying that it is incumbent on international civil servants to comply with all instructions designed to protect their safety.

Personal conduct

38. The private life of international civil servants is their own concern and organizations should not intrude upon it. There can be situations, however, in which the behaviour of an international civil servant can reflect on the organization. International civil servants must therefore bear in mind that their conduct and activities outside the workplace, even if unrelated to official duties, can compromise the image and the interests of the organization. This can also result from the conduct of members of international civil servants' households and it is the responsibility of international civil servants to make sure that their households are fully aware of this.

39. The privileges and immunities that international civil servants enjoy are conferred upon them solely in the interests of the organizations. They do not exempt international civil servants from observing local laws, nor do they provide an excuse for ignoring private legal or financial obligations. It should be remembered that only the executive head is competent to waive the immunity accorded to international civil servants or to determine its scope.

40. Violations of law can range from serious criminal activities to trivial offences, and organizations may be called upon to exercise judgement in the light of the nature and circumstances of individual cases. A conviction by a national court will usually, although not always, be persuasive evidence of the act for which an international civil servant was prosecuted, and acts that are generally recognized as offences by national criminal laws will normally also be violations of the standards of conduct for the international civil service.

Outside employment and activities

41. The primary obligation of international civil servants is to devote their energies to the work of their organizations. It is therefore improper for international civil servants to engage, without prior authorization, in any outside activity, whether remunerated or not, that interferes with that obligation or is incompatible with their status or conicts with the interests of the organization. Any questions about this should be referred to the executive head.

42. Subject to the above, outside activities may, of course, be beneficial both to staff members and to their organizations. Organizations should allow, encourage and facilitate the participation of international civil servants in professional activities that foster contacts with private and public bodies and thus serve to maintain and enhance their professional and technical competencies.

43. International civil servants on leave, whether with or without pay, should bear in mind that they remain international civil servants in the employ of their organization and are still subject to its rules. They may, therefore, only accept employment, paid or unpaid, during their leave with proper authorization.

44. In view of the independence and impartiality that they must maintain, international civil servants, while retaining the right to vote, should not participate in political activities, such as standing for or holding local or national political office. This does not, however, preclude participation in local community or civic activities, provided that such participation is consistent with the oath of service in the United Nations system. It is necessary for international civil servants to exercise discretion in their support for a political party or campaign, and they should not accept or solicit funds, write articles or make public speeches or make statements to the press. These cases require the exercise of judgement and, where there is any doubt, should be referred to the executive head.

45. The significance of membership in a political party varies from country to country and it is difficult to formulate standards that will apply in all cases. In general, international civil servants may be members of a political party provided its prevailing views and the obligations imposed on its members are consistent with the oath of service in the United Nations system.

Gifts, honours and remuneration from outside sources

46. To protect the international civil service from any appearance of impropriety, international civil servants must not accept, without authorization from the executive head, any honour, decoration, gift, remuneration, favour or economic benefit of more than nominal value from any source external to their organizations; it is understood that this includes Governments as well as commercial firms and other entities.

47. It is not proper for international civil servants to accept supplementary payments or other subsidies from a Government or any other source prior to, during or after their assignment with an international organization if the payment is

related to that assignment. Balancing this requirement, it is understood that Governments or other entities should not make or offer such payments, recognizing that they are at variance with the spirit of the Charter and the constitutions of the organizations of the United Nations system.

Conclusion

48. The attainment of the standards of conduct for the international civil service requires the highest commitment of all parties. International civil servants must be committed to the values, principles and standards set forth here. They are expected to take a positive and active approach in upholding them. They should feel responsible for contributing to the broad ideals to which they dedicated themselves in joining the United Nations system. International organizations have a particular responsibility to ensure that the necessary guidance or rules are adopted to implement these standards. For their part, member States are expected, through their allegiance to the Charter and other constituent instruments, to preserve the independence and impartiality of the international civil service.

49. For these standards to be effectively applied, it is essential that they be widely disseminated, and that measures be taken to ensure that their scope and importance are understood throughout the international civil service, the member States and the organizations of the United Nations system.

50. Respect for these standards assures that the international civil service will continue to be an effective instrument in fulfilling its responsibilities and in meeting the aspirations of the peoples of the world.

ANNEX II

IMF Code of Conduct for Staff

I. Preamble

1. The goals of the International Monetary Fund require that all who work for the institution observe the highest standards of professional ethics. We all have a responsibility to contribute to the good governance of the Fund and to help maintain its reputation for probity, integrity, and impartiality.

2. This code presents guidelines for staff conduct, which are intended to be consistent with the specific standards of conduct applicable to Fund staff members pursuant to the Fund's N-Rules and Regulations.

3. The code outlines obligations of Fund staff. However, the Fund as employer also has the obligation to assist staff in these matters by providing information and advice and by being responsive to staff concerns about ethical issues. Ethical conduct is not a passive process, but requires you to make conscious choices and decisions, and to exercise good judgment, consistent with the ethical values of the organization embodied in this code. A few basic guidelines to keep in mind:

- always act honestly and impartially when carrying out your duties;
- never make private use of, nor disclose without authorization, any confidential information you obtain through your work for the Fund;
- avoid outside activity that could reasonably be perceived as a conflict of interest; and
- always treat others in a courteous and professional manner.

4. You may sometimes find that the proper conduct in a given situation is not self-evident. This code can help you decide what to do in many, but not all, situations. When you are in doubt about the ethical implications of an action, seek advice before you act. Consult the documents posted on the IMF Web Service under the heading "Ethics and Staff Conduct." Address any questions to your supervisor or to the Staff Development Division of the Administration Department. And ask yourself these questions:

> Is it legal?
> Does it feel right?
> Will it reflect negatively or positively on me or the Fund?
> What would a reasonable person think about my action?
> Would I be embarrassed if others knew I took this action?
> Is there an alternative action that does not pose an ethical conflict?

5. Failure to observe the Fund's Rules and Regulations may be grounds for disciplinary action by the Fund, which may include termination of employment in the case of serious violations. Disciplinary action may be imposed for such misconduct depending on factors such as the nature and seriousness of the violation

and the staff member's prior record of conduct. Before disciplinary action is imposed, staff will be given the opportunity to present his/her views on the alleged misconduct, and, in case of disagreement with the action, may appeal it.

II. Basic Standard of Conduct

6. As a staff member, you are expected to observe the highest standards of ethical conduct, consistent with the values of integrity, impartiality and discretion. You should strive to avoid even the appearance of impropriety in your conduct. In the performance of your duties, you have a duty of exclusive loyalty to the Fund, and to its objectives, purposes, and principles.

Integrity

7. You are expected to act with integrity in all your official activities, avoiding any behavior that would reflect adversely on you or on the Fund. Integrity encompasses honesty, probity, and loyalty. You are expected to provide accurate and complete information needed by the Fund for the administration of personnel matters, and you must promptly report changes in your personal circumstances that affect your eligibility for benefits and allowances.

8. The Fund respects the privacy of staff members and does not wish to interfere with their personal lives and behavior outside the workplace. However, the status of an international civil servant carries certain obligations as regards conduct, both at work and elsewhere. The Fund attaches great importance to the observance of local laws by staff members, as well as the avoidance of actions that could be perceived as an abuse of the privileges and immunities conferred on the Fund and its staff, as the failure to do so would reflect adversely on the Fund. For example, staff members are expected to meet their private legal obligations to pay child support and alimony, and to comply with applicable laws concerning the treatment of G-5 domestic employees, as this program is available as a special privilege for international organization personnel. The Fund would also be seriously concerned about notoriously disgraceful conduct by a staff member involving domestic violence or abuse of family members.

9. The Fund is not in a position to investigate allegations that a staff member has violated local law. However, if concerns about a staff member's behavior outside the workplace are brought to its attention by third parties, it is both appropriate and prudent that the staff member be informed about the matter. It is not the Fund's role to determine whether local laws have been violated by a staff member, as that is for the domestic courts to decide. However, if the Fund receives a lawful order from a court or other governmental authority instructing it to withhold an amount of salary to be paid to a staff member to satisfy an outstanding legal obligation, the Fund will not allow the staff member to take undue advantage of the fact that it is immune from such orders.

Impartiality

10. You are expected to act with impartiality. You should take care that your expression of personal views and convictions does not compromise or appear to compromise the performance of your official duties or the interests of the Fund. Your official conduct must at all times be characterized by objectivity and professionalism. You should not allow personal relationships or considerations, including bias or favoritism, to influence the performance of your official duties and you should avoid situations that create a conflict of interest.

Discretion

11. You should exercise the utmost discretion in your actions and show tact and reserve in your pronouncements in a manner that is consistent with your status as an international civil servant. You should refrain from participating in any activity that is in conflict with the interests of the Fund or would damage the Fund's reputation. You must respect and safeguard the confidentiality of information which is available or known to you by reason of your official functions.

III. Conduct within the Fund

12. The basic values of impartiality, integrity, and discretion should govern all aspects of your conduct in your work.

Duty of loyalty

13. By accepting appointment at the Fund, you have promised to discharge your functions under the sole authority of the Managing Director. You must respect the international character of your position and maintain your independence by not accepting any instructions relating to the performance of your official duties from any national government or from any other sources external to the Fund.

Courtesy and respect

14. You should treat your colleagues, whether supervisors, peers, or subordinates, with courtesy and respect, without harassment, or physical or verbal abuse. You should at all times avoid behavior at the workplace that, although not rising to the level of harassment or abuse, may nonetheless create an atmosphere of hostility or intimidation.

Diversity

15. In view of the international character of the Fund and the value that the Fund attaches to diversity, you are expected to act with tolerance, sensitivity, respect, and impartiality toward other persons' cultures and backgrounds.

Accountability

16. You must act within the scope of your authority at all times. You remain accountable for tasks you delegate to others and you are expected to exercise adequate control and supervision over matters for which you are responsible.

Use of Fund property, facilities, and supplies

17. You have a responsibility to ensure that Fund resources are used for the official business of the Fund and you are expected to devote your time during working hours to the official activities of the Fund.

18. A rule of reason applies to the personal use of Fund premises or equipment.

Conflict resolution

19. Managers have a responsibility to make themselves available to staff members who may wish to raise concerns in confidence and to deal with such situations in an impartial and sensitive manner. Managers should endeavor to create an atmosphere in which staff feel free to use, without fear of reprisal, the existing institutional channels for conflict resolution,[1] and to express concerns about situations which are, or have the potential to be, conflictive.

IV. Use and Disclosure of Information

Use and disclosure of confidential information

20. You have a responsibility to protect the security of any confidential information provided to, or generated by, the Fund.[2] Accordingly, to avoid any unauthorized disclosure, you should be careful how you handle confidential information. The basic principle of the rules and guidelines on information security is that confidential information may be communicated among staff only in accordance with the rules/guidelines of document classification and must not be communicated to outsiders without authorization. Such authorization may take the form of either direct instructions from management to individuals or departments, or general policies established by management and the Executive Board. In addition, you must not use any such confidential information for your own advantage, for example, in your private business dealings (see Section V).

Press relations, public statements and publications[3]

21. You should not, without authorization, provide to the news media, publish, or make public statements relating to the policies or activities of the Fund or to

[1] For example, supervisors, Administrative Officers, Senior Personnel Managers, Harassment Advisors, or the Ombudsperson and the Grievance Committee.
[2] Confidential means not cleared/released by the Fund for public use.
[3] Based on revised GAO 34, to be proposed for issuance.

any national political question.[4] You are free to publish and speak about other subjects, but you should avoid any public communication not in keeping with your position as an international civil servant, which calls for reserve and tact.

22. Special procedures have been established for handling news media contacts in the Fund. Normally, before responding to or initiating a press contact related to the policies or activities of the Fund or a national political question, you should consult your supervisor, who in turn may need to consult the head of your department and the External Relations Department before you proceed with the contact.

23. The Fund owns the copyright for all written material you produce as part of your official duties, and has the right to publish such work in a manner it deems appropriate. If the Fund does not choose to publish your work, you may, with the approval of your department and EXR, publish your work elsewhere. The same joint approval is required for works (including public statements) prepared on your own time, or prior to joining the Fund staff, if the subject of the work relates to the Fund or its activities, or to any national political question. In contrast, no approval is required if the subject is unrelated to the Fund, its activities, or national political questions.

V. Conflicts of Interest, Including Personal Financial Affairs

Conflicts of interest

24. You should avoid any situation involving a conflict, or the appearance of a conflict, between your personal interests and performance of your official duties. In dealings with member country authorities, suppliers, and other parties, you should act in the best interest of the Fund to the exclusion of any personal advantage. To avoid potential conflicts of interest, the Fund will seek to avoid assigning nationals to work on policy issues relating specifically to Fund relations with their home country, unless needed for linguistic or other reasons. This would also apply to non-nationals who, given their individual circumstances, may have a particular conflict of interest vis-à-vis the country or its authorities. If a potential conflict exists, you should make prompt and full disclosure to your supervisor and seek his or her views as to whether you should recuse yourself from the situation that is creating the conflict or the appearance of conflict.

- If you are engaged in Fund procurement activities and if you have, or are considering having, any direct or indirect outside interests, financial or

[4] Rule N-5 requires Fund staff to obtain authorization before publishing or speaking publicly with respect to the policies and activities of the Fund or "any national political question." Such questions have not been further defined in the Fund's rules. It is the intention that the term will be narrowly interpreted so as to allow staff to express their personal views, as long as this would not prove to be embarrassing to the Fund nor could reasonably be perceived as interfering with domestic political matters. However, this concept is obviously judgmental, and its application in individual cases will depend on the context, including the nature of the issue involved and its particular sensitivity at a given time.

otherwise, which might conflict or appear to conflict with the interests of the Fund, you should make this situation known to your supervisor and seek his/her view on whether you should withdraw from participating in the procurement activity.

- If you are negotiating for, or have an arrangement concerning, prospective employment outside the Fund, you should maintain an arms-length relationship with the prospective employer in all matters relating to the work of the Fund. For example, you should recuse yourself from involvement in sensitive member country matters that could benefit, or could be perceived to benefit, the prospective employer. Similar conduct is expected of staff who are on temporary secondments to the Fund from their parent institution.

Personal financial affairs

25. You are generally free to conduct your personal financial affairs as you see fit with two exceptions:

a. because of the Fund's role in exchange rate surveillance, all staff members are prohibited from engaging in short-term trading (i.e., a combination of buying and selling within six months) in gold, foreign currencies and closely related financial instruments, for speculative purposes. The term "combination" does not include one way transactions, such as the selling or buying of foreign exchange for household expenses, education or travel expenses;

b. staff members are prohibited from using, or providing to others, confidential information to which they have access for purposes of carrying out private financial transactions.

26. As many diverse situations may arise where the general principle mentioned in paragraph 25(b) above could be subject to various interpretations, further guidance is provided below. If you remain unsure on how to proceed in a given situation, you should seek the assistance of the officer designated to this effect by management.

- Confidential information includes market-sensitive information relating to pending Fund or government actions that, when disclosed, are likely to have a material impact on the market value of currency or other investment vehicles. Examples of such market-sensitive information may include information about pending exchange rate or interest rate changes, major fiscal or economic policy changes or initiatives, and, in some cases, pending changes in top government officials or developments in relations with the Fund (e.g., calendar of missions or Board meetings).
- The prohibitions above apply to financial transactions effected by yourselves and by your immediate family members, i.e., spouse and dependents.
- The prohibitions above do not apply to pre-existing financial holdings. However, if you hold prior investments in financial assets of a country or group of countries to which you have been newly assigned and with respect to which you are likely to have access to confidential information, you should seek the views of the officer designated to this effect by management who would advise you whether you should divest these assets or refrain from effecting changes in asset positions during your assignment.

Disclosures

27. You should disclose any financial or business interests that you or your immediate family members have that might be in actual or apparent conflict with your Fund duties. You should make this disclosure to your supervisor or to the officer designated by management for such matters. Supervisors and the officers designated by management should make a written record of the disclosure for the protection of the staff member.

28. All staff members shall certify, according to a periodicity and in a form to be prescribed by the Managing Director, that they have read the policy on conflicts of interest and that they are in compliance. If a staff member is unsure about the extent of his/her compliance, he/she should provide further explanations as provided for in the certification form. In addition, the Managing Director may require certain categories of staff members to file a confidential statement of financial interests and activities, according to a periodicity and in a form prescribed by the Managing Director. These statements shall be filed with and examined by an officer designated by the Managing Director.

VI. External Activities

Outside employment

29. You need permission from the Fund to engage in any outside employment, occupation, business activity, or profession. The Fund would not object to your engaging in such an activity, provided that (i) it does not interfere with your ability to perform your regular work for the Fund; (ii) it is compatible with the Fund's rules on staff conduct; (iii) it does not create a conflict of interest; and (iv) it does not violate applicable immigration rules. Your request should be cleared with your department and forwarded to ADM, with the endorsement of your department. In some cases, especially activities related to outside publications and speeches, your request will need to be cleared by EXR also.

30. You may participate in volunteer activities of a community or charitable nature without advance clearance. However, if you are in doubt as to whether an activity you are contemplating would run counter to the criteria in (i)–(iv) above, you should seek advice from the Staff Development Division, ADM.

Political activities

31. Staff members need permission to engage in political activities, except for activities such as voting, making legal political contributions, and participating at the local, grass roots, or community level. Staff members may not run for elected public office without obtaining permission. A staff member who accepts a political appointment must offer to resign from the Fund staff. The rules for public statements apply if, for example, you wish to make a public statement endorsing a national political candidate.

Acceptance of gifts, decorations and honors

32. You should never solicit gifts or favors in connection with your Fund duties. Gifts that are offered should normally be declined. However, you may accept a small gift when it would create an embarrassment to refuse it. Under current rules, if its value is clearly less than $100, you may keep it and need not report it. If the value of the gift could exceed $100, you should report it, along with your estimate of its value. The gift may have to be turned in for an appraisal if there is a question about its value.

33. You are not allowed to accept any honors or decorations given to you in connection with your official duties with the Fund. If there is no advance notice of the honor or decoration, and it is impossible to refuse it, then you may accept it on behalf of the Fund and then report it to the Fund. However, in cases where the honor or decoration is in recognition of services unrelated to the Fund, the Fund will permit acceptance of such recognition.

Post-Fund employment

34. Staff members who separate from the Fund, or are on leave status, including leave without pay, are expected to observe the respective Fund rules on use or disclosure of confidential information. In particular, staff members who separate from the Fund should not use or disclose confidential information known to them by reason of their service with the Fund and should not contact former colleagues to obtain confidential information. Fund employees are prohibited from providing confidential information to former colleagues, who should be treated like any other outside party.

Basic Standard of Conduct

1. *A staff member fails to pay his or her spousal or child support obligations, notwithstanding a court order to do so. Does this violate the Fund's standards of conduct?*

   Yes. Staff members may not take improper advantage of the fact that the Fund is not subject to mandatory wage garnishments in order to avoid such obligations.

2. *A staff member fails to comply with domestic violence laws or a court order regarding visitation rights. Does this violate the Fund's standards of conduct?*

   Yes. Staff members are required to comply with laws against domestic violence. This includes not only physical assault, but also violent acts and the threat of violent acts to those in the staff member's household. While the Fund will not become involved in purely domestic disputes, as an international organization the Fund has an interest in ensuring that its staff members do not abuse any immunities, engage in acts of cruelty against household members, or violate court orders.

3. *A staff member receives a traffic ticket in the operation of a motor vehicle. Does this violate the Fund's standards of conduct?*

> No. The type of unlawful conduct that would violate the Fund's standards on private conduct is conduct that is so serious, under the circumstances, that it would embarrass the Fund or call into question a staff member's ability to perform official duties. By contrast, fraud and theft would be serious unlawful acts in violation of the Fund's standards of conduct.

Conduct within the Fund

1. *I am taking orders for Girl Scout cookies on behalf of my daughter. May I ask colleagues whether they wish to place an order?*

> Yes, so long as there is no coercion or pressure placed on colleagues to make a purchase.

2. *I am aware that my colleagues have made false claims on their travel claims following a mission. Should I report this?*

> You are not under any formal obligation to report unethical behavior by colleagues. However, should you decide to report an ethical breach by another staff member, you should do so without fear of reprisal. You may also consider raising privately with the colleague your concern about the unethical behavior. Under no circumstances should you actively participate in, or facilitate the commitment of, an ethical violation by another staff member. Staff should also be aware that malicious and unfounded whistle blowing is not acceptable behavior.

3. *A staff member hangs a reproduction in his/her office of a famous painting of a nude. Another employee in an adjacent office reports that this picture makes him/her uncomfortable. Should the staff member be required to remove the painting?*

> Although not all norms of behavior constitute mandatory rules of conduct, it is nevertheless expected that staff members will avoid actions that could reasonably be deemed to create a hostile work environment or make others uncomfortable in the office. Assuming that this situation meets these criteria, the staff member should be respectful of his/her colleague's feelings and remove the painting.

4. *My daughter is away at a university abroad. In order to cut down on the cost of telephone calls, I occasionally send her e-mails from the Fund. Is this a violation of the Fund's rules on conduct?*

> The primary purpose of the E-mail facilities is for official communications. The use of E-mail at headquarters for personal purposes is permitted as long as this does not encroach on work time, overburden the electronic network, or involve a significant extra expense for the Fund.

5. *I am organizing a series of sermons to be delivered in my church by outside speakers. In this connection, I need to make and receive some phone calls. Can I do this from my office?*

> Yes, as long as the number and duration of such calls are limited and do not interfere with the performance of your duties. Generally, spending a small amount of time on personal calls is permitted within the constraints established by the supervisor. If significant time has to be spent on personal matters, you should make up the time by staying later in the office or you should make the calls during the lunch break. You are required to pay for any long distance calls.

Use and Disclosure of Information

1. *You receive a call from outside the Fund, requesting data on the balance of payments of Country X, as reported in the Recent Economic Developments (RED) for the last Article IV consultation. How do you respond?*

> You could refer the caller to EXR's public information number (623–7300) or you may provide the data if you know it is in the public domain.

2. *You are the desk economist for Country Y, and receive a request from an international bank for information on the status of negotiations on a new Fund arrangement with Country Y. How do you answer?*

> You may disclose information about the negotiations only to the extent you have been authorized to do so. If you are uncertain as to how far such authorization extends or what is appropriate in the circumstances, you could pass the inquiry to either EXR or to the mission chief (or other senior officer in your area department), who can determine how much information should be disclosed.

3. *You are working on Country Z, which has both an arrangement with the Fund and a Structural Adjustment Loan with the World Bank. Your Bank counterpart, seeking clarification of the monetary targets, specifically asks for a copy of the Board paper that incorporates the monetary projections, which he says have been published in a national newspaper in Country Z. How do you respond?*

> You may not give confidential Fund documents to outsiders, including the World Bank, without prior authorization. The fact that the paper has reportedly been leaked is irrelevant – it is a Fund document, and only the Executive Board can authorize its publication. Your best course of action is to seek guidance from the mission chief, or another senior officer of your department.

4. *You are an expert on tax policy and would like to write a letter to the editor of a newspaper regarding a national sales tax. Does your letter need Fund clearance?*

> Whether your letter to the editor requires Fund clearance depends upon the issues covered and the context in which the letter is being written. This includes whether the author is identified as a Fund staff member, whether

the letter could reasonably be expected to have an adverse effect on the policies or activities of the Fund, and whether a national sales tax is a significant issue in the Fund's relations with the country in question (the presumption is that it could be a significant issue).

5. *You have expertise (acquired outside the Fund) on the problem of inadequate child care in your city and a local journalist would like to interview you. Do you need to clear this press contact in the Fund?*

No, so long as you avoid commenting directly upon national policy issues such as controversies over national budget outlays for child care. If you do intend to touch on such controversies, you may need to seek Fund clearance for your comments in advance depending upon the issue.

6. *I am invited to give a talk on the international agreement to ban land mines. Do I need to clear my outline within the Fund?*

If this is currently a matter of national political controversy considering the context of the talk, and the content is such that it may reasonably be expected to embarrass the Fund or have an adverse effect on Fund policies and activities, you would need clearance from the Fund before accepting the invitation.

Conflicts of Interest, Including Personal Financial Affairs

1. *I work on emerging Country X, may I acquire mutual funds specialized in:*
   a. *this country?*
   b. *this region?*

You may not if you make this acquisition on the basis of confidential information that you have obtained in the course of your work. For instance, you are prohibited from buying mutual funds if this decision is based on the information of a pending change in interest rates that you have learned about during confidential discussions with the authorities of the country to which you are assigned. In addition to this prohibition, you should not be perceived by a reasonable outsider to have acted on the basis of your access to confidential information in making an acquisition. This is why such acquisitions are generally discouraged. If in doubt, consult the officer designated to that effect by management before undertaking such investment.

2. *I work on Country X desk. Do the rules above mean that I may not hold Country X mutual funds, equities, or Treasury bills?*

No, they do not prohibit such holdings. They require that you refrain from conducting financial transactions which an outsider could reasonably consider to be influenced by your access to confidential information. As an example, selling Country X Treasury bills shortly after you have been discussing interest rate prospects with the authorities of Country X for your Article IV surveillance work could reasonably be perceived by an outsider to be influenced by confidential information obtained in the course of your work.

3. *May I sell gold?*

In general, you may, as long as you do not trade in gold. You may not, of course, make use of confidential information obtained in the course of your duties in the Fund as the basis for initiating a sale. Therefore, if you learned, for example, that the Fund was planning to sell gold, you would be prohibited from selling gold prior to the public announcement of a sale of gold by the Fund.

4. *May I sell French Francs forward to protect the U.S. dollar value of the proceeds that I am expecting to repatriate to Washington following the sale of my house in France?*

Yes, you may. The prohibition stated in paragraph 25(a) (combination of buying and selling within six months) does not apply in this case.

5. *I have recently been involved in the assessment of the financial sector of Country X where I came to learn about the financial situation of some commercial banks. Is it all right for me to take either a short or long position in their traded bonds or stocks?*

No, it is not. You would be taking advantage of confidential information that you might have obtained in the course of your duties. Even if you had not been entrusted with any such information, others could reasonably perceive you as having been and, for that reason, you should abstain from such trading.

6. *A staff member has been recruited by an investment bank. Before his departure, he is asked to participate in a Fund mission to a country that is undergoing a financial crisis. In the course of this mission, he will no doubt come across confidential information that will be useful to his next employer. Should he go or should he recuse himself?*

No, he should not go. This situation creates the appearance of impropriety in light of his imminent plans and it would be difficult or impossible for him to refrain from using information learned during the mission in his next job. He should bring this conflict of interest to the attention of his supervisor, who would be expected not to send him on the mission.

7. *I learned through my brother-in-law, who works for a software firm, of a new product of that firm that may be useful for the Fund. May I arrange a meeting between the software firm and representatives of the Fund?*

Yes, so long as you do nothing to influence the Fund's decision whether to acquire the software or otherwise use the products of this firm, as you would have a conflict of interest in dealing with such matters.

External Activities

1. *I have been invited by a university located in the U.S. to teach a course on macroeconomics, for which I will be paid $5,000. Can I accept the invitation?*

You can accept this invitation, provided that it is approved by your department, EXR, and ADM and that the work, including preparation, is not done on office time. If prohibited by U.S. law, you may not accept remuneration for the work if you are not a U.S. national or Permanent Resident. (Currently, under U.S. law G-4 staff can accept "honoraria" of not more than $500 per occasion (no more than two occasions per year)).

2. *I am a Resident Representative in Country X and I have been asked by a private investment fund to provide advice on a strategic plan for investment and to receive remuneration for this service. Can I accept this offer?*

No. This would create at least the perception of a conflict of interest and perhaps also an actual conflict of interest because you have access to confidential information.

3. *I own an apartment that is currently rented to generate some income. Must I report it to the Fund to avoid violating the rules on outside activities?*

No. You may rent your properties without advance clearance, as long as the rental has not become an organized business.

4. *May I participate in a lawful public demonstration on an issue not closely related to the work of the Fund, for example, abortion policy or nuclear disarmament, without obtaining advance clearance?*

Yes, provided that you participate in a manner that does not publicly identify your connection to the Fund. If, however, you intend to make a public statement on a "national political question," advance clearance is required (see paragraphs 21 through 23 above).

5. *May I join and participate in the activities of a non-governmental environmental, animal rights, religious, or civic organization?*

You may join both formal and informal clubs and non-governmental organizations, if you can join and participate without identifying yourself in connection with the Fund, and without bringing embarrassment to the Fund or adversely affecting its interests.

6. *May I sign a petition supporting a particular political candidate or endorse a candidate for elected office in my country?*

You may sign a petition supporting a political candidate or endorse a candidate for elected office in the country in which you are qualified to vote, or join a political party, if you can do so without publicly identifying yourself in connection with the Fund and without bringing embarrassment to the Fund or adversely affecting its interests.

7. *I am invited to accept an honorary degree in connection with my alumni activities and other services unrelated to the Fund. May I accept?*

You should seek clearance from the Fund, which will grant permission to staff members to accept honorary degrees awarded in recognition of achievements and services unrelated to the Fund.

ANNEX III

UNHCR
Code of Conduct

INTRODUCTION

UNHCR's capacity to ensure the protection of and assistance to refugees and other persons of concern depends on the ability of its staff to uphold and promote the highest standards of ethical and professional conduct. We, the staff members of UNHCR, are personally and collectively responsible for maintaining these standards. Managers have a particular responsibility to uphold these standards, to set a good example, and to create a working environment that supports and empowers staff.

It is recognised that UNHCR's work often puts its staff in positions of power in relation to its beneficiaries. Staff have an obligation not to abuse this power.

This Code of Conduct is intended to serve as an illustrative guide for staff to make ethical decisions in their professional lives, and at times in their private lives. It is a moral code that does not have the force of law. It is designed to assist staff to better understand the obligations placed upon their conduct by the Charter of the United Nations and the Staff Regulations and Rules, which remain the only legal instruments that determine acceptable conduct in UNHCR. Signing the Code does not take away any acquired rights of UNHCR Staff.

While acknowledging that local laws and customs may differ from one country to another, the Code of Conduct is based on international legal standards. For example, children are defined as those under the age of 18. Guidance on appropriate interpretation can be found in the Notes to the Code of Conduct.

The Code applies to all UNHCR staff members, who will be requested to sign it. Persons holding a UNHCR consultant contract and interns will also receive the Code and be requested to confirm that they uphold its standards as far as applicable to their status. Governmental and non-governmental organisations and companies which, through their employees, work for UNHCR, will be requested to make the principles contained in the Code known to those persons in an appropriate manner.

All UNHCR staff are responsible for encouraging, advocating and promoting the dissemination of the Code of Conduct. They also have a role in implementing, monitoring and enforcing its standards. Staff are also urged to encourage partners to adhere to these standards and to join UNHCR staff in upholding them.

Core Values and Guiding Principles

UNHCR staff are committed to the following fundamental values and principles:

- As staff working within the United Nations system, we will ensure that our conduct is consistent with and reflects the values enshrined in the Charter of the United Nations: respect for fundamental human rights, social justice and human dignity, and respect for the equal rights of men and women. We will assist UNHCR to actively promote adherence to the principles of international refugee law, international human rights law and international humanitarian law. We will be guided by the core values of the United Nations system, including professionalism, integrity and respect for diversity, and will maintain an international perspective at all times.

- As UNHCR staff, our primary commitment is to ensure the protection of and assistance to refugees and other persons of concern, in accordance with the mandate of the Office. We are committed to supporting the fullest possible participation of refugees and other persons of concern – as individuals, families and communities – in decisions that affect their lives.
- We will respect the dignity and worth of every individual, will promote and practise understanding, respect, compassion and tolerance, and will demonstrate discretion and maintain confidentiality as required. We will aim to build constructive and respectful working relations with our humanitarian partners, will continuously seek to improve our performance, and will foster a climate that encourages learning, supports positive change, and applies the lessons learned from our experience.
- We will show respect for all persons equally without distinction whatsoever of race, gender, religion, colour, national or ethnic origin, language, marital status, sexual orientation, age, socio-economic status, disability, political conviction, or any other distinguishing feature. We will strive to remove all barriers to equality.
- We will respect the cultures, customs and traditions of all peoples, and will strive to avoid behaving in ways that are not acceptable in a particular cultural context. However, when the tradition or practice is considered by the relevant organ of the United Nations to be directly contrary to an international human rights instrument or standard, we will be guided by the applicable human rights instrument or standard.

Commitment to UNHCR Code of Conduct

As a staff member of UNHCR, I commit myself to:

1. Treat all refugees and other persons of concern fairly, and with respect and dignity.

I will always seek to understand the difficult experiences that refugees and other persons of concern to UNHCR have faced and survived, as well as the disadvantaged position in which they – particularly on the basis of gender, age or disability – may find themselves in relation to those who hold power or influence over aspects of their lives.

I will always seek to care for and protect the rights of children, and act in a manner that ensures that their best interests shall be the paramount consideration.

If my job involves direct work with refugees or other persons of concern, I will meet with them regularly, in order to fully understand their experiences and needs, and to explain the role of UNHCR and the scope of its work.

I will keep myself informed about UNHCR's policies, objectives and activities and about refugee concerns, and will do my utmost to support the Office's protection and assistance work.

2. Uphold the integrity of UNHCR, by ensuring that my personal and professional conduct is, and is seen to be, of the highest standard.

I will demonstrate integrity, truthfulness, dedication and honesty in my actions. I will be patient, respectful and courteous to all persons with whom I deal in an official capacity, including refugees and other persons of concern, representatives of operational and implementing partners, governments and donors.

I will observe local laws, will meet all my private legal and financial obligations, and will not seek to take personal advantage of any privileges or immunities that have been conferred on me in the interest of the United Nations. I will do my utmost to ensure that the conduct of members of my household does not reflect unfavourably on the integrity of UNHCR.

3. Perform my official duties and conduct my private affairs in a manner that avoids conflicts of interest, thereby preserving and enhancing public confidence in UNHCR.

My actions will be free of any consideration of personal gain, and I will resist any undue political pressure in decision-making. I will neither seek nor accept instructions regarding the performance of my duties from any government, including my national authorities, or from any authority external to the United Nations.

In accordance with Staff Regulations and Rules, I will not accept any honour, decoration, favour gift, remuneration, from any government; nor will I accept these from any other source external to the United Nations without prior authorisation. I will not engage in any outside occupation or employment without prior authorisation. I will not accept supplementary payments or subsidies from a government or any other source, or participate in certain political activities such as standing for or holding public office.

I will avoid assisting private persons or companies in their undertakings with UNHCR where this might lead to actual or perceived preferential treatment. I will never participate in activities related to procurement of goods or services, or in human resource activities, where a conflict of interests may arise.

4. Contribute to building a harmonious workplace based on team spirit, mutual respect and understanding.

I will show respect to all colleagues, regardless of status or position, and will allow all colleagues the opportunity to have their views heard, and to contribute from their knowledge and experience to team efforts. I will communicate openly and share relevant information (subject to confidentiality requirements) with other colleagues, and will endeavour to respond in a timely manner to queries.

I will respect my colleagues' privacy, and avoid misinformation. I will seek to resolve differences and solve problems when they arise. I will contribute to building constructive dialogue, guided by mutual respect and an open, positive approach, between management and staff representatives.

As a manager/supervisor I will be open to the views of all team members. I will provide timely feedback on the performance of each team member through guidance, motivation and full recognition of their merits.

5. Promote the safety, health and welfare of all UNHCR staff as a necessary condition for effective and consistent performance.

I will remain aware of and comply with all instructions designed to protect my health, welfare and safety. I will always consider the safety of staff in operational decisions. If I have doubts regarding an instruction that I consider threatening to my safety or the safety of other persons, I will bring this immediately to the attention of my supervisor.

As a manager/supervisor, I will endeavour to ensure that the health and well-being of staff and their families are not subjected to undue risk. I will promote a healthy work-life balance for staff, and will respect staff entitlements.

6. Safeguard and make responsible use of the information and resources to which I have access by reason of my employment with UNHCR.

I will exercise due care in all matters of official business, and not divulge any confidential information about refugees, colleagues and other work-related matters in accordance with the staff regulations and rules and current guidelines.

I will protect, manage and utilise UNHCR human, financial and material resources efficiently and effectively, bearing in mind that these resources have been placed at UNHCR's disposal for the benefit of refugees and other persons of concern.

7. Prevent, oppose and combat all exploitation and abuse of refugees and other persons of concern.

I undertake not to abuse the power and influence that I have by virtue of my position over the lives and well-being of refugees and other persons of concern.

I will never request any service or favour from refugees or other persons of concern in return for protection or assistance. I will never engage in any exploitative relationships – sexual, emotional, financial or employment-related – with refugees or other persons of concern.

Should I find myself in such a relationship with a beneficiary that I consider non-exploitative and consensual, I will report this to my supervisor for appropriate guidance in the knowledge that this matter will be treated with due discretion. I understand that both my supervisor and I have available to us normal consultative and recourse mechanisms on these issues.

I will act responsibly when hiring or otherwise engaging refugees or other persons of concern for private services. I will report in writing on the nature and conditions of this employment to my supervisor.

8. Refrain from any involvement in criminal or unethical activities, activities that contravene human rights, or activities that compromise the image and interests of UNHCR.

I will neither support nor take part in any form of illegal, exploitative or abusive activities, including, for example, child labour, and trafficking of human beings and commodities.

As UNHCR is committed to the highest standards of protection and care for children, I am aware that I am expected not to engage in sexual activities with any person under the age of 18. (Further guidance is given in the Notes to this Code of Conduct).

9. Refrain from any form of harassment, discrimination, physical or verbal abuse, intimidation or favouritism in the workplace.

I will not engage in or tolerate any form of harassment in the workplace, including sexual harassment and abuse of power.

As a manager/supervisor, I will not solicit favours, loans or gifts from staff, nor will I accept unsolicited ones that are of more than token value.

I recognise that there is an inherent conflict of interest and potential abuse of power in having sexual relations with staff under my supervision. Should I find myself in such a relationship, I will resolve this conflict of interest without delay.

ANNEX IV

Code of Conduct of the European Central Bank[1] in accordance with Article 11.3 of the Rules of Procedure of the European Central Bank

1. Preliminary statements

This Code of Conduct (hereinafter referred to as the "Code") gives guidance in matters of professional ethics to all persons employed by the European Central Bank (hereinafter referred to as the "Addressees") and serves as a reference for the public with regard to the standard of conduct that third parties are entitled to expect in their dealings with the European Central Bank (ECB). The Code makes explicit the ethical conventions and standards by which the ECB considers it necessary for the Addressees to abide and clarifies the benchmarks against which fulfilment of the obligations already assumed by the Addressees will be measured. The Code draws on, and is without prejudice to, the terms of individual contracts of the members of the Executive Board, the Conditions of Employment for Staff of the European Central Bank (hereinafter referred to as the "Conditions of Employment") and all texts implementing them. Similarly, the Code gives guidance to and sets ethical conventions, standards and benchmarks for the members of the Executive Board of the ECB.

2. Basic principles

The Addressees are expected to act with exclusive loyalty to the ECB, honestly, independently, impartially, with discretion and without regard to self-interest or national interests, to subscribe to high standards of professional ethics, and to avoid any situation liable to give rise to a conflict of interest.

The Addressees are encouraged in their inter-personal relationships within the ECB to behave as Europeans and citizens of the European Union, with no national bias, drawing on the cross-cultural heritage of the Member States, and achieving a level of teamwork and team spirit which goes beyond cultural differences.

2.1 Equal treatment and non-discrimination

The Addressees should avoid any form of discrimination and, in particular, any discrimination based on race, nationality, gender, age, physical disability, sexual preference, political opinions, philosophical views or religious convictions.

Sexual harassment or psychological or physical bullying of any kind whatsoever will not be tolerated by the ECB. Community legislation defines sexual harassment as "unwanted conduct of a sexual nature, or other conduct based on sex affecting the dignity of women and men at work. This can include unwelcome

[1] OJ C 76, 8.3.2001, p. 11.

physical, verbal or non-verbal conduct".[2] The Addressees need both to show sensitivity to and respect for others and to stop any behaviour seen as offensive by another person at his/her first indication. None of the Addressees shall be prejudiced in any way whatsoever for preventing or reporting harassment or bullying.

2.2 Diligence, efficiency, responsibility

The Addressees are expected always to carry out diligently, efficiently and to the best of their abilities the responsibilities and the duties entrusted to them. They are expected to be mindful of the importance of their duties and responsibilities, to take into account the expectations of the public concerning their moral behaviour, to conduct themselves in a way that maintains and boosts the public's trust in the ECB, and to contribute to the efficiency of the administration of the ECB.

2.3 Legal compliance

According to the Protocol on the privileges and immunities of the European Communities, the privileges and immunities enjoyed by the Addressees are accorded solely in the interests of the ECB. These privileges and immunities shall in no way exempt the Addressees from fulfilling their private obligations or from complying with the applicable national laws. In particular, the criminal laws and police regulations in force in Germany are to be respected in full by the Addressees.

3. Relations with the outside world

3.1 Independence

3.1.1 Avoidance of external influence

The principle of independence is laid down in Article 7 of the Statute of the European System of Central Banks and of the European Central Bank (hereinafter referred to as the "Statute"). In all external relations the Addressees should support the commitment of the ECB to act in accordance with the principle of independence. Accordingly, Addressees should not seek or take instructions from any government, authority, organisation or person outside the ECB.

3.1.2 Negotiating prospective employment outside the ECB

The Addressees should behave with integrity and discretion in respect of both any negotiations concerning prospective employment and the acceptance of professional positions after they have ceased to hold office at the ECB, in particular if such positions are taken with a financial institution or with one of the ECB's suppliers. As soon as any such negotiations are under way or such a perspective

[2] Commission Recommendation of 27 November 1991 on the protection of the dignity of women and men at work, OJ L 49, 24/02/1992, pp. 1–8.

exists, the Addressees concerned are expected to abstain from any matter that may relate to the prospective employer, if the continuation of such relationship may lead to their being reproached for a conflict of interest or for having misused their position at the ECB.

3.1.3 Gifts and honours

Respect of the principle of independence is incompatible with applying for, receiving or accepting from any source outside the ECB or from subordinates any benefits, rewards, remuneration or gifts in excess of a customary or negligible amount, whether financial or non-financial, which are connected in any way whatsoever with an Addressee's activity within the ECB.

As regards the acceptance of honours or decorations granted to Addressees by national authorities on the grounds of services to the ECB, Addressees should give prior notification to and seek clearance by the President of the ECB.

3.1.4 External activities

Addressees may undertake non-remunerated and non-financial activities outside working hours in domains such as culture, science, education, sports, charity, religion, social work or other benevolent work, on condition that such activities do not have a negative impact on the Addressees' obligations with regard to the ECB. Remunerated activities of this nature and other activities outside working hours require prior approval in accordance with the Conditions of Employment.

The Addressees are requested to employ prudence and caution in any political activities so as to preserve the independence and neutrality of the ECB. In particular, the ECB is not in favour of senior management acquiring or maintaining any prominent position in political parties. The Addressees should not carry out political activities within working hours, using the facilities of the ECB, or on its premises.

The Addressees may associate with academic societies and contribute to their material and scientific development. In particular, the Addressees may engage in research, deliver lectures, write articles or books or pursue any other similar activities involving a subject matter related to topics covered by their work, subject to the approval of the Executive Board. However, it must be made clear that such scientific or academic contributions by the Addressees are made in a personal capacity and do not involve the ECB. The Addressees should in no way appear to represent an institutional position held by the ECB, unless they have been authorised to the contrary in advance.

The Addressees shall neither solicit nor receive remuneration – whether financial or of any other kind – for any external activities carried out in the performance of their duties, except where strictly required to cover their expenses, unless duly authorised to do so by the Executive Board.

3.2 Confidentiality and public access to documentation

Professional secrecy, provided for in Article 38 of the Statute, in the Conditions of Employment and in all texts implementing them, requires the non-divulgence of confidential information obtained by the Addressees in the performance of their duties. Permission to give evidence, whether as a witness in legal proceedings or otherwise, shall be requested and it shall be granted whenever a refusal to give evidence would involve the Addressee in criminal proceedings. Permission shall not, however, be required in the event of an Addressee being summoned to give evidence before the Court of Justice of the European Communities in a case between the ECB and a current or former member of its staff.

The obligations with regard to professional secrecy do not prevent public access to information and documents as determined in the ECB Decision of 3 November 1998 (ECB/1998/12 and subsequent modifications).

3.2 Relations with the public

3.2.1 Basic principles

Accessibility, efficiency, correctness and courtesy should guide the Addressees in their relations with the public. The Addressees shall ensure, to the extent possible, that members of the public are provided with the information they request. Such information, as well as any reason not to provide the information, shall be clear and understandable.

3.2.2 Data protection

Addressees dealing with personal data concerning individual citizens shall respect the principles laid down in the Directive 95/46/EC of the European Parliament and of the Council of 24 October 1995 on the protection of individuals with regard to the processing of personal data and on the free movement of such data.[3] Such Addressees shall, in particular, avoid processing personal data for non-legitimate purposes or the transmission of such data to non-authorised persons.

3.2.3 Appeals

Addressees should ensure that any decision of the ECB which may have an adverse effect on the rights or interests of a third party shall contain an indication of the options available to challenge the decision, as well as the competent appeal bodies and time-limits required for the exercise of such options.

3.4 Contacts with the media

Addressees should refrain from giving interviews or supplying off-the-record information (i.e. information that is not available in the public domain) on their own initiative or upon invitation to the media without prior authorisation. When meeting members of the media on a social basis, Addressees shall exercise the utmost degree of discretion with regard to matters related to the European System of Central Banks (ESCB).

[3] Directive 95/46/EC of the European Parliament and of the Council of 24 October 1995 on the protection of individuals with regard to the processing of personal data and on the free movement of such data, OJ L 281, 23/11/1995, p. 31 ff.

3.5 Relations with national Central banks

A spirit of close mutual co-operation should govern the relations between the Addressees and their colleagues at the national central banks (NCBs) forming part of the ESCB. Such co-operation with the NCBs should be guided by the principles of non-discrimination, equal treatment and the avoidance of national bias. It should be without prejudice to the maintenance of confidentiality wherever appropriate. In this context it has to be borne in mind that not all members of the ESCB form part of the Eurosystem, which has institutional implications for the extent of this co-operation.

In any relationship with an NCB, the Addressees should bear in mind their obligations with regard to loyalty to the ECB and the impartial role of the ECB within the ESCB.

3.6 European institutions and bodies and national authorities

Contacts, whether formal or informal, with representatives of European institutions, other European bodies and national authorities should always reflect the position of the ECB if and when such a position exists; in the absence of an established ECB position, the Addressees should explicitly reserve any ECB position on a given matter when advancing personal views. Contacts with European institutions and bodies require special attention and a high level of accessibility, while the independence of the ECB and the maintenance of professional secrecy as provided for in the Statute should be ensured.

Addressees should inform their superiors of any attempt to influence the ECB in the performance of its tasks in an improper manner.

3.7 Private financial activities and conflicts of interest

The tasks and activities of the ECB involve financial transactions with financial institutions as well as a diverse set of other business relationships. They also involve the analysis for and the preparation of decisions which may have an impact on market developments. In these and other professional activities, the Addressees should be in a position to act with full independence and impartially.

3.7.1 Avoidance of potential conflicts of interest

The Addressees should avoid any situation liable to give rise to a conflict of interest. Conflicts of interest arise where the Addressees have private or personal interests which may influence or appear to influence the impartial and objective performance of their duties. Private or personal interests mean any potential advantage for themselves, their families, their other relatives or their circle of friends and acquaintances.

3.7.2 Information on Tenders for Goods and Services

During tender procedures the Addressees should communicate only through the official channels and avoid providing information orally.

3.7.3 Insider trading

Addressees shall comply with the rules on insider trading established by the Executive Board.

3.8 Relations with interest groups

Relations with interest groups should be built upon the basic rules of professional ethics. The Addressees should ensure that all representatives of interest groups identify themselves as such, clearly state the capacity in which they are acting and give the names of any other Addressee whom they have contacted on the same subject.

4. In-house relations

4.1 Loyalty and co-operation

For the Addressees, loyalty implies not only the fulfilment of the tasks entrusted to them by their superiors and compliance with the latters' instructions and with the applicable reporting lines, but also assistance, advice, openness and transparency in all dealings with superiors and colleagues. In particular, the Addressees should keep other concerned colleagues informed with regard to work in progress and enable them to contribute to it. Withholding information that may affect the conduct of business from superiors or colleagues, particularly in order to gain a personal advantage, providing false, inaccurate or exaggerated information, refusing to co-operate with colleagues or demonstrating any obstructive behaviour would be contrary to the form of loyalty expected of the Addressees.

Any communication should demonstrate due respect for the reporting channels. Documents should be copied to any colleagues concerned. Managers shall instruct the Addressees working with them in a clear and understandable manner, whether orally or in writing.

4.2 Use of the ECB's resources

The Addressees are expected to respect and protect the ECB's property and not to allow third parties to make use of the ECB's services and/or facilities. All equipment and facilities, whatever their nature, are provided to the Addressees by the ECB for official use only, unless private use is permitted either according to relevant internal rules or practices or on a discretionary basis.

The Addressees are also expected to take all reasonable and appropriate measures to limit the costs and expenses of the ECB wherever possible, so that the available resources can be employed in the most efficient manner.

5. Implementation

5.1 Role of the Addressees

Proper implementation of this Code depends first and foremost on the professionalism, conscience and common sense of the Addressees.

In addition to the vigilance which Addressees in positions of authority are expected to demonstrate, they are also expected to behave in an exemplary fashion with regard to the adherence to the principles and rules laid down in this Code.

5.2 Ethics Adviser

Addressees who have any questions on the application of the Code of Conduct should discuss the matter with the Ethics Adviser mentioned in the Staff Rules. Conduct that is fully in conformity with the advice and interpretative ethical rules developed by the Ethics Adviser shall not give rise to a disciplinary procedure for non-compliance by the Addressee with his/her obligations vis-à-vis the ECB. Such advice shall, however, not release the Addressee from his/her external liability.

5.3 Distribution and publication

A copy of this Code shall be distributed to each Addressee. It shall be published in the Official Journal of the European Communities.

ANNEX V

Extract of ECB Staff Rules containing the Rules on Professional Conduct and Professional Secrecy[1]

1.2 Professional conduct and professional secrecy

The provisions of Articles 4(b), 4(c), 4(f) and 5(b) of the Conditions of Employment are applied as follows:

1.2.1 The Executive Board shall appoint an Ethics Adviser. The Ethics Adviser shall provide guidance on all aspects of professional conduct and professional secrecy. Without prejudice to such obligation, the Ethics Adviser shall provide advice and adopt interpretative ethical criteria. The Ethics Adviser shall be subject to an obligation of strict confidentiality in performing his/her duties. The advice and interpretative ethical criteria shall be published in a generalised format on the ECB's intranet.

The Ethics Adviser shall in particular ensure a consistent interpretation of the ECB's insider trading rules. The Ethics Adviser shall immediately inform the ECB's External Auditor in full of the advice and interpretative ethical criteria developed concerning the insider trading rules.

1.2.2 "Remuneration, rewards or gifts" means any financial benefit and/or any non-financial benefit.

1.2.3 A member of staff who is invited to attend an event in his/her official capacity may not accept a fee of any kind.

1.2.4 Normal hospitality and token gifts may be accepted to avoid causing offence.

1.2.5 Where there is any doubt, a member of staff shall obtain the approval of his/her Director General/Director before accepting any gift or hospitality or, where this is not possible, report to him/her immediately any gift or hospitality received.

1.2.6 Without the prior permission of the Executive Board, members of staff shall not publish any work or articles or give any lectures relating to the ECB or its activities.

1.2.7 In view of the position held by the ECB and the general economic and financial importance of the issues with which it deals, members of staff shall maintain professional secrecy concerning information relating to issues dealt with by the ECB.

---

[1] OJ C 92, 16.4.2004, p. 31.

1.2.8 Information relating to issues dealt with by the ECB (inside information) shall mean information; (i) which is known to a member of staff; and (ii) which relates to the administration of the ECB or to transactions of any kind (including proposed transactions) arising in connection with the implementation of the objectives and tasks of the ECB; and (iii) which is confidential; or (iv) which is or might be perceived as being relevant to decisions to be made by the ECB. Inside information relating to issues dealt with by the ECB can comprise a broad range of information and may originate from any country or business area within the ECB. Therefore, the following items are examples only and shall not be exhaustive:

- changes in the monetary or exchange rate policies of the Eurosystem or of other central banks internationally;
- movements in monthly monetary aggregates, balance of payment data or foreign currency reserves or any other market-sensitive economic or financial data;
- impending regulatory changes;
- market-sensitive information related to discussions and negotiations in international fora;
- internal administrative decisions taken by the ECB.

The disclosure of information in the regular course of employment does not constitute a breach of these rules.

1.2.9 Members of staff are prohibited from using, whether directly or indirectly via third parties, inside information to which they have access, irrespective of whether such information is used in any kind of private financial transaction conducted at their own risk and for their own account, or at the risk and for the account of third parties. The term "third party" shall include, but is not limited to, spouses, recognised partners, parents, children, other family members, colleagues, and legal persons.

1.2.10 Members of staff are specifically prohibited from taking advantage, whether directly or indirectly via third parties, of their position and functions at the ECB or of inside information to which they have access by acquiring or disposing of, whether at their own risk and for their own account, or at the risk and for the account of a third party as defined in Article 1.2.9, any assets (including transferable securities, foreign currency and gold) or rights (including rights under derivative contracts or closely related financial instruments) to which that information is closely related. This prohibition applies to any kind of financial (investment) transactions, including but not limited to the following:

- investment in securities (shares, bonds, warrants, options, futures or any other securities in the broadest sense of the term, as well as contracts to subscribe to, acquire or dispose of such securities);
- index contracts based on such securities;
- interest rate transactions;
- foreign exchange transactions;
- commodity transactions.

1.2.11 Short-term trading (i.e. a combination of buying and selling within a period of one month) for speculative purposes in any assets (including transferable securities, foreign currency, and gold) or rights (including rights under derivatives contracts or closely related financial instruments) is prohibited unless the member of staff concerned is able objectively to demonstrate the non-speculative nature of and the rationale for such trading.

1.2.12 Members of staff shall be prohibited from using any component of the technical infrastructure dedicated to the financial operations of the ESCB when conducting any personal financial transactions at their own risk and for their own account or at the risk and for the account of third parties as defined in Article 1.2.9.

The term "technical infrastructure dedicated to financial operations of the ESCB" shall encompass the Bosch dealing telephones, the telex system, connections with agencies or wire services such as Bloomberg and Reuters, TOP, BI, EBS, Finance KIT and S.W.I.F.T., as well as any subsequent replacements thereof.

Moreover, the use of mobile telephones in the Market Room and in the premises of the Back Office and the Investment Division shall be prohibited, except as an emergency measure in accordance with ECB contingency procedures.

1.2.13 The Executive Board shall determine those members of staff who, by virtue of the exercise of their employment, profession or duties, have access to inside information concerning the financial operations of the ESCB. Such a decision by the Executive Board shall automatically become part of the Staff Rules. Any such members of staff shall refrain from conducting on the same day as an ESCB transaction, whether directly or indirectly, any transactions concerning assets (including transferable securities, foreign currency, and gold) or rights (including rights under derivatives contracts or closely related financial instruments) that have the same generic characteristics (currency, issuer and similar maturity) as those traded on that day by the ESCB, whether at their own risk and for their own account, or at the risk and for the account of third parties as defined in Article 1.2.9.

1.2.14 The Executive Board shall determine those members of staff who, by virtue of the exercise of their employment, profession or duties, are deemed to have access to inside information concerning the monetary or exchange rate policies of the ECB or the financial operations of the ESCB. Such a decision by the Executive Board shall automatically become part of the Staff Rules.

Those members of staff shall, at the request of the Director General Administration provide the following information:

- a list of his/her bank accounts, including custody accounts and accounts with stock brokers;
- a list of any powers of attorney which third parties have conferred upon

him/her in connection with their bank accounts, including custody accounts;
- his/her general directives or guidelines to third parties to whom responsibility for managing his/her investment portfolio has been delegated.[2]

Those members of staff shall at their own initiative and without delay provide details of any changes to the information above. The information and any updates shall be provided in sealed envelopes and kept in the custody of the Director General Administration, who shall pass it to the ECB's External Auditor at the latter's request.

At the annual request of the ECB's External Auditor, those members of staff shall in addition provide the following documentation for a period of six consecutive months, as specified in the annual request:

- any sale or purchase of assets (including transferable securities, foreign currency, and gold) or rights (including rights under derivatives contracts or closely related financial instruments) conducted by the member of staff at his/her own risk and for his/her own account, or conducted by him/her at the risk and for the account of third parties as defined in Article 1.2.9;
- statements of bank accounts, including custody accounts and accounts with stock brokers; the conclusion or the amendment of mortgages or other loans at his/her own risk and for his/her own account, or by him/her at the risk and for the account of third parties as defined in Article 1.2.9;
- his/her dealings in relation to retirement plans, including the ECB retirement plan;

All information shall be provided in sealed envelopes and kept in the custody of the Director General Administration, who shall pass on the information to the ECB's External Auditor at the latter's request. All information received by the ECB's External Auditor shall remain confidential. In derogation from the abovementioned rule, a report by the ECB's External Auditor to the ECB's Directorate Internal Audit for the further investigation of a specific case in accordance with Article 1.2.16 shall contain the information received from the member of staff concerned.

1.2.15 In the event that the ECB's External Auditor has reasonable grounds to believe that the above-mentioned rules, including the advice and interpretative ethical rules developed by the Ethics Adviser have not been respected, he/she shall have the right to ask any of the ECB's members of staff to provide him/her with full information thereon. The member of staff concerned shall provide full information on a confidential basis to the ECB's External Auditor at the latter's reasoned request regarding the following:

---

[2] Members of staff identified in accordance with Article 1.2.14 may wish to consider taking the opportunity to delegate the management of their investment portfolios to third parties, such as "blind trusts", mutual funds, etc.

- all his/her bank accounts, including custody accounts and accounts with stock brokers; the conclusion or the amendment of mortgages or other loans at his/her own risk and for his/her own account, or by him/her at the risk and for the account of third parties as defined in Article 1.2.9;
- all his/her investment transactions concerning assets (including transferable securities, foreign currency, and gold) or rights (including rights under derivatives contracts or closely related financial instruments) that he/she has performed at his/her own risk and for his/her own account, or at the risk and for the account of third parties as defined in Article 1.2.9, during the period indicated by the ECB's External Auditor;
- his/her dealings in relation to retirement plans including the ECB retirement plan;
- a list of any powers of attorney which third parties have conferred upon members of staff in connection with their bank accounts, including custody accounts.

The information shall be provided in sealed envelopes via the Director General Administration to the ECB's External Auditor. All information received by the ECB's External Auditor shall remain confidential. In derogation to the above-mentioned rule, a report by the ECB's External Auditor to the ECB's Directorate Internal Audit for the further investigation of a specific case in accordance with Article 1.2.16 shall contain the information received from the member of staff concerned.

1.2.16 The ECB's External Auditor shall report any cases of non-compliance with the above-mentioned rules to the ECB's Directorate Internal Audit, which shall further investigate compliance with these rules. Private financial activities carried out in full conformity with the advice and interpretative ethical rules developed by the Ethics Adviser shall not give rise to such a report by the ECB's External Auditor. The member of staff concerned shall be informed of such a report by the ECB's External Auditor, and he/she shall have the right to make his/her views on the report to the ECB's External Auditor.

A report prepared by the ECB's External Auditor, including the information therein supplied by the member of staff concerned, may be used in a disciplinary procedure as set out in Part 8 of the Conditions of Employment for the Staff of the European Central Bank and, to the extent required by applicable law, in any prosecution by external authorities regarding alleged violations of national criminal laws.

1.2.17 A member of staff with any questions on the application of these rules (e.g. whether a private financial transaction he/she may be contemplating would involve a misuse of inside information) should discuss the matter with the Ethics Adviser. The conduct of private financial transactions that is fully in conformity with the advice and interpretative ethical rules developed by the Ethics Adviser shall not give rise to a disciplinary procedure for non-compliance by the member of staff with his/her obligations. Such advice shall, however, not release the member of staff from his/her external liability.

1.2.18 The obligations of members of staff provided for in Articles 1.2.14 to 1.2.15 shall continue to apply beyond the termination of their employment with the ECB for six months following such termination. The request for information by the External Auditor shall refer to a period ending one month after the termination of employment.

ANNEX VI

The Charter of Values of the European Space Agency

General Introduction

I. Background

Over the last few years, partly in response to the need for greater public accountability on the part of large and influential institutions, growing numbers of professional, commercial, governmental and intergovernmental organisations worldwide have produced corporate charters of values.

The adoption of such charters – also referred to as "codes of ethics" – has meant that the ethical yardstick that guides an institution's activities and underlies its standards has been made public. Publicising the ethical principles on which an institution relies reflects an aspiration to attain greater transparency and therefore to maintain or increase public faith and accountability. Certainly, adopting a code of ethics constitutes a public affirmation of *bona fides* that gives confidence to the public at large regarding the organisation's integrity and honesty. For an international organisation entrusted with implementing public policy, a charter of values codifies a set of core principles that individuals representing that organisation adhere to jointly as staff members.

Internally, the aim of these codes is to highlight personal responsibility as the fundamental and most effective element in the functioning of an organisation.

II. The Charter

The Charter of Values establishes a framework which, though it does not have force of law, is morally binding. It seeks to promote the standards of conduct expected from ESA as an international organisation and from ESA staff in their internal and external relations.

By officially promulgating a Charter of Values, the Agency is able to make a solemn declaration of its profound attachment to the ethical principles and values that have continuously inspired its activities. The Charter initiative puts in writing what are already commonly considered as central standards of conduct. In so doing, the Charter seeks to reaffirm the very identity of the European Space Agency and brings greater transparency to its activities.

The Charter of Values concerns and applies to:

- ESA as a legal entity endowed with legal personality,
- all ESA staff, including the Director General, regardless of grade or seniority,
- Member State delegates acting in their official ESA capacities and thus playing an integral part in the work of the Agency.

Because the Convention of the European Space Agency describes our mandate, and in essence, what we stand for, it is the spirit of the Convention that has guided the drafting of the Charter and that must guide its implementation and interpretation.

Moreover, as a European organisation, ESA feels strongly committed to fundamental European principles and values, which are the foundation of democratic societies, such as Council of Europe Treaties, the European Social Charter and above all, the European Convention for the Protection of Human Rights and Fundamental Freedoms (European Convention on Human Rights) and its Protocols. In that spirit, the Agency has produced, in addition to the Charter of Values, a document entitled "the Values of the European Space Agency" (ESA/C(2002)91 Annex 1). This document, directed at the public at large, recalls the fundamental values (ethics, European identity, investment in people, professionalism and technical innovation) that go to make up ESA's identity, rooted in our mandate to serve European citizens and guide our future activities. Although directed at different audiences, the Charter of Values and the Values of the European Space Agency form a common philosophy, through which the Agency's ethical standards and values are given expression.

By its very nature as an ethical commitment, the Charter of Values does not provide for new rules or legal obligations, neither does it in any way supersede or amend the contractual obligations of staff members under the Staff Regulations, Rules and Instructions. Unlike the Staff Regulations, Rules and Instructions, the Charter of Values is not legally binding, as its sole purpose is to set common standards for ethical behaviour.

Contents

Our Shared Values

1. THE AGENCY'S PRINCIPLES AND VALUES

1.1. Professionalism

1.1.1. The Agency owes its success primarily to the competence and professionalism of its staff.

1.1.2. In the Agency's activities, there is no room for unprofessional behaviour. Tasks at all levels should be performed thoroughly and rigorously.

1.1.3. Our programmes are funded by the Member States' governments and, through them, millions of European taxpayers. Competence is therefore vital, at all levels, to ensure that those programmes are carried out to the highest standards, meeting the needs of European society and its governments, and that funding received from the Member States is used responsibly and to good purpose.

1.2. Integrity

1.2.1. The Agency aims to be an exemplary institution. Consequently, professional integrity is an essential value. Professional integrity calls for honesty and realism in stating claims or estimates based on available data.

1.2.2. Staff should seek, accept and offer honest criticism of work, acknowledge and correct errors, and give proper credit to the contributions of others. Professional integrity also entails open discussion and the reporting of divergent views particularly between different layers of management.

1.3. Fostering of professional competence

1.3.1. Staff competence is fostered throughout a staff member's entire career, beginning with recruitment and continuing throughout the career development process and the provision of appropriate training.

1.3.2. The professional development of individual staff members and optimum use of their abilities in the Agency call for participation, initiative, and personal commitment. Each staff member should strive to improve his or her competence.

1.4. Fair and equal treatment

1.4.1. The Agency sees it as a duty to treat all staff members with dignity and fairness in an embodiment of its commitment to refrain from all discrimination on grounds of race, ethnic origin, nationality, political, philosophical or religious opinions, health, disability, gender or sexual orientation.

1.4.2. In recruitment and promotion, the Agency rejects nepotism and all other forms of favouritism. As its rules dictate, the only criteria taken into consideration are ability, dedication and professional qualities.

1.4.3. Equality of opportunity in the recruitment, personal and professional development and promotion of all staff having equal qualifications, without discrimination, is a fundamental Agency principle. Regardless of whether they are men or women, and notwithstanding Agency diversity policies, only merit and length of service count.

1.5. Environment and health

1.5.1. The Agency has environmental and health responsibilities and makes decisions consistent with the safety, health and welfare of the public. It measures the potential consequences of its specific activities and takes all necessary steps to contain them, in line with the principles established for protecting its staff, the public and the environment.

1.5.2. The Agency is committed to the prompt disclosure of any information concerning a potential danger to the public or the environment.

1.6. Social dialogue

The Agency is committed to respecting, in a transparent way, the prerogatives of the bodies representing its staff by conducting an ongoing constructive dialogue with them. By involving staff representatives in all major developments affecting the life of the Agency and its working conditions, it seeks to cement the loyalty of staff in support of its objectives.

1.7. Transparency

1.7.1. The Agency shall ensure that technical, programmatic, financial and other information is both accurate and pertinent. It has a duty to maintain transparency.

1.7.2. All staff members, at all levels of the hierarchy, must make sure that the documents they produce are rigorous, authentic, sound and accurate.

1.7.3. At the same time, staff are bound by a duty of discretion and confidentiality with regard to specific Agency activities.

1.8. The Agency's image

1.8.1. All members of staff must be mindful of their contribution to, and responsibility for the image of the Agency, which strives to be an exemplary institution in its areas of competence through technical and scientific excellence, and in its internal and external relationships through its ethical standards and values.

1.8.2. Each staff member has to be aware that casual attitudes to duty, even on matters that may seem trivial or inconsequential, are damaging to the Agency.

2. INTERPERSONAL RELATIONS

2.1. Working environment

2.1.1. The Agency's cultural diversity is a "natural resource" which needs to be fostered by a working climate conducive to fulfilment in which each person receives recognition and encouragement for his or her efforts.

2.1.2. The working environment needs to be built on mutual respect, team spirit, and continuous dialogue, so as to create a positive, relaxed atmosphere, free from all forms of harassment, pressure or duress.

2.1.3. There has to be frank and constructive discussion about the performance of all staff members. It has to be possible to be completely candid with a colleague when expressing disapproval or dissatisfaction with his or her work – without this being taken as unkind criticism. By the same token, the colleague must be able to respond without offence being caused, particularly in the context of hierarchical relations.

2.1.4. Building human relations involves listening to colleagues, appreciating and even anticipating their expectations.

2.2. Team spirit

2.2.1. The Agency seeks to develop team spirit at all levels.

2.2.2. Effective teamwork begins with the establishment and acceptance of common goals. In order to achieve these goals, all skills, energies and diversities have to be pooled. Coordinating activities, encouraging initiative and listening to suggestions are the best ways of promoting creative solidarity and unity.

2.2.3. Team spirit calls for active listening, mutual help and putting knowledge at the disposal of colleagues. It involves sharing and exchanging experience, passing on know-how and showing generosity.

2.2.4. Furthermore, it entails assisting colleagues and co-workers in their professional development. All staff members have to be involved, but line managers have a special responsibility towards their team members.

2.3. Mutual respect and discretion

2.3.1. Every individual is entitled to respect and consideration from colleagues. Mutual help and loyalty are values to be absorbed by all, for the well-being of all.

2.3.2. We are all different from one another and entitled to respect for our individuality. It is therefore unacceptable to make hurtful comments or tasteless jokes about colleagues or groups represented within the Agency. Publicly questioning their integrity or good faith in the performance of their duties with the sole purpose of undermining them can give serious offence.

2.3.3. Spreading unsubstantiated gossip or lending credence to rumours from unknown sources, often without being able to weigh the consequences for the individuals concerned or for the Agency, is behaviour falling short of the standards of probity, credibility and *esprit de corps* expected of staff members.

2.4. Respect for staff members' private lives

2.4.1. Personal information gathered by the Agency on staff members, such as medical details, CVs, assessment marks or disciplinary measures, is confidential. It may not be disclosed, within or outside the Agency, without the consent of the person concerned except when legal or regulatory obligations so dictate.

2.4.2. Staff members handling personal information on colleagues must take all steps necessary to ensure that it remains strictly confidential.

2.5. Entitlement to consideration

2.5.1. The Agency is committed to respect for the individual. It is attentive to the needs of its staff and is conscious of the duty of consideration that it owes them. It does all it can to take account of the legitimate interests and expectations of its staff.

2.5.2. The Agency trusts its staff and encourages initiative, and innovative approaches to problem solving. In that spirit, it is aware that mistakes can be made involuntarily.

2.5.3. Without excusing negligence or recklessness, the Agency calls for indulgence and consideration towards honest mistakes made in good faith, which should not attract disciplinary measures. They must however be reported immediately in the appropriate manner – without fear of the consequences.

3. COMMITMENTS AND RESPONSIBILITIES

On the part of the Agency

3.1. Health and safety at work

The Agency has an obligation to comply with the health and safety rules and procedures applicable in the workplace. Each staff member is also under a duty to contribute to the maintenance of safe and healthy working conditions.

3.2. In-service training and personal development

3.2.1. The Agency undertakes to maintain satisfactory conditions of employment for its staff and to develop their technical capabilities on the basis of equal opportunities. To this end, it ensures that a diverse range of training is available to improve the skills of its staff.

3.2.2. The personal development of individual staff members and best use of their capabilities in- and outside the Agency also call for a proactive approach and personal commitment.

3.3. Protection of staff members

3.3.1. The Agency protects staff members from all forms of discrimination, harassment (sexual, psychological or otherwise) in the context of their work.

3.3.2. The Agency lends support and assistance to any staff member suffering malicious treatment, denigration or infringement of his or her rights or interests.

3.3.3. Staff members may decline work on moral grounds (e.g. projects connected to security/defence) without prejudicing their careers.

On the part of staff members

3.4. Staff availability

3.4.1. The Agency is not in favour of systematic, strict checks on attendance, apart from for safety and security reasons, as it trusts staff members fully to assume their responsibilities and to manage their working time efficiently in accordance with the applicable Agency instructions.

3.4.2. Staff are required to devote a specified amount of time to their duties at the Agency under the terms of the Staff Regulations, Rules and Instructions. For work outside normal working hours, the Agency must be able to rely on staff members to perform their duties to the best of their abilities. At the same time, the Agency must respect the personal and social environment of the staff members concerned.

3.5. Compliance with laws and regulations

3.5.1. Agency staff must maintain rigorous standards of professional conduct. They must all behave responsibly and in accordance with applicable rules when discharging their duties.

3.5.2. The status of international civil servant implies certain obligations as regards conduct, both at work and elsewhere. Outside the scope of official functions and duties, the Agency attaches great importance to the strict observance of applicable local laws by staff members as well as the avoidance of actions that could be perceived as an abuse of the privileges and immunities conferred on the Agency and its staff members.

3.6. Observance of ethical behaviour

3.6.1. The observance of ethical behaviour involves ensuring compliance with the ethical standards and values defined in this document, on both a personal and a collective level. To this end, it is particularly important to help colleagues, where difficulties arise, to maintain ethical behaviour. Each staff member should contribute to awareness of a sense of belonging to a workplace where honesty and integrity prevail.

3.6.2. The Agency protects staff members against all forms of reprisal or retaliatory measures taken in response to the promotion of ethical behaviour.

3.7. Protection of Agency property

The Agency provides its staff with costly equipment and they are expected to take good care of it. It is accepted practice for staff to make personal use of their telephones, PCs, faxes or photocopiers as long as this is exceptional, limited in time and does not interfere with the smooth running of Agency business. Agency equipment must not be used to collect or distribute offensive material.

4. CONFLICTS OF INTEREST AND OUTSIDE ACTIVITIES

4.1. Use of the Agency's name for personal purposes

The Agency's image and name must never be used to serve personal interests. Employment by the Agency should therefore never be mentioned by any staff member in an undue promotional way other than for the exclusive benefit of the Agency itself.

4.2. Invitations and gifts

4.2.1. Honesty and integrity are essential qualities in the eyes of the Agency. Staff members must under no circumstances offer or receive commission payments in the course of transactions with the Agency's partners. It is nevertheless accepted practice in professional relations for gifts to be offered and invitations extended. It is all a matter of proportion.

4.2.2. Without encouraging them, the Agency is able to accept these practices as long as they amount to no more than gestures of courtesy and as long as they do not affect the independence of Agency staff.

4.3. Confidentiality and duty of discretion

4.3.1. Prudence must be exercised in the use of information technologies such as e-mail, the Internet, Intranet, teleconferencing etc. Agency information must be kept secure and confidential.

4.3.2. Staff members are under a duty to behave with discretion towards all governments, organisations or enterprises that are partners of the Agency. Moreover, staff must exercise discretion with the media, and in personal contacts, in conversations among friends or colleagues, in public places etc. as involuntary disclosure of confidential information can be extremely damaging to the Agency.

5. RIGHT TO ENGAGE IN POLITICAL ACTIVITIES

The Agency recognises the right of staff members to engage in political activities outside the context of their work. However, their public political engagement should be in compliance with the Agency's ethical standards and values as defined in this document.

6. RELATIONS WITH THE AGENCY'S PARTNERS

6.1. Openness with industrial and institutional partners is a fundamental Agency value on the basis of which positive working relationships can be established.

6.2. The Agency is committed to the principle of open competition and fair dealing with all its partners.

6.3. In their relations with the Agency's various partners, staff members must have regard for the interests of the Agency alone, to which they owe loyalty in all circumstances.

6.4. In addition, staff members are under a duty to behave with discretion towards all the Agency's partners.

7. RELATIONS WITH NATIONAL DELEGATIONS

7.1. The staff of the Agency enjoy the status of international civil servants under the sole authority of the Director General. They naturally retain links with their countries of origin but must not receive any instructions from their own or any other government relating to the discharge of their duties. They must not seek to prevail on Delegations to oppose decisions or positions taken by the Director General.

7.2. Staff members should not undermine the credibility of colleagues when dealing with Delegations.

ANNEX VII A

WTO
Understanding on Rules and Procedures Governing the Settlement of Disputes

Members hereby *agree* as follows:

Article 1

Coverage and Application

1. The rules and procedures of this Understanding shall apply to disputes brought pursuant to the consultation and dispute settlement provisions of the agreements listed in Appendix 1 to this Understanding (referred to in this Understanding as the "covered agreements"). The rules and procedures of this Understanding shall also apply to consultations and the settlement of disputes between Members concerning their rights and obligations under the provisions of the Agreement Establishing the World Trade Organization (referred to in this Understanding as the "WTO Agreement") and of this Understanding taken in isolation or in combination with any other covered agreement.

2. The rules and procedures of this Understanding shall apply subject to such special or additional rules and procedures on dispute settlement contained in the covered agreements as are identified in Appendix 2 to this Understanding. To the extent that there is a difference between the rules and procedures of this Understanding and the special or additional rules and procedures set forth in Appendix 2, the special or additional rules and procedures in Appendix 2 shall prevail. In disputes involving rules and procedures under more than one covered agreement, if there is a conflict between special or additional rules and procedures of such agreements under review, and where the parties to the dispute cannot agree on rules and procedures within 20 days of the establishment of the panel, the Chairman of the Dispute Settlement Body provided for in paragraph 1 of Article 2 (referred to in this Understanding as the "DSB"), in consultation with the parties to the dispute, shall determine the rules and procedures to be followed within 10 days after a request by either Member. The Chairman shall be guided by the principle that special or additional rules and procedures should be used where possible, and the rules and procedures set out in this Understanding should be used to the extent necessary to avoid conflict.

Article 2

Administration

1. The Dispute Settlement Body is hereby established to administer these rules and procedures and, except as otherwise provided in a covered agreement, the

consultation and dispute settlement provisions of the covered agreements. Accordingly, the DSB shall have the authority to establish panels, adopt panel and Appellate Body reports, maintain surveillance of implementation of rulings and recommendations, and authorize suspension of concessions and other obligations under the covered agreements. With respect to disputes arising under a covered agreement which is a Plurilateral Trade Agreement, the term "Member" as used herein shall refer only to those Members that are parties to the relevant Plurilateral Trade Agreement. Where the DSB administers the dispute settlement provisions of a Plurilateral Trade Agreement, only those Members that are parties to that Agreement may participate in decisions or actions taken by the DSB with respect to that dispute.

2. The DSB shall inform the relevant WTO Councils and Committees of any developments in disputes related to provisions of the respective covered agreements.

3. The DSB shall meet as often as necessary to carry out its functions within the time-frames provided in this Understanding.

4. Where the rules and procedures of this Understanding provide for the DSB to take a decision, it shall do so by consensus.[1]

Article 3

General Provisions

1. Members affirm their adherence to the principles for the management of disputes heretofore applied under Articles XXII and XXIII of GATT 1947, and the rules and procedures as further elaborated and modified herein.

2. The dispute settlement system of the WTO is a central element in providing security and predictability to the multilateral trading system. The Members recognize that it serves to preserve the rights and obligations of Members under the covered agreements, and to clarify the existing provisions of those agreements in accordance with customary rules of interpretation of public international law. Recommendations and rulings of the DSB cannot add to or diminish the rights and obligations provided in the covered agreements.

3. The prompt settlement of situations in which a Member considers that any benefits accruing to it directly or indirectly under the covered agreements are being impaired by measures taken by another Member is essential to the effective functioning of the WTO and the maintenance of a proper balance between the rights and obligations of Members.

---

[1] The DSB shall be deemed to have decided by consensus on a matter submitted for its consideration, if no Member, present at the meeting of the DSB when the decision is taken, formally objects to the proposed decision.

4. Recommendations or rulings made by the DSB shall be aimed at achieving a satisfactory settlement of the matter in accordance with the rights and obligations under this Understanding and under the covered agreements.

5. All solutions to matters formally raised under the consultation and dispute settlement provisions of the covered agreements, including arbitration awards, shall be consistent with those agreements and shall not nullify or impair benefits accruing to any Member under those agreements, nor impede the attainment of any objective of those agreements.

6. Mutually agreed solutions to matters formally raised under the consultation and dispute settlement provisions of the covered agreements shall be notified to the DSB and the relevant Councils and Committees, where any Member may raise any point relating thereto.

7. Before bringing a case, a Member shall exercise its judgement as to whether action under these procedures would be fruitful. The aim of the dispute settlement mechanism is to secure a positive solution to a dispute. A solution mutually acceptable to the parties to a dispute and consistent with the covered agreements is clearly to be preferred. In the absence of a mutually agreed solution, the first objective of the dispute settlement mechanism is usually to secure the withdrawal of the measures concerned if these are found to be inconsistent with the provisions of any of the covered agreements. The provision of compensation should be resorted to only if the immediate withdrawal of the measure is impracticable and as a temporary measure pending the withdrawal of the measure which is inconsistent with a covered agreement. The last resort which this Understanding provides to the Member invoking the dispute settlement procedures is the possibility of suspending the application of concessions or other obligations under the covered agreements on a discriminatory basis vis-à-vis the other Member, subject to authorization by the DSB of such measures.

8. In cases where there is an infringement of the obligations assumed under a covered agreement, the action is considered *prima facie* to constitute a case of nullification or impairment. This means that there is normally a presumption that a breach of the rules has an adverse impact on other Members parties to that covered agreement, and in such cases, it shall be up to the Member against whom the complaint has been brought to rebut the charge.

9. The provisions of this Understanding are without prejudice to the rights of Members to seek authoritative interpretation of provisions of a covered agreement through decision-making under the WTO Agreement or a covered agreement which is a Plurilateral Trade Agreement.

10. It is understood that requests for conciliation and the use of the dispute settlement procedures should not be intended or considered as contentious acts and that, if a dispute arises, all Members will engage in these procedures in good faith in an effort to resolve the dispute. It is also understood that complaints and counter-complaints in regard to distinct matters should not be linked.

11. This Understanding shall be applied only with respect to new requests for consultations under the consultation provisions of the covered agreements made on or after the date of entry into force of the WTO Agreement. With respect to disputes for which the request for consultations was made under GATT 1947 or under any other predecessor agreement to the covered agreements before the date of entry into force of the WTO Agreement, the relevant dispute settlement rules and procedures in effect immediately prior to the date of entry into force of the WTO Agreement shall continue to apply.[2]

12. Notwithstanding paragraph 11, if a complaint based on any of the covered agreements is brought by a developing country Member against a developed country Member, the complaining party shall have the right to invoke, as an alternative to the provisions contained in Articles 4, 5, 6 and 12 of this Understanding, the corresponding provisions of the Decision of 5 April 1966 (BISD 14S/18), except that where the Panel considers that the time-frame provided for in paragraph 7 of that Decision is insufficient to provide its report and with the agreement of the complaining party, that time-frame may be extended. To the extent that there is a difference between the rules and procedures of Articles 4, 5, 6 and 12 and the corresponding rules and procedures of the Decision, the latter shall prevail.

Article 4

Consultations

1. Members affirm their resolve to strengthen and improve the effectiveness of the consultation procedures employed by Members.

2. Each Member undertakes to accord sympathetic consideration to and afford adequate opportunity for consultation regarding any representations made by another Member concerning measures affecting the operation of any covered agreement taken within the territory of the former.[3]

3. If a request for consultations is made pursuant to a covered agreement, the Member to which the request is made shall, unless otherwise mutually agreed, reply to the request within 10 days after the date of its receipt and shall enter into consultations in good faith within a period of no more than 30 days after the date of receipt of the request, with a view to reaching a mutually satisfactory solution. If the Member does not respond within 10 days after the date of receipt of the request, or does not enter into consultations within a period of no more

[2] This paragraph shall also be applied to disputes on which panel reports have not been adopted or fully implemented.

[3] Where the provisions of any other covered agreement concerning measures taken by regional or local governments or authorities within the territory of a Member contain provisions different from the provisions of this paragraph, the provisions of such other covered agreement shall prevail.

than 30 days, or a period otherwise mutually agreed, after the date of receipt of the request, then the Member that requested the holding of consultations may proceed directly to request the establishment of a panel.

4. All such requests for consultations shall be notified to the DSB and the relevant Councils and Committees by the Member which requests consultations. Any request for consultations shall be submitted in writing and shall give the reasons for the request, including identification of the measures at issue and an indication of the legal basis for the complaint.

5. In the course of consultations in accordance with the provisions of a covered agreement, before resorting to further action under this Understanding, Members should attempt to obtain satisfactory adjustment of the matter.

6. Consultations shall be confidential, and without prejudice to the rights of any Member in any further proceedings.

7. If the consultations fail to settle a dispute within 60 days after the date of receipt of the request for consultations, the complaining party may request the establishment of a panel. The complaining party may request a panel during the 60-day period if the consulting parties jointly consider that consultations have failed to settle the dispute.

8. In cases of urgency, including those which concern perishable goods, Members shall enter into consultations within a period of no more than 10 days after the date of receipt of the request. If the consultations have failed to settle the dispute within a period of 20 days after the date of receipt of the request, the complaining party may request the establishment of a panel.

9. In cases of urgency, including those which concern perishable goods, the parties to the dispute, panels and the Appellate Body shall make every effort to accelerate the proceedings to the greatest extent possible.

10. During consultations Members should give special attention to the particular problems and interests of developing country Members.

11. Whenever a Member other than the consulting Members considers that it has a substantial trade interest in consultations being held pursuant to paragraph 1 of Article XXII of GATT 1994, paragraph 1 of Article XXII of GATS, or the corresponding provisions in other covered agreements,[4] such Member may notify

[4] The corresponding consultation provisions in the covered agreements are listed hereunder: Agreement on Agriculture, Article 19; Agreement on the Application of Sanitary and Phytosanitary Measures, paragraph 1 of Article 11; Agreement on Textiles and Clothing, paragraph 4 of Article 8; Agreement on Technical Barriers to Trade, paragraph 1 of Article 14; Agreement on Trade-Related Investment Measures, Article 8; Agreement on Implementation of Article VI of GATT 1994, paragraph 2 of Article 17; Agreement on Implementation of Article VII of GATT 1994, paragraph 2 of Article 19; Agreement on Preshipment Inspection, Article 7; Agreement on Rules of Origin,

the consulting Members and the DSB, within 10 days after the date of the circulation of the request for consultations under said Article, of its desire to be joined in the consultations. Such Member shall be joined in the consultations, provided that the Member to which the request for consultations was addressed agrees that the claim of substantial interest is well-founded. In that event they shall so inform the DSB. If the request to be joined in the consultations is not accepted, the applicant Member shall be free to request consultations under paragraph 1 of Article XXII or paragraph 1 of Article XXIII of GATT 1994, paragraph 1 of Article XXII or paragraph 1 of Article XXIII of GATS, or the corresponding provisions in other covered agreements.

Article 5

Good Offices, Conciliation and Mediation

1. Good offices, conciliation and mediation are procedures that are undertaken voluntarily if the parties to the dispute so agree.

2. Proceedings involving good offices, conciliation and mediation, and in particular positions taken by the parties to the dispute during these proceedings, shall be confidential, and without prejudice to the rights of either party in any further proceedings under these procedures.

3. Good offices, conciliation or mediation may be requested at any time by any party to a dispute. They may begin at any time and be terminated at any time. Once procedures for good offices, conciliation or mediation are terminated, a complaining party may then proceed with a request for the establishment of a panel.

4. When good offices, conciliation or mediation are entered into within 60 days after the date of receipt of a request for consultations, the complaining party must allow a period of 60 days after the date of receipt of the request for consultations before requesting the establishment of a panel. The complaining party may request the establishment of a panel during the 60-day period if the parties to the dispute jointly consider that the good offices, conciliation or mediation process has failed to settle the dispute.

5. If the parties to a dispute agree, procedures for good offices, conciliation or mediation may continue while the panel process proceeds.

6. The Director-General may, acting in an *ex officio* capacity, offer good offices, conciliation or mediation with the view to assisting Members to settle a dispute.

Article 7; Agreement on Import Licensing Procedures, Article 6; Agreement on Subsidies and Countervailing Measures, Article 30; Agreement on Safeguards, Article 14; Agreement on Trade-Related Aspects of Intellectual Property Rights, Article 64.1; and any corresponding consultation provisions in Plurilateral Trade Agreements as determined by the competent bodies of each Agreement and as notified to the DSB.

Article 6

Establishment of Panels

1. If the complaining party so requests, a panel shall be established at the latest at the DSB meeting following that at which the request first appears as an item on the DSB's agenda, unless at that meeting the DSB decides by consensus not to establish a panel.[5]

2. The request for the establishment of a panel shall be made in writing. It shall indicate whether consultations were held, identify the specific measures at issue and provide a brief summary of the legal basis of the complaint sufficient to present the problem clearly. In case the applicant requests the establishment of a panel with other than standard terms of reference, the written request shall include the proposed text of special terms of reference.

Article 7

Terms of Reference of Panels

1. Panels shall have the following terms of reference unless the parties to the dispute agree otherwise within 20 days from the establishment of the panel:

> To examine, in the light of the relevant provisions in (name of the covered agreement(s) cited by the parties to the dispute), the matter referred to the DSB by (name of party) in document . . . and to make such findings as will assist the DSB in making the recommendations or in giving the rulings provided for in that/those agreement(s).

2. Panels shall address the relevant provisions in any covered agreement or agreements cited by the parties to the dispute.

3. In establishing a panel, the DSB may authorize its Chairman to draw up the terms of reference of the panel in consultation with the parties to the dispute, subject to the provisions of paragraph 1. The terms of reference thus drawn up shall be circulated to all Members. If other than standard terms of reference are agreed upon, any Member may raise any point relating thereto in the DSB.

---

[5] If the complaining party so requests, a meeting of the DSB shall be convened for this purpose within 15 days of the request, provided that at least 10 days' advance notice of the meeting is given.

Article 8

Composition of Panels

1. Panels shall be composed of well-qualified governmental and/or non-governmental individuals, including persons who have served on or presented a case to a panel, served as a representative of a Member or of a contracting party to GATT 1947 or as a representative to the Council or Committee of any covered agreement or its predecessor agreement, or in the Secretariat, taught or published on international trade law or policy, or served as a senior trade policy official of a Member.

2. Panel members should be selected with a view to ensuring the independence of the members, a sufficiently diverse background and a wide spectrum of experience.

3. Citizens of Members whose governments[6] are parties to the dispute or third parties as defined in paragraph 2 of Article 10 shall not serve on a panel concerned with that dispute, unless the parties to the dispute agree otherwise.

4. To assist in the selection of panelists, the Secretariat shall maintain an indicative list of governmental and non-governmental individuals possessing the qualifications outlined in paragraph 1, from which panelists may be drawn as appropriate. That list shall include the roster of non-governmental panelists established on 30 November 1984 (BISD 31S/9), and other rosters and indicative lists established under any of the covered agreements, and shall retain the names of persons on those rosters and indicative lists at the time of entry into force of the WTO Agreement. Members may periodically suggest names of governmental and non-governmental individuals for inclusion on the indicative list, providing relevant information on their knowledge of international trade and of the sectors or subject matter of the covered agreements, and those names shall be added to the list upon approval by the DSB. For each of the individuals on the list, the list shall indicate specific areas of experience or expertise of the individuals in the sectors or subject matter of the covered agreements.

5. Panels shall be composed of three panelists unless the parties to the dispute agree, within 10 days from the establishment of the panel, to a panel composed of five panelists. Members shall be informed promptly of the composition of the panel.

6. The Secretariat shall propose nominations for the panel to the parties to the dispute. The parties to the dispute shall not oppose nominations except for compelling reasons.

---

[6] In the case where customs unions or common markets are parties to a dispute, this provision applies to citizens of all member countries of the customs unions or common markets.

7. If there is no agreement on the panelists within 20 days after the date of the establishment of a panel, at the request of either party, the Director-General, in consultation with the Chairman of the DSB and the Chairman of the relevant Council or Committee, shall determine the composition of the panel by appointing the panelists whom the Director-General considers most appropriate in accordance with any relevant special or additional rules or procedures of the covered agreement or covered agreements which are at issue in the dispute, after consulting with the parties to the dispute. The Chairman of the DSB shall inform the Members of the composition of the panel thus formed no later than 10 days after the date the Chairman receives such a request.

8. Members shall undertake, as a general rule, to permit their officials to serve as panelists.

9. Panelists shall serve in their individual capacities and not as government representatives, nor as representatives of any organization. Members shall therefore not give them instructions nor seek to influence them as individuals with regard to matters before a panel.

10. When a dispute is between a developing country Member and a developed country Member the panel shall, if the developing country Member so requests, include at least one panelist from a developing country Member.

11. Panelists' expenses, including travel and subsistence allowance, shall be met from the WTO budget in accordance with criteria to be adopted by the General Council, based on recommendations of the Committee on Budget, Finance and Administration.

Article 9

Procedures for Multiple Complainants

1. Where more than one Member requests the establishment of a panel related to the same matter, a single panel may be established to examine these complaints taking into account the rights of all Members concerned. A single panel should be established to examine such complaints whenever feasible.

2. The single panel shall organize its examination and present its findings to the DSB in such a manner that the rights which the parties to the dispute would have enjoyed had separate panels examined the complaints are in no way impaired. If one of the parties to the dispute so requests, the panel shall submit separate reports on the dispute concerned. The written submissions by each of the complainants shall be made available to the other complainants, and each complainant shall have the right to be present when any one of the other complainants presents its views to the panel.

3. If more than one panel is established to examine the complaints related to the same matter, to the greatest extent possible the same persons shall serve as pan-

elists on each of the separate panels and the timetable for the panel process in such disputes shall be harmonized.

Article 10

Third Parties

1. The interests of the parties to a dispute and those of other Members under a covered agreement at issue in the dispute shall be fully taken into account during the panel process.

2. Any Member having a substantial interest in a matter before a panel and having notified its interest to the DSB (referred to in this Understanding as a "third party") shall have an opportunity to be heard by the panel and to make written submissions to the panel. These submissions shall also be given to the parties to the dispute and shall be reflected in the panel report.

3. Third parties shall receive the submissions of the parties to the dispute to the first meeting of the panel.

4. If a third party considers that a measure already the subject of a panel proceeding nullifies or impairs benefits accruing to it under any covered agreement, that Member may have recourse to normal dispute settlement procedures under this Understanding. Such a dispute shall be referred to the original panel wherever possible.

Article 11

Function of Panels

The function of panels is to assist the DSB in discharging its responsibilities under this Understanding and the covered agreements. Accordingly, a panel should make an objective assessment of the matter before it, including an objective assessment of the facts of the case and the applicability of and conformity with the relevant covered agreements, and make such other findings as will assist the DSB in making the recommendations or in giving the rulings provided for in the covered agreements. Panels should consult regularly with the parties to the dispute and give them adequate opportunity to develop a mutually satisfactory solution.

Article 12

Panel Procedures

1. Panels shall follow the Working Procedures in Appendix 3 unless the panel decides otherwise after consulting the parties to the dispute.

2. Panel procedures should provide sufficient flexibility so as to ensure high-quality panel reports, while not unduly delaying the panel process.

3. After consulting the parties to the dispute, the panelists shall, as soon as practicable and whenever possible within one week after the composition and terms of reference of the panel have been agreed upon, fix the timetable for the panel process, taking into account the provisions of paragraph 9 of Article 4, if relevant.

4. In determining the timetable for the panel process, the panel shall provide sufficient time for the parties to the dispute to prepare their submissions.

5. Panels should set precise deadlines for written submissions by the parties and the parties should respect those deadlines.

6. Each party to the dispute shall deposit its written submissions with the Secretariat for immediate transmission to the panel and to the other party or parties to the dispute. The complaining party shall submit its first submission in advance of the responding party's first submission unless the panel decides, in fixing the timetable referred to in paragraph 3 and after consultations with the parties to the dispute, that the parties should submit their first submissions simultaneously. When there are sequential arrangements for the deposit of first submissions, the panel shall establish a firm time-period for receipt of the responding party's submission. Any subsequent written submissions shall be submitted simultaneously.

7. Where the parties to the dispute have failed to develop a mutually satisfactory solution, the panel shall submit its findings in the form of a written report to the DSB. In such cases, the report of a panel shall set out the findings of fact, the applicability of relevant provisions and the basic rationale behind any findings and recommendations that it makes. Where a settlement of the matter among the parties to the dispute has been found, the report of the panel shall be confined to a brief description of the case and to reporting that a solution has been reached.

8. In order to make the procedures more efficient, the period in which the panel shall conduct its examination, from the date that the composition and terms of reference of the panel have been agreed upon until the date the final report is issued to the parties to the dispute, shall, as a general rule, not exceed six months. In cases of urgency, including those relating to perishable goods, the panel shall aim to issue its report to the parties to the dispute within three months.

9. When the panel considers that it cannot issue its report within six months, or within three months in cases of urgency, it shall inform the DSB in writing of the reasons for the delay together with an estimate of the period within which it will issue its report. In no case should the period from the establishment of the panel to the circulation of the report to the Members exceed nine months.

10. In the context of consultations involving a measure taken by a developing country Member, the parties may agree to extend the periods established in paragraphs 7 and 8 of Article 4. If, after the relevant period has elapsed, the con-

sulting parties cannot agree that the consultations have concluded, the Chairman of the DSB shall decide, after consultation with the parties, whether to extend the relevant period and, if so, for how long. In addition, in examining a complaint against a developing country Member, the panel shall accord sufficient time for the developing country Member to prepare and present its argumentation. The provisions of paragraph 1 of Article 20 and paragraph 4 of Article 21 are not affected by any action pursuant to this paragraph.

11. Where one or more of the parties is a developing country Member, the panel's report shall explicitly indicate the form in which account has been taken of relevant provisions on differential and more-favourable treatment for developing country Members that form part of the covered agreements which have been raised by the developing country Member in the course of the dispute settlement procedures.

12. The panel may suspend its work at any time at the request of the complaining party for a period not to exceed 12 months. In the event of such a suspension, the time-frames set out in paragraphs 8 and 9 of this Article, paragraph 1 of Article 20, and paragraph 4 of Article 21 shall be extended by the amount of time that the work was suspended. If the work of the panel has been suspended for more than 12 months, the authority for establishment of the panel shall lapse.

Article 13

Right to Seek Information

1. Each panel shall have the right to seek information and technical advice from any individual or body which it deems appropriate. However, before a panel seeks such information or advice from any individual or body within the jurisdiction of a Member it shall inform the authorities of that Member. A Member should respond promptly and fully to any request by a panel for such information as the panel considers necessary and appropriate. Confidential information which is provided shall not be revealed without formal authorization from the individual, body, or authorities of the Member providing the information.

2. Panels may seek information from any relevant source and may consult experts to obtain their opinion on certain aspects of the matter. With respect to a factual issue concerning a scientific or other technical matter raised by a party to a dispute, a panel may request an advisory report in writing from an expert review group. Rules for the establishment of such a group and its procedures are set forth in Appendix 4.

Article 14

Confidentiality

1. Panel deliberations shall be confidential.

2. The reports of panels shall be drafted without the presence of the parties to the dispute in the light of the information provided and the statements made.

3. Opinions expressed in the panel report by individual panelists shall be anonymous.

Article 15

Interim Review Stage

1. Following the consideration of rebuttal submissions and oral arguments, the panel shall issue the descriptive (factual and argument) sections of its draft report to the parties to the dispute. Within a period of time set by the panel, the parties shall submit their comments in writing.

2. Following the expiration of the set period of time for receipt of comments from the parties to the dispute, the panel shall issue an interim report to the parties, including both the descriptive sections and the panel's findings and conclusions. Within a period of time set by the panel, a party may submit a written request for the panel to review precise aspects of the interim report prior to circulation of the final report to the Members. At the request of a party, the panel shall hold a further meeting with the parties on the issues identified in the written comments. If no comments are received from any party within the comment period, the interim report shall be considered the final panel report and circulated promptly to the Members.

3. The findings of the final panel report shall include a discussion of the arguments made at the interim review stage. The interim review stage shall be conducted within the time-period set out in paragraph 8 of Article 12.

Article 16

Adoption of Panel Reports

1. In order to provide sufficient time for the Members to consider panel reports, the reports shall not be considered for adoption by the DSB until 20 days after the date they have been circulated to the Members.

2. Members having objections to a panel report shall give written reasons to explain their objections for circulation at least 10 days prior to the DSB meeting at which the panel report will be considered.

3. The parties to a dispute shall have the right to participate fully in the consideration of the panel report by the DSB, and their views shall be fully recorded.

4. Within 60 days after the date of circulation of a panel report to the Members, the report shall be adopted at a DSB meeting[7] unless a party to the dispute formally notifies the DSB of its decision to appeal or the DSB decides by consensus not to adopt the report. If a party has notified its decision to appeal, the report by the panel shall not be considered for adoption by the DSB until after completion of the appeal. This adoption procedure is without prejudice to the right of Members to express their views on a panel report.

Article 17

Appellate Review

Standing Appellate Body

1. A standing Appellate Body shall be established by the DSB. The Appellate Body shall hear appeals from panel cases. It shall be composed of seven persons, three of whom shall serve on any one case. Persons serving on the Appellate Body shall serve in rotation. Such rotation shall be determined in the working procedures of the Appellate Body.

2. The DSB shall appoint persons to serve on the Appellate Body for a four-year term, and each person may be reappointed once. However, the terms of three of the seven persons appointed immediately after the entry into force of the WTO Agreement shall expire at the end of two years, to be determined by lot. Vacancies shall be filled as they arise. A person appointed to replace a person whose term of office has not expired shall hold office for the remainder of the predecessor's term.

3. The Appellate Body shall comprise persons of recognized authority, with demonstrated expertise in law, international trade and the subject matter of the covered agreements generally. They shall be unaffiliated with any government. The Appellate Body membership shall be broadly representative of membership in the WTO. All persons serving on the Appellate Body shall be available at all times and on short notice, and shall stay abreast of dispute settlement activities and other relevant activities of the WTO. They shall not participate in the consideration of any disputes that would create a direct or indirect conflict of interest.

4. Only parties to the dispute, not third parties, may appeal a panel report. Third parties which have notified the DSB of a substantial interest in the matter pursuant to paragraph 2 of Article 10 may make written submissions to, and be given an opportunity to be heard by, the Appellate Body.

---

[7] If a meeting of the DSB is not scheduled within this period at a time that enables the requirements of paragraphs 1 and 4 of Article 16 to be met, a meeting of the DSB shall be held for this purpose.

5. As a general rule, the proceedings shall not exceed 60 days from the date a party to the dispute formally notifies its decision to appeal to the date the Appellate Body circulates its report. In fixing its timetable the Appellate Body shall take into account the provisions of paragraph 9 of Article 4, if relevant. When the Appellate Body considers that it cannot provide its report within 60 days, it shall inform the DSB in writing of the reasons for the delay together with an estimate of the period within which it will submit its report. In no case shall the proceedings exceed 90 days.

6. An appeal shall be limited to issues of law covered in the panel report and legal interpretations developed by the panel.

7. The Appellate Body shall be provided with appropriate administrative and legal support as it requires.

8. The expenses of persons serving on the Appellate Body, including travel and subsistence allowance, shall be met from the WTO budget in accordance with criteria to be adopted by the General Council, based on recommendations of the Committee on Budget, Finance and Administration.

Procedures for Appellate Review

9. Working procedures shall be drawn up by the Appellate Body in consultation with the Chairman of the DSB and the Director-General, and communicated to the Members for their information.

10. The proceedings of the Appellate Body shall be confidential. The reports of the Appellate Body shall be drafted without the presence of the parties to the dispute and in the light of the information provided and the statements made.

11. Opinions expressed in the Appellate Body report by individuals serving on the Appellate Body shall be anonymous.

12. The Appellate Body shall address each of the issues raised in accordance with paragraph 6 during the appellate proceeding.

13. The Appellate Body may uphold, modify or reverse the legal findings and conclusions of the panel.

Adoption of Appellate Body Reports

14. An Appellate Body report shall be adopted by the DSB and unconditionally accepted by the parties to the dispute unless the DSB decides by consensus not to adopt the Appellate Body report within 30 days following its circulation to the Members.[8] This adoption procedure is without prejudice to the right of Members to express their views on an Appellate Body report.

---

[8] If a meeting of the DSB is not scheduled during this period, such a meeting of the DSB shall be held for this purpose.

Article 18

Communications with the Panel or Appellate Body

1. There shall be no *ex parte* communications with the panel or Appellate Body concerning matters under consideration by the panel or Appellate Body.

2. Written submissions to the panel or the Appellate Body shall be treated as confidential, but shall be made available to the parties to the dispute. Nothing in this Understanding shall preclude a party to a dispute from disclosing statements of its own positions to the public. Members shall treat as confidential information submitted by another Member to the panel or the Appellate Body which that Member has designated as confidential. A party to a dispute shall also, upon request of a Member, provide a non-confidential summary of the information contained in its written submissions that could be disclosed to the public.

Article 19

Panel and Appellate Body Recommendations

1. Where a panel or the Appellate Body concludes that a measure is inconsistent with a covered agreement, it shall recommend that the Member concerned[9] bring the measure into conformity with that agreement.[10] In addition to its recommendations, the panel or Appellate Body may suggest ways in which the Member concerned could implement the recommendations.

2. In accordance with paragraph 2 of Article 3, in their findings and recommendations, the panel and Appellate Body cannot add to or diminish the rights and obligations provided in the covered agreements.

Article 20

Time-frame for DSB Decisions

Unless otherwise agreed to by the parties to the dispute, the period from the date of establishment of the panel by the DSB until the date the DSB considers the panel or appellate report for adoption shall as a general rule not exceed nine months where the panel report is not appealed or 12 months where the report is appealed. Where either the panel or the Appellate Body has acted, pursuant to paragraph 9 of Article 12 or paragraph 5 of Article 17, to extend the time for providing its report, the additional time taken shall be added to the above periods.

---

[9] The "Member concerned" is the party to the dispute to which the panel or Appellate Body recommendations are directed.

[10] With respect to recommendations in cases not involving a violation of GATT 1994 or any other covered agreement, see Article 26.

Article 21

Surveillance of Implementation of Recommendations and Rulings

1. Prompt compliance with recommendations or rulings of the DSB is essential in order to ensure effective resolution of disputes to the benefit of all Members.

2. Particular attention should be paid to matters affecting the interests of developing country Members with respect to measures which have been subject to dispute settlement.

3. At a DSB meeting held within 30 days[11] after the date of adoption of the panel or Appellate Body report, the Member concerned shall inform the DSB of its intentions in respect of implementation of the recommendations and rulings of the DSB. If it is impracticable to comply immediately with the recommendations and rulings, the Member concerned shall have a reasonable period of time in which to do so. The reasonable period of time shall be:

(a) the period of time proposed by the Member concerned, provided that such period is approved by the DSB; or, in the absence of such approval,
(b) a period of time mutually agreed by the parties to the dispute within 45 days after the date of adoption of the recommendations and rulings; or, in the absence of such agreement,
(c) a period of time determined through binding arbitration within 90 days after the date of adoption of the recommendations and rulings.[12] In such arbitration, a guideline for the arbitrator[13] should be that the reasonable period of time to implement panel or Appellate Body recommendations should not exceed 15 months from the date of adoption of a panel or Appellate Body report. However, that time may be shorter or longer, depending upon the particular circumstances.

4. Except where the panel or the Appellate Body has extended, pursuant to paragraph 9 of Article 12 or paragraph 5 of Article 17, the time of providing its report, the period from the date of establishment of the panel by the DSB until the date of determination of the reasonable period of time shall not exceed 15 months unless the parties to the dispute agree otherwise. Where either the panel or the Appellate Body has acted to extend the time of providing its report, the additional time taken shall be added to the 15-month period; provided that unless the parties to the dispute agree that there are exceptional circumstances, the total time shall not exceed 18 months.

---

[11] If a meeting of the DSB is not scheduled during this period, such a meeting of the DSB shall be held for this purpose.
[12] If the parties cannot agree on an arbitrator within ten days after referring the matter to arbitration, the arbitrator shall be appointed by the Director-General within ten days, after consulting the parties.
[13] The expression "arbitrator" shall be interpreted as referring either to an individual or a group.

5. Where there is disagreement as to the existence or consistency with a covered agreement of measures taken to comply with the recommendations and rulings such dispute shall be decided through recourse to these dispute settlement procedures, including wherever possible resort to the original panel. The panel shall circulate its report within 90 days after the date of referral of the matter to it. When the panel considers that it cannot provide its report within this time frame, it shall inform the DSB in writing of the reasons for the delay together with an estimate of the period within which it will submit its report.

6. The DSB shall keep under surveillance the implementation of adopted recommendations or rulings. The issue of implementation of the recommendations or rulings may be raised at the DSB by any Member at any time following their adoption. Unless the DSB decides otherwise, the issue of implementation of the recommendations or rulings shall be placed on the agenda of the DSB meeting after six months following the date of establishment of the reasonable period of time pursuant to paragraph 3 and shall remain on the DSB's agenda until the issue is resolved. At least 10 days prior to each such DSB meeting, the Member concerned shall provide the DSB with a status report in writing of its progress in the implementation of the recommendations or rulings.

7. If the matter is one which has been raised by a developing country Member, the DSB shall consider what further action it might take which would be appropriate to the circumstances.

8. If the case is one brought by a developing country Member, in considering what appropriate action might be taken, the DSB shall take into account not only the trade coverage of measures complained of, but also their impact on the economy of developing country Members concerned.

Article 22

Compensation and the Suspension of Concessions

1. Compensation and the suspension of concessions or other obligations are temporary measures available in the event that the recommendations and rulings are not implemented within a reasonable period of time. However, neither compensation nor the suspension of concessions or other obligations is preferred to full implementation of a recommendation to bring a measure into conformity with the covered agreements. Compensation is voluntary and, if granted, shall be consistent with the covered agreements.

2. If the Member concerned fails to bring the measure found to be inconsistent with a covered agreement into compliance therewith or otherwise comply with the recommendations and rulings within the reasonable period of time determined pursuant to paragraph 3 of Article 21, such Member shall, if so requested, and no later than the expiry of the reasonable period of time, enter into negotiations with any party having invoked the dispute settlement procedures, with a view to developing mutually acceptable compensation. If no satisfactory compensation has

been agreed within 20 days after the date of expiry of the reasonable period of time, any party having invoked the dispute settlement procedures may request authorization from the DSB to suspend the application to the Member concerned of concessions or other obligations under the covered agreements.

3. In considering what concessions or other obligations to suspend, the complaining party shall apply the following principles and procedures:

(a) the general principle is that the complaining party should first seek to suspend concessions or other obligations with respect to the same sector(s) as that in which the panel or Appellate Body has found a violation or other nullification or impairment;
(b) if that party considers that it is not practicable or effective to suspend concessions or other obligations with respect to the same sector(s), it may seek to suspend concessions or other obligations in other sectors under the same agreement;
(c) if that party considers that it is not practicable or effective to suspend concessions or other obligations with respect to other sectors under the same agreement, and that the circumstances are serious enough, it may seek to suspend concessions or other obligations under another covered agreement;
(d) in applying the above principles, that party shall take into account:

  (i) the trade in the sector or under the agreement under which the panel or Appellate Body has found a violation or other nullification or impairment, and the importance of such trade to that party;
  (ii) the broader economic elements related to the nullification or impairment and the broader economic consequences of the suspension of concessions or other obligations;

(e) if that party decides to request authorization to suspend concessions or other obligations pursuant to subparagraphs (b) or (c), it shall state the reasons therefor in its request. At the same time as the request is forwarded to the DSB, it also shall be forwarded to the relevant Councils and also, in the case of a request pursuant to subparagraph (b), the relevant sectoral bodies;
(f) for purposes of this paragraph, "sector" means:

  (i) with respect to goods, all goods;
  (ii) with respect to services, a principal sector as identified in the current "Services Sectoral Classification List" which identifies such sectors;[14]
  (iii) with respect to trade-related intellectual property rights, each of the categories of intellectual property rights covered in Section 1, or Section 2, or Section 3, or Section 4, or Section 5, or Section 6, or Section 7 of Part II, or the obligations under Part III, or Part IV of the Agreement on TRIPS;

[14] The list in document MTN.GNS/W/120 identifies eleven sectors.

(g) for purposes of this paragraph, "agreement" means:

(i) with respect to goods, the agreements listed in Annex 1A of the WTO Agreement, taken as a whole as well as the Plurilateral Trade Agreements in so far as the relevant parties to the dispute are parties to these agreements;

(ii) with respect to services, the GATS;

(iii) with respect to intellectual property rights, the Agreement on TRIPS.

4. The level of the suspension of concessions or other obligations authorized by the DSB shall be equivalent to the level of the nullification or impairment.

5. The DSB shall not authorize suspension of concessions or other obligations if a covered agreement prohibits such suspension.

6. When the situation described in paragraph 2 occurs, the DSB, upon request, shall grant authorization to suspend concessions or other obligations within 30 days of the expiry of the reasonable period of time unless the DSB decides by consensus to reject the request. However, if the Member concerned objects to the level of suspension proposed, or claims that the principles and procedures set forth in paragraph 3 have not been followed where a complaining party has requested authorization to suspend concessions or other obligations pursuant to paragraph 3(b) or (c), the matter shall be referred to arbitration. Such arbitration shall be carried out by the original panel, if members are available, or by an arbitrator[15] appointed by the Director-General and shall be completed within 60 days after the date of expiry of the reasonable period of time. Concessions or other obligations shall not be suspended during the course of the arbitration.

7. The arbitrator[16] acting pursuant to paragraph 6 shall not examine the nature of the concessions or other obligations to be suspended but shall determine whether the level of such suspension is equivalent to the level of nullification or impairment. The arbitrator may also determine if the proposed suspension of concessions or other obligations is allowed under the covered agreement. However, if the matter referred to arbitration includes a claim that the principles and procedures set forth in paragraph 3 have not been followed, the arbitrator shall examine that claim. In the event the arbitrator determines that those principles and procedures have not been followed, the complaining party shall apply them consistent with paragraph 3. The parties shall accept the arbitrator's decision as final and the parties concerned shall not seek a second arbitration. The DSB shall be informed promptly of the decision of the arbitrator and shall upon request, grant authorization to suspend concessions or other obligations where the request is consistent with the decision of the arbitrator, unless the DSB decides by consensus to reject the request.

---

[15] The expression"arbitrator" shall be interpreted as referring either to an individual or a group.

[16] The expression "arbitrator" shall be interpreted as referring either to an individual or a group or to the members of the original panel when serving in the capacity of arbitrator.

8. The suspension of concessions or other obligations shall be temporary and shall only be applied until such time as the measure found to be inconsistent with a covered agreement has been removed, or the Member that must implement recommendations or rulings provides a solution to the nullification or impairment of benefits, or a mutually satisfactory solution is reached. In accordance with paragraph 6 of Article 21, the DSB shall continue to keep under surveillance the implementation of adopted recommendations or rulings, including those cases where compensation has been provided or concessions or other obligations have been suspended but the recommendations to bring a measure into conformity with the covered agreements have not been implemented.

9. The dispute settlement provisions of the covered agreements may be invoked in respect of measures affecting their observance taken by regional or local governments or authorities within the territory of a Member. When the DSB has ruled that a provision of a covered agreement has not been observed, the responsible Member shall take such reasonable measures as may be available to it to ensure its observance. The provisions of the covered agreements and this Understanding relating to compensation and suspension of concessions or other obligations apply in cases where it has not been possible to secure such observance.[17]

Article 23

Strengthening of the Multilateral System

1. When Members seek the redress of a violation of obligations or other nullification or impairment of benefits under the covered agreements or an impediment to the attainment of any objective of the covered agreements, they shall have recourse to, and abide by, the rules and procedures of this Understanding.

2. In such cases, Members shall:

(a) not make a determination to the effect that a violation has occurred, that benefits have been nullified or impaired or that the attainment of any objective of the covered agreements has been impeded, except through recourse to dispute settlement in accordance with the rules and procedures of this Understanding, and shall make any such determination consistent with the findings contained in the panel or Appellate Body report adopted by the DSB or an arbitration award rendered under this Understanding;
(b) follow the procedures set forth in Article 21 to determine the reasonable period of time for the Member concerned to implement the recommendations and rulings; and

[17] Where the provisions of any covered agreement concerning measures taken by regional or local governments or authorities within the territory of a Member contain provisions different from the provisions of this paragraph, the provisions of such covered agreement shall prevail.

(c) follow the procedures set forth in Article 22 to determine the level of suspension of concessions or other obligations and obtain DSB authorization in accordance with those procedures before suspending concessions or other obligations under the covered agreements in response to the failure of the Member concerned to implement the recommendations and rulings within that reasonable period of time.

Article 24

Special Procedures Involving Least-Developed Country Members

1. At all stages of the determination of the causes of a dispute and of dispute settlement procedures involving a least-developed country Member, particular consideration shall be given to the special situation of least-developed country Members. In this regard, Members shall exercise due restraint in raising matters under these procedures involving a least-developed country Member. If nullification or impairment is found to result from a measure taken by a least-developed country Member, complaining parties shall exercise due restraint in asking for compensation or seeking authorization to suspend the application of concessions or other obligations pursuant to these procedures.

2. In dispute settlement cases involving a least-developed country Member, where a satisfactory solution has not been found in the course of consultations the Director-General or the Chairman of the DSB shall, upon request by a least-developed country Member offer their good offices, conciliation and mediation with a view to assisting the parties to settle the dispute, before a request for a panel is made. The Director-General or the Chairman of the DSB, in providing the above assistance, may consult any source which either deems appropriate.

Article 25

Arbitration

1. Expeditious arbitration within the WTO as an alternative means of dispute settlement can facilitate the solution of certain disputes that concern issues that are clearly defined by both parties.

2. Except as otherwise provided in this Understanding, resort to arbitration shall be subject to mutual agreement of the parties which shall agree on the procedures to be followed. Agreements to resort to arbitration shall be notified to all Members sufficiently in advance of the actual commencement of the arbitration process.

3. Other Members may become party to an arbitration proceeding only upon the agreement of the parties which have agreed to have recourse to arbitration. The parties to the proceeding shall agree to abide by the arbitration award. Arbitration awards shall be notified to the DSB and the Council or Committee of any relevant agreement where any Member may raise any point relating thereto.

4. Articles 21 and 22 of this Understanding shall apply *mutatis mutandis* to arbitration awards.

Article 26

1. *Non-Violation Complaints of the Type Described in Paragraph 1(b) of Article XXIII of GATT 1994*

Where the provisions of paragraph 1(b) of Article XXIII of GATT 1994 are applicable to a covered agreement, a panel or the Appellate Body may only make rulings and recommendations where a party to the dispute considers that any benefit accruing to it directly or indirectly under the relevant covered agreement is being nullified or impaired or the attainment of any objective of that Agreement is being impeded as a result of the application by a Member of any measure, whether or not it conflicts with the provisions of that Agreement. Where and to the extent that such party considers and a panel or the Appellate Body determines that a case concerns a measure that does not conflict with the provisions of a covered agreement to which the provisions of paragraph 1(b) of Article XXIII of GATT 1994 are applicable, the procedures in this Understanding shall apply, subject to the following:

(a) the complaining party shall present a detailed justification in support of any complaint relating to a measure which does not conflict with the relevant covered agreement;
(b) where a measure has been found to nullify or impair benefits under, or impede the attainment of objectives, of the relevant covered agreement without violation thereof, there is no obligation to withdraw the measure. However, in such cases, the panel or the Appellate Body shall recommend that the Member concerned make a mutually satisfactory adjustment;
(c) notwithstanding the provisions of Article 21, the arbitration provided for in paragraph 3 of Article 21, upon request of either party, may include a determination of the level of benefits which have been nullified or impaired, and may also suggest ways and means of reaching a mutually satisfactory adjustment; such suggestions shall not be binding upon the parties to the dispute;
(d) notwithstanding the provisions of paragraph 1 of Article 22, compensation may be part of a mutually satisfactory adjustment as final settlement of the dispute.

2. *Complaints of the Type Described in Paragraph 1(c) of Article XXIII of GATT 1994*

Where the provisions of paragraph 1(c) of Article XXIII of GATT 1994 are applicable to a covered agreement, a panel may only make rulings and recommendations where a party considers that any benefit accruing to it directly or indirectly under the relevant covered agreement is being nullified or impaired or the attainment of any objective of that Agreement is being impeded as a result of the existence of any situation other than those to which the provisions of paragraphs 1(a) and 1(b) of Article XXIII of GATT 1994 are applicable. Where and to the extent that such party considers and a panel determines that the matter is covered by this paragraph, the procedures of this Understanding shall apply only up to and including the point in the proceedings where the panel report has been circulated to the Members. The dispute settlement rules and procedures contained in the Decision of 12 April 1989 (BISD 36S/61–67) shall apply to consideration for adoption, and surveillance and implementation of recommendations and rulings. The following shall also apply:

(a) the complaining party shall present a detailed justification in support of any argument made with respect to issues covered under this paragraph;
(b) in cases involving matters covered by this paragraph, if a panel finds that cases also involve dispute settlement matters other than those covered by this paragraph, the panel shall circulate a report to the DSB addressing any such matters and a separate report on matters falling under this paragraph.

Article 27

Responsibilities of the Secretariat

1. The Secretariat shall have the responsibility of assisting panels, especially on the legal, historical and procedural aspects of the matters dealt with, and of providing secretarial and technical support.

2. While the Secretariat assists Members in respect of dispute settlement at their request, there may also be a need to provide additional legal advice and assistance in respect of dispute settlement to developing country Members. To this end, the Secretariat shall make available a qualified legal expert from the WTO technical cooperation services to any developing country Member which so requests. This expert shall assist the developing country Member in a manner ensuring the continued impartiality of the Secretariat.

3. The Secretariat shall conduct special training courses for interested Members concerning these dispute settlement procedures and practices so as to enable Members' experts to be better informed in this regard.

APPENDIX 1

Agreements Covered by the Understanding

(A) Agreement Establishing the World Trade Organization
(B) Multilateral Trade Agreements

Annex 1A: Multilateral Agreements on Trade in Goods
Annex 1B: General Agreement on Trade in Services
Annex 1C: Agreement on Trade-Related Aspects of Intellectual Property Rights
Annex 2: Understanding on Rules and Procedures Governing the Settlement of Disputes

(C) Plurilateral Trade Agreements

Annex 4: Agreement on Trade in Civil Aircraft
Agreement on Government Procurement
International Dairy Agreement
International Bovine Meat Agreement

The applicability of this Understanding to the Plurilateral Trade Agreements shall be subject to the adoption of a decision by the parties to each agreement setting out the terms for the application of the Understanding to the individual agreement, including any special or additional rules or procedures for inclusion in Appendix 2, as notified to the DSB.

APPENDIX 2

Special or Additional Rules and Procedures contained in the Covered Agreements

Agreement	*Rules and Procedures*
Agreement on the Application of Sanitary and Phytosanitary Measures	11.2
Agreement on Textiles and Clothing	2.14, 2.21, 4.4, 5.2, 5.4, 5.6, 6.9, 6.10, 6.11, 8.1 through 8.12
Agreement on Technical Barriers to Trade	14.2 through 14.4, Annex 2
Agreement on Implementation of Article VI of GATT 1994	17.4 through 17.7
Agreement on Implementation of Article VII of GATT 1994	19.3 through 19.5, Annex II.2(f), 3, 9, 21
Agreement on Subsidies and Countervailing Measures	4.2 through 4.12, 6.6, 7.2 through 7.10, 8.5, footnote 35, 24.4, 27.7, Annex V
General Agreement on Trade in Services	XXII:3, XXIII:3
Annex on Financial Services	4
Annex on Air Transport Services	4
Decision on Certain Dispute Settlement Procedures for the GATS	1 through 5

The list of rules and procedures in this Appendix includes provisions where only a part of the provision may be relevant in this context.

Any special or additional rules or procedures in the Plurilateral Trade Agreements as determined by the competent bodies of each agreement and as notified to the DSB.

APPENDIX 3

Working Procedures

1. In its proceedings the panel shall follow the relevant provisions of this Understanding. In addition, the following working procedures shall apply.

2. The panel shall meet in closed session. The parties to the dispute, and interested parties, shall be present at the meetings only when invited by the panel to appear before it.

3. The deliberations of the panel and the documents submitted to it shall be kept confidential. Nothing in this Understanding shall preclude a party to a dispute from disclosing statements of its own positions to the public. Members shall treat as confidential information submitted by another Member to the panel which that Member has designated as confidential. Where a party to a dispute submits a confidential version of its written submissions to the panel, it shall also, upon request of a Member, provide a non-confidential summary of the information contained in its submissions that could be disclosed to the public.

4. Before the first substantive meeting of the panel with the parties, the parties to the dispute shall transmit to the panel written submissions in which they present the facts of the case and their arguments.

5. At its first substantive meeting with the parties, the panel shall ask the party which has brought the complaint to present its case. Subsequently, and still at the same meeting, the party against which the complaint has been brought shall be asked to present its point of view.

6. All third parties which have notified their interest in the dispute to the DSB shall be invited in writing to present their views during a session of the first substantive meeting of the panel set aside for that purpose. All such third parties may be present during the entirety of this session.

7. Formal rebuttals shall be made at a second substantive meeting of the panel. The party complained against shall have the right to take the floor first to be followed by the complaining party. The parties shall submit, prior to that meeting, written rebuttals to the panel.

8. The panel may at any time put questions to the parties and ask them for explanations either in the course of a meeting with the parties or in writing.

9. The parties to the dispute and any third party invited to present its views in accordance with Article 10 shall make available to the panel a written version of their oral statements.

10. In the interest of full transparency, the presentations, rebuttals and statements referred to in paragraphs 5 to 9 shall be made in the presence of the parties.

Moreover, each party's written submissions, including any comments on the descriptive part of the report and responses to questions put by the panel, shall be made available to the other party or parties.

11. Any additional procedures specific to the panel.

12. Proposed timetable for panel work:

(a) Receipt of first written submissions of the parties:		
(1) complaining Party:	_______	3–6 weeks
(2) Party complained against:	_______	2–3 weeks
(b) Date, time and place of first substantive meeting with the parties; third party session:	_______	1–2 weeks
(c) Receipt of written rebuttals of the parties:	_______	2–3 weeks
(d) Date, time and place of second substantive meeting with the parties:	_______	1–2 weeks
(e) Issuance of descriptive part of the report to the parties:	_______	2–4 weeks
(f) Receipt of comments by the parties on the descriptive part of the report:	_______	2 weeks
(g) Issuance of the interim report, including the findings and conclusions, to the parties:	_______	2–4 weeks
(h) Deadline for party to request review of part(s) of report:	_______	1 week
(i) Period of review by panel, including possible additional meeting with parties:	_______	2 weeks
(j) Issuance of final report to parties to dispute:	_______	2 weeks
(k) Circulation of the final report to the Members:	_______	3 weeks

The above calendar may be changed in the light of unforeseen developments. Additional meetings with the parties shall be scheduled if required.

APPENDIX 4

Expert Review Groups

The following rules and procedures shall apply to expert review groups established in accordance with the provisions of paragraph 2 of Article 13.

1. Expert review groups are under the panel's authority. Their terms of reference and detailed working procedures shall be decided by the panel, and they shall report to the panel.

2. Participation in expert review groups shall be restricted to persons of professional standing and experience in the field in question.

3. Citizens of parties to the dispute shall not serve on an expert review group without the joint agreement of the parties to the dispute, except in exceptional circumstances when the panel considers that the need for specialized scientific expertise cannot be fulfilled otherwise. Government officials of parties to the dispute shall not serve on an expert review group. Members of expert review groups shall serve in their individual capacities and not as government representatives, nor as representatives of any organization. Governments or organizations shall therefore not give them instructions with regard to matters before an expert review group.

4. Expert review groups may consult and seek information and technical advice from any source they deem appropriate. Before an expert review group seeks such information or advice from a source within the jurisdiction of a Member, it shall inform the government of that Member. Any Member shall respond promptly and fully to any request by an expert review group for such information as the expert review group considers necessary and appropriate.

5. The parties to a dispute shall have access to all relevant information provided to an expert review group, unless it is of a confidential nature. Confidential information provided to the expert review group shall not be released without formal authorization from the government, organization or person providing the information. Where such information is requested from the expert review group but release of such information by the expert review group is not authorized, a non-confidential summary of the information will be provided by the government, organization or person supplying the information.

6. The expert review group shall submit a draft report to the parties to the dispute with a view to obtaining their comments, and taking them into account, as appropriate, in the final report, which shall also be issued to the parties to the dispute when it is submitted to the panel. The final report of the expert review group shall be advisory only.

ANNEX VII B

WTO
Rules of Conduct for the Understanding on Rules and Procedures Governing the Settlement of Disputes[1]

I. Preamble

Members,

Recalling that on 15 April 1994 in Marrakesh, Ministers welcomed the stronger and clearer legal framework they had adopted for the conduct of international trade, including a more effective and reliable dispute settlement mechanism;

Recognizing the importance of full adherence to the Understanding on Rules and Procedures Governing the Settlement of Disputes ("DSU") and the principles for the management of disputes applied under Articles XXII and XXIII of GATT 1947, as further elaborated and modified by the DSU;

Affirming that the operation of the DSU would be strengthened by rules of conduct designed to maintain the integrity, impartiality and confidentiality of proceedings conducted under the DSU thereby enhancing confidence in the new dispute settlement mechanism;

Hereby establish the following Rules of Conduct.

II. Governing Principle

1. Each person covered by these Rules (as defined in paragraph 1 of Section IV below and hereinafter called "covered person") shall be independent and impartial, shall avoid direct or indirect conflicts of interest and shall respect the confidentiality of proceedings of bodies pursuant to the dispute settlement mechanism, so that through the observance of such standards of conduct the integrity and impartiality of that mechanism are preserved. These Rules shall in no way modify the rights and obligations of Members under the DSU nor the rules and procedures therein.

III. Observance of the Governing Principle

1. To ensure the observance of the Governing Principle of these Rules, each covered person is expected (1) to adhere strictly to the provisions of the DSU; (2) to

[1] Adopted 15 November 1996.

disclose the existence or development of any interest, relationship or matter that that person could reasonably be expected to know and that is likely to affect, or give rise to justifiable doubts as to, that person's independence or impartiality; and (3) to take due care in the performance of their duties to fulfil these expectations, including through avoidance of any direct or indirect conflicts of interest in respect of the subject matter of the proceedings.

2. Pursuant to the Governing Principle, each covered person, shall be independent and impartial, and shall maintain confidentiality. Moreover, such persons shall consider only issues raised in, and necessary to fulfil their responsibilities within, the dispute settlement proceeding and shall not delegate this responsibility to any other person. Such person shall not incur any obligation or accept any benefit that would in anyway interfere with, or which could give rise to, justifiable doubts as to the proper performance of that person's dispute settlement duties.

IV. Scope

1. These Rules shall apply, as specified in the text, to each person serving: (a) on a panel; (b) on the Standing Appellate Body; (c) as an arbitrator pursuant to the provisions mentioned in Annex "1a"; or (d) as an expert participating in the dispute settlement mechanism pursuant to the provisions mentioned in Annex "1b". These Rules shall also apply, as specified in this text and the relevant provisions of the Staff Regulations, to those members of the Secretariat called upon to assist the panel in accordance with Article 27.1 of the DSU or to assist in formal arbitration proceedings pursuant to Annex "1a"; to the Chairman of the Textiles Monitoring Body (hereinafter called "TMB") and other members of the TMB Secretariat called upon to assist the TMB in formulating recommendations, findings or observations pursuant to the WTO Agreement on Textiles and Clothing; and to Standing Appellate Body support staff called upon to provide the Standing Appellate Body with administrative or legal support in accordance with Article 17.7 of the DSU (hereinafter "Member of the Secretariat or Standing Appellate Body support staff"), reflecting their acceptance of established norms regulating the conduct of such persons as international civil servants and the Governing Principle of these Rules.

2. The application of these Rules shall not in any way impede the Secretariat's discharge of its responsibility to continue to respond to Members' requests for assistance and information.

3. These Rules shall apply to the members of the TMB to the extent prescribed in Section V.

V. Textiles Monitoring Body

1. Members of the TMB shall discharge their functions on an *ad personam* basis,

in accordance with the requirement of Article 8.1 of the Agreement on Textiles and Clothing, as further elaborated in the working procedures of the TMB, so as to preserve the integrity and impartiality of its proceedings.[2]

VI. Self-Disclosure Requirements by Covered Persons

1. (a) Each person requested to serve on a panel, on the Standing Appellate Body, as an arbitrator, or as an expert shall, at the time of the request, receive from the Secretariat these Rules, which include an Illustrative List (Annex 2) of examples of the matters subject to disclosure.

(b) Any member of the Secretariat described in paragraph IV:1, who may expect to be called upon to assist in a dispute, and Standing Appellate Body support staff, shall be familiar with these Rules.

2. As set out in paragraph VI:4 below, all covered persons described in paragraph VI.1(a) and VI.1(b) shall disclose any information that could reasonably be expected to be known to them at the time which, coming within the scope of the Governing Principle of these Rules, is likely to affect or give rise to justifiable doubts as to their independence or impartiality. These disclosures include the type of information described in the Illustrative List, if relevant.

3. These disclosure requirements shall not extend to the identification of matters whose relevance to the issues to be considered in the proceedings would be insignificant. They shall take into account the need to respect the personal privacy of those to whom these Rules apply and shall not be so administratively burdensome as to make it impracticable for otherwise qualified persons to serve on panels, the Standing Appellate Body, or in other dispute settlement roles.

4. (a) All panelists, arbitrators and experts, prior to confirmation of their appointment, shall complete the form at Annex 3 of these Rules. Such information would be disclosed to the Chair of the Dispute Settlement Body ("DSB") for consideration by the parties to the dispute.

(b) (i) Persons serving on the Standing Appellate Body who, through rotation, are selected to hear the appeal of a particular panel case, shall review the factual portion of the Panel report and complete the form at Annex 3. Such information would be disclosed to the Standing Appellate Body for its consideration

[2] These working procedures, as adopted by the TMB on 26 July 1995 (G/TMB/R/1), currently include, *inter alia*, the following language in paragraph 1.4: "In discharging their functions in accordance with paragraph 1.1 above, the TMB members and alternates shall undertake not to solicit, accept or act upon instructions from governments, nor to be influenced by any other organisations or undue extraneous factors. They shall disclose to the Chairman any information that they may consider likely to impede their capacity to discharge their functions on an *ad personam* basis. Should serious doubts arise during the deliberations of the TMB regarding the ability of a TMB member to act on an *ad personam* basis, they shall be communicated to the Chairman. The Chairman shall deal with the particular matter as necessary".

whether the member concerned should hear a particular appeal.

(ii) Standing Appellate Body support staff shall disclose any relevant matter to the Standing Appellate Body, for its consideration in deciding on the assignment of staff to assist in a particular appeal.

(c) When considered to assist in a dispute, members of the Secretariat shall disclose to the Director-General of the WTO the information required under paragraph VI:2 of these Rules and any other relevant information required under the Staff Regulations, including the information described in the footnote.[3]

5. During a dispute, each covered person shall also disclose any new information relevant to paragraph VI:2 above at the earliest time they become aware of it.

6. The Chair of the DSB, the Secretariat, parties to the dispute, and other individuals involved in the dispute settlement mechanism shall maintain the confidentiality of any information revealed through this disclosure process, even after the panel process and its enforcement procedures, if any, are completed.

VII. Confidentiality

1. Each covered person shall at all times maintain the confidentiality of dispute settlement deliberations and proceedings together with any information identified by a party as confidential. No covered person shall at any time use such information acquired during such deliberations and proceedings to gain personal advantage or advantage for others.

2. During the proceedings, no covered person shall engage in *ex parte* contacts concerning matters under consideration. Subject to paragraph VII:1, no covered person shall make any statements on such proceedings or the issues in dispute in which that person is participating, until the report of the panel or the Standing Appellate Body has been derestricted.

---

[3] Pending adoption of the Staff Regulations, members of the Secretariat shall make disclosures to the Director-General in accordance with the following draft provision to be included in the Staff Regulations:

When paragraph VI:4(c) of the Rules of Conduct for the DSU is applicable, members of the Secretariat would disclose to the Director-General of the WTO the information required in paragraph VI:2 of those Rules, as well as any information regarding their participation in earlier formal consideration of the specific measure at issue in a dispute under any provisions of the WTO Agreement, including through formal legal advice under Article 27.2 of the DSU, as well as any involvement with the dispute as an official of a WTO Member government or otherwise professionally, before having joined the Secretariat.

The Director-General shall consider any such disclosures in deciding on the assignment of members of the Secretariat to assist in a dispute.

When the Director-General, in the light of his consideration, including of available Secretariat resources, decides that a potential conflict of interest is not sufficiently material to warrant non-assignment of a particular member of the Secretariat to assist in a dispute, the Director-General shall inform the panel of his decision and of the relevant supporting information.

VIII. Procedures Concerning Subsequent Disclosure and Possible Material Violations

1. Any party to a dispute, conducted pursuant to the WTO Agreement, who possesses or comes into possession of evidence of a material violation of the obligations of independence, impartiality or confidentiality or the avoidance of direct or indirect conflicts of interest by covered persons which may impair the integrity, impartiality or confidentiality of the dispute settlement mechanism, shall at the earliest possible time and on a confidential basis, submit such evidence to the Chair of the DSB, the Director-General or the Standing Appellate Body, as appropriate according to the respective procedures detailed in paragraphs VIII:5 to VIII:17 below, in a written statement specifying the relevant facts and circumstances. Other Members who possess or come into possession of such evidence, may provide such evidence to the parties to the dispute in the interest of maintaining the integrity and impartiality of the dispute settlement mechanism.

2. When evidence as described in paragraph VIII:1 is based on an alleged failure of a covered person to disclose a relevant interest, relationship or matter, that failure to disclose, as such, shall not be a sufficient ground for disqualification unless there is also evidence of a material violation of the obligations of independence, impartiality, confidentiality or the avoidance of direct or indirect conflicts of interests and that the integrity, impartiality or confidentiality of the dispute settlement mechanism would be impaired thereby.

3. When such evidence is not provided at the earliest practicable time, the party submitting the evidence shall explain why it did not do so earlier and this explanation shall be taken into account in the procedures initiated in paragraph VIII:1.

4. Following the submission of such evidence to the Chair of the DSB, the Director-General of the WTO or the Standing Appellate Body, as specified below, the procedures outlined in paragraphs VIII:5 to VIII:17 below shall be completed within fifteen working days.

Panelists, Arbitrators, Experts

5. If the covered person who is the subject of the evidence is a panelist, an arbitrator or an expert, the party shall provide such evidence to the Chair of the DSB.

6. Upon receipt of the evidence referred to in paragraphs VIII:1 and VIII:2, the Chair of the DSB shall forthwith provide the evidence to the person who is the subject of such evidence, for consideration by the latter.

7. If, after having consulted with the person concerned, the matter is not resolved, the Chair of the DSB shall forthwith provide all the evidence, and any additional information from the person concerned, to the parties to the dispute. If the person concerned resigns, the Chair of the DSB shall inform the parties to the dispute and, as the case may be, the panelists, the arbitrator(s) or experts.

8. In all cases, the Chair of the DSB, in consultation with the Director-General and a sufficient number of Chairs of the relevant Council or Councils to provide an odd number, and after having provided a reasonable opportunity for the views of the person concerned and the parties to the dispute to be heard, would decide whether a material violation of these Rules as referred to in paragraphs VIII:1 and VIII:2 above has occurred. Where the parties agree that a material violation of these Rules has occurred, it would be expected that, consistent with maintaining the integrity of the dispute settlement mechanism, the disqualification of the person concerned would be confirmed.

9. The person who is the subject of the evidence shall continue to participate in the consideration of the dispute unless it is decided that a material violation of these Rules has occurred.

10. The Chair of the DSB shall thereafter take the necessary steps for the appointment of the person who is the subject of the evidence to be formally revoked, or excused from the dispute as the case may be, as of that time.

Secretariat

11. If the covered person who is the subject of the evidence is a member of the Secretariat, the party shall only provide the evidence to the Director-General of the WTO, who shall forthwith provide the evidence to the person who is the subject of such evidence and shall further inform the other party or parties to the dispute and the panel.

12. It shall be for the Director-General to take any appropriate action in accordance with the Staff Regulations.[4]

13. The Director-General shall inform the parties to the dispute, the panel and the Chair of the DSB of his decision, together with relevant supporting information.

Standing Appellate Body

14. If the covered person who is the subject of the evidence is a member of the Standing Appellate Body or of the Standing Appellate Body support staff, the party shall provide the evidence to the other party to the dispute and the evidence shall thereafter be provided to the Standing Appellate Body.

15. Upon receipt of the evidence referred to in paragraphs VIII:1 and VIII:2 above, the Standing Appellate Body shall forthwith provide it to the person who is the subject of such evidence, for consideration by the latter.

---

[4] Pending adoption of the Staff Regulations, the Director-General would act in accordance with the following draft provision for the Staff Regulations: "If paragraph VIII:11 of the Rules of Conduct for the DSU governing the settlement of disputes is invoked, the Director-General shall consult with the person who is the subject of the evidence and the panel and shall, if necessary, take appropriate disciplinary action".

16. It shall be for the Standing Appellate Body to take any appropriate action after having provided a reasonable opportunity for the views of the person concerned and the parties to the dispute to be heard.

17. The Standing Appellate Body shall inform the parties to the dispute and the Chair of the DSB of its decision, together with relevant supporting information.

* * *

18. Following completion of the procedures in paragraphs VIII:5 to VIII:17, if the appointment of a covered person, other than a member of the Standing Appellate Body, is revoked or that person is excused or resigns, the procedures specified in the DSU for initial appointment shall be followed for appointment of a replacement, but the time periods shall be half those specified in the DSU.[5] The member of the Standing Appellate Body who, under that Body's rules, would next be selected through rotation to consider the dispute, would automatically be assigned to the appeal. The panel, members of the Standing Appellate Body hearing the appeal, or the arbitrator, as the case may be, may then decide after consulting with the parties to the dispute, on any necessary modifications to their working procedures or proposed timetable.

19. All covered persons and Members concerned shall resolve matters involving possible material violations of these Rules as expeditiously as possible so as not to delay the completion of proceedings, as provided in the DSU.

20. Except to the extent strictly necessary to carry out this decision, all information concerning possible or actual material violations of these Rules shall be kept confidential.

IX. Review

1. These Rules of Conduct shall be reviewed within two years of their adoption and a decision shall be taken by the DSB as to whether to continue, modify or terminate these Rules.

---

[5] Appropriate adjustments would be made in the case of appointments pursuant to the Agreement on Subsidies and Countervailing Measures.

ANNEX 1A

Arbitrators acting pursuant to the following provisions:

- Articles 21.3(c); 22.6 and 22.7; 26.1(c) and 25 of the DSU;
- Article 8.5 of the Agreement on Subsidies and Countervailing Measures;
- Articles XXI.3 and XXII.3 of the General Agreement on Trade in Services.

ANNEX 1B

Experts advising or providing information pursuant to the following provisions:

- Article 13.1; 13.2 of the DSU;
- Article 4.5 of the Agreement on Subsidies and Countervailing Measures;
- Article 11.2 of the Agreement on the Application of Sanitary and Phytosanitary Measures;
- Article 14.2; 14.3 of the Agreement on Technical Barriers to Trade.

ANNEX 2

Illustrative List of Information to be Disclosed

This list contains examples of information of the type that a person called upon to serve in a dispute should disclose pursuant to the Rules of Conduct for the Understanding on Rules and Procedures Governing the Settlement of Disputes.

Each covered person, as defined in Section IV:1 of these Rules of Conduct has a continuing duty to disclose the information described in Section VI:2 of these Rules which may include the following:

(a) financial interests (e.g. investments, loans, shares, interests, other debts); business interests (e.g. directorship or other contractual interests); and property interests relevant to the dispute in question;
(b) professional interests (e.g. a past or present relationship with private clients, or any interests the person may have in domestic or international proceedings, and their implications, where these involve issues similar to those addressed in the dispute in question);
(c) other active interests (e.g. active participation in public interest groups or other organisations which may have a declared agenda relevant to the dispute in question);
(d) considered statements of personal opinion on issues relevant to the dispute in question (e.g. publications, public statements);
(e) employment or family interests (e.g. the possibility of any indirect advantage or any likelihood of pressure which could arise from their employer, business associates or immediate family members).

ANNEX 3

Dispute Number: ________

WORLD TRADE ORGANIZATION
DISCLOSURE FORM

I have read the Understanding on Rules and Procedures Governing the Settlement of Disputes (DSU) and the Rules of Conduct for the DSU. I understand my continuing duty, while participating in the dispute settlement mechanism, and until such time as the Dispute Settlement Body (DSB) makes a decision on adoption of a report relating to the proceeding or notes its settlement, to disclose herewith and in future any information likely to affect my independence or impartiality, or which could give rise to justifiable doubts as to the integrity and impartiality of the dispute settlement mechanism; and to respect my obligations regarding the confidentiality of dispute settlement proceedings.

Signed: Dated:

ANNEX VIII

United Nations General Assembly: Resolution 59/283

Fifty-ninth session
Agenda items 108 and 120

Resolution adopted by the General Assembly
[*on the report of the Fifth Committee (A/59/773)*]

59/283. Administration of justice at the United Nations

The General Assembly,

Recalling its resolutions 57/307 of 15 April 2003 and 59/266 of 23 December 2004,

Stressing that the system of justice in the United Nations as a whole should be independent, transparent, effective, efficient and fair,

Stressing also the importance of increased transparency in decision-making and increased accountability of managers for the system,

Noting that the existing system should respect the principle of due process and provide for appropriate peer review,

Noting with concern the continuing backlog of appeals in various parts of the system,

Emphasizing the necessity of informal mechanisms for the early and swift resolution of disputes in the Secretariat, in particular through a direct dialogue between managers and staff,

Emphasizing also the importance for the United Nations to have an efficient and effective system of internal justice so as to ensure that individuals and the Organization are held accountable for their actions in accordance with relevant resolutions and regulations,

Welcoming the increased focus on training for all participants in the system of administration of justice,

Recognizing that a transparent, impartial and effective system of administration of justice is a necessary condition for ensuring fair and just treatment of United Nations staff and important for the success of human resources reform in the Organization,

Having considered the reports of the Secretary-General on the administration of justice in the Secretariat,[1] on the role of the Panels on Discrimination and Other Grievances,[2] on the outcome of the work of the Joint Appeals Board during 2001 and 2002[3] and on the outcome of the work of the Joint Appeals Board during 2002 and 2003,[4] the comprehensive report of the United Nations Administrative

---

[1] A/59/449.
[2] A/59/414.
[3] A/58/300.
[4] A/59/70.

Tribunal on its activities,[5] the reports of the Secretary-General on the possibility of the financial independence of the United Nations Administrative Tribunal from the Office of Legal Affairs[6] and on measures to prevent discrimination on the basis of nationality, race, gender, religion or language in the United Nations,[7] the note by the Secretary-General transmitting the report of the Office of Internal Oversight Services on the management review of the appeals process at the United Nations,[8] the report of the Secretary-General containing the cost implications of the recommendations of the Office of Internal Oversight Services following its management review of the appeals process,[9] the note by the Secretary-General transmitting the report of the Joint Inspection Unit entitled "Administration of justice: harmonization of the statutes of the United Nations Administrative Tribunal and the International Labour Organization Administrative Tribunal",[10] the note by the Secretary-General containing his comments on the report of the Joint Inspection Unit,[11] the note by the Secretary-General on compensation for members of the United Nations Administrative Tribunal,[12] the letter dated 18 November 2003 from the President of the United Nations Administrative Tribunal addressed to the Chairman of the Fifth Committee[13] and the interim report of the Advisory Committee on Administrative and Budgetary Questions,[14]

Regretting that the present system of administration of justice in the Secretariat continues to be slow, cumbersome and costly,

Regretting also that the related reports were not introduced at its fifty-eighth session, as requested in its resolution 57/307, and that, in addition, they were submitted and issued late at its fifty-ninth session,

1. *Notes* the importance of having a strong administration of justice mechanism that avoids duplication and overlap within the formal processes;

2. *Regrets* the continued serious delays in the appeals process, and stresses the need to implement measures to improve the appeals process to make it more efficient;

I. Cross-cutting issues – general guidelines

3. *Takes note* of the reports of the Secretary-General on the administration of justice in the Secretariat,[1] the role of the Panels on Discrimination and Other Grievances,[2] the outcome of the work of the Joint Appeals Board during 2001 and 2002,[3] the outcome of the work of the Joint Appeals Board during 2002 and

[5] A/58/680.
[6] A/59/78.
[7] A/59/211.
[8] A/59/408.
[9] A/59/706.
[10] A/59/280 and Corr. 1.
[11] A/59/280/Add. 1.
[12] A/C.5/59/12.
[13] A/C.5/58/16.
[14] A/59/715.

2003,[4] the possibility of the financial independence of the United Nations Administrative Tribunal from the Office of Legal Affairs,[6] measures to prevent discrimination on the basis of nationality, race, gender, religion or language in the United Nations[7] and his report containing the cost implications of the recommendations of the Office of Internal Oversight Services following its management review of the appeals process;[9]

4. *Takes note with interest* of the report of the Office of Internal Oversight Services on the management review of the appeals process at the United Nations;[8]

5. *Endorses* the conclusions and recommendations of the Advisory Committee on Administrative and Budgetary Questions set out in its report,[14] subject to the provisions of the present resolution;

6. *Stresses* that the administrative law framework of the Organization should allow all levels of United Nations staff to obtain due process, regardless of their location, grade or contractual arrangement;

7. *Appreciates* the efforts made by staff volunteering their services in the system of justice of the United Nations, and stresses the need to provide them with further training;

8. *Takes note with interest* of the option described in paragraph 30 of the report of the Secretary-General,[1] and requests the Secretary-General to explore the implications of this option and to report thereon in the context of his annual report on the administration of justice in the Secretariat;

9. *Affirms* that the functions of staff members selected to serve under the new system are official in nature, and requests the Secretary-General to ensure that those staff members are given sufficient time off from their substantive responsibilities to perform their functions;

10. *Recognizes* that the system of administration of justice, being heavily dependent on volunteers, requires frequent and comprehensive training of participants, and calls upon the Secretary-General to organize periodic training at each of the headquarters duty stations for all staff involved in the system of administration of justice;

11. *Stresses* the importance of the proper implementation of a sound performance appraisal system as a potential means of avoiding conflict;

12. *Also stresses* the need to provide training in managerial skills to improve conflict resolution skills of managers;

13. *Further stresses* the need to link the ability of managers to respond in the course of a proceeding with their own individual performance appraisal;

14. *Notes* that staff rule 112.3, which relates to the financial liability of managers, has yet to be implemented, also notes the issuance of the Secretary-General's bulletin ST/SGB/2004/14, and requests the Secretary-General to report on its implementation to the General Assembly at its sixty-first session;

15. *Requests* the Secretary-General to expeditiously implement the recommendations of the Office of Internal Oversight Services, subject to the provisions of the present resolution;

16. *Decides* that the time limits recommended by the Office of Internal Oversight Services will be mandatory within the appeals process once adequate capacity is in place, and no later than 1 January 2006;

17. *Also decides* that measures should be taken to eliminate the appearance of conflict of interest, and towards this end requests the Secretary-General to proceed with the transfer of the responsibility for formulating decisions on appeals from

the Department of Management of the Secretariat to the Office of the Secretary-General;

II. The informal mechanism of administration of justice

Ombudsman

18. *Stresses* the importance of the Office of the Ombudsman as the primary means of informal dispute resolution, and reaffirms General Assembly resolution 56/253 of 24 December 2001 on the establishment of the Office;

19. *Requests* that the Office of the Ombudsman continue and expand its outreach activities, in particular to local, national and General Service staff, in order to facilitate equal access and awareness-raising, bearing in mind the structure, activities and operational environment of the Organization;

20. *Requests* the Secretary-General to submit proposals for strengthening the Office of the Ombudsman through improved access to it for staff serving in different locations;

21. *Invites* the Office of the Ombudsman to reduce all possible delays in responding to the requests of staff in order to ensure that staff are encouraged to seek resolution of conflict in an informal way;

22. *Requests* the Secretary-General to submit, in the context of his annual report on the administration of justice in the Secretariat, information on the activities of the Ombudsman, including general statistical information and information on trends and comments on policies, procedures and practices that have come to the attention of the Ombudsman;

III. The formal mechanisms of administration of justice

Panel of Counsel

23. *Takes note* of the role of the Coordinator of the Panel of Counsel, in preliminary consultations before initiation of the formal appeals process, to support an informal resolution at an early stage;

24. *Stresses* the role of staff representatives in advising and assisting staff in addressing issues informally and formally;

25. *Recognizes* the need to strengthen the capacities of the Panels of Counsel by increasing the opportunity for training on the United Nations Staff Regulations and Rules, policies, procedures or precedents for staff serving on the Panels, in view of the urgent need to strengthen legal advice and administrative support for staff members submitting an appeal;

26. *Invites* staff representatives to explore the possibility of establishing a staff-funded scheme in the Organization that provides legal advice and support to the staff; staff representatives may consult with the Secretary-General as they deem appropriate;

27. *Invites* the Secretary-General to consider appropriate incentives to be built into the system to encourage staff members to serve on the Panels;

28. *Encourages* the Panel of Counsel to increase outreach activities, and requests

the Secretary-General to consider the inclusion of travel costs in section 28A, Office of the Under-Secretary-General for Management, of the proposed programme budget for the biennium 2006–2007, for this purpose;

Administrative Law Unit

29. *Notes* that the Administrative Law Unit has the multiple functions of administrative review, appeals, disciplinary matters and advisory services;

30. *Requests* the Secretary-General to submit to the General Assembly by the end of its fifty-ninth session proposals to separate the above-mentioned functions, through the redeployment of resources, in order to avoid conflicts of interest, taking into account the following needs:

(*a*) To ensure the necessary means to collect evidence;

(*b*) To advise both the appellant and the respondent;

(*c*) To ensure the uniform application of administrative decisions;

(*d*) To ensure appropriate consultation with the Office of Human Resources Management of the Department of Management and legal experts;

(*e*) To relay all necessary information to the Office of Human Resources Management;

31. *Stresses* that increased accountability by managers would contribute to the elimination of the backlog of appeals cases, as stated in the report of the Secretary-General,[15] and decides that as a means to facilitate early consideration of cases, the following procedures should be adopted:

(*a*) Staff members wishing to appeal an administrative decision should send a copy of their request to the executive head of their department;

(*b*) The Administrative Law Unit should clarify with managers the requirements for the respondent's reply and the contributions expected from managers, as well as time limits;

32. *Requests* the Secretary-General to ensure that written explanations by managers to the Administrative Law Unit are submitted within eight weeks with no possibility of extension, and decides that compliance with this responsibility shall constitute part of the performance appraisal of managers;

33. *Decides* to amend staff rule 111.2 (*a*) to provide that staff wishing to appeal an administrative decision shall submit to the executive head of their department, office, fund or programme a copy of the letter addressed to the Secretary-General requesting a review of the case;

Joint Appeals Board

34. *Stresses* the particular importance of providing adequate training to the members of the Joint Appeals Board;

---

[15] A/59/449, para. 27.

United Nations Administrative Tribunal

35. *Recalls* paragraph 5 of its resolution 57/307, and regrets that the steps necessary to separate the secretariat of the United Nations Administrative Tribunal from the Office of Legal Affairs were not undertaken;

36. *Endorses* the proposal of the Secretary-General to transfer the resources of the Tribunal from section 8, Legal affairs, of the proposed programme budget to section 1, Overall policy-making, direction and coordination, effective from the beginning of the biennium 2006–2007;

37. *Reaffirms* paragraph 5 of its resolution 57/307, and requests the Secretary-General to guarantee the immediate independence of the Tribunal, including through ensuring the provision of administrative and logistical services that are exclusive to the secretariat of the Tribunal;

38. *Recalls* the recent amendment to the statute of the Tribunal, which provides that members shall possess judicial or other relevant legal experience in the field of administrative law or its equivalent within their national jurisdiction;

39. *Acknowledges* the need for the further strengthening of professionalism in the Tribunal by increasing membership of professional judges;

40. *Decides* to amend article 3, paragraph 1, of the statute of the Tribunal, with effect from 1 January 2006, to read:

> The Tribunal shall be composed of seven members, no two of whom may be nationals of the same State. Members shall possess judicial experience in the field of administrative law or its equivalent within their national jurisdiction. Only three members shall sit in any particular case.;

41. *Also decides* that the amendment to article 3 will be applied in the election of new members of the Tribunal with effect from 1 January 2006;

42. *Requests* the Secretary-General to submit proposals on compensation for the members of the Tribunal once all its members meet the criteria set out in article 3 of the statute as amended in the present resolution;

43. *Notes* that the vast majority of appeals against administrative decisions concern termination of employment or non-renewal of employment contracts, and decides, with reference to recommendation 5 of the Office of Internal Oversight Services,[16] to revert to the question of amendment of article 7 of the statute of the Tribunal following receipt of the report of the panel as described in section IV of the present resolution;

44. *Also notes* the report of the Joint Inspection Unit on administration of justice;[17]

45. *Stresses* the importance of the eventual harmonization of the statutes of the United Nations Administrative Tribunal and the International Labour Organization Administrative Tribunal;

46. *Requests* the United Nations Administrative Tribunal to review the rules, practices and procedures of similar tribunals with a view towards enhanced effective management of caseloads;

---

[16] See A/59/408, para. 65.

[17] See A/59/280 and Corr. 1.

IV. Review of the internal justice system

47. *Decides* that the Secretary-General shall form a panel of external and independent experts to consider redesigning the system of administration of justice;

48. *Also decides* that the panel shall be composed of a pre-eminent judge or former judge with administrative law experience, an expert in alternative dispute resolution methods, a leading legal academic in international law, a person with senior management and administrative experience in an international organization and a person with United Nations field experience;

49. *Further decides* that the terms of reference of the redesign panel shall be as follows:

(*a*) The redesign panel shall propose a model for a new system for resolving staff grievances in the United Nations that is independent, transparent, effective, efficient and adequately resourced and that ensures managerial accountability; the model should involve guiding principles and procedures that clearly articulate the participation of staff and management within reasonable time frames and time limits;

(*b*) The redesign panel shall:

(i) Consider the relevant resolutions of the General Assembly;

(ii) Receive and review information from all the relevant stakeholders regarding existing mechanisms for the administration of justice in the Organization;

(iii) Consult with United Nations staff, including individual staff members, the Staff Union and managers, in order to form an opinion as to how and why some aspects of the system function effectively while other aspects do not;

(*c*) The redesign panel shall, in particular:

(i) Consider alternative systems for resolving staff grievances by considering other models of organizational dispute resolution, while acknowledging the uniqueness of the United Nations system, in particular the immunity of United Nations staff from national laws and thus the lack of recourse to national courts;

(ii) In proposing a model, consider the value of creating an effective system for handling staff complaints that involves alternative forms of dispute resolution by which cases can be settled by mutual consent, such as mediation, conciliation, arbitration and/or an ombudsman;

(iii) Consider the peer review;

(iv) Identify proactive measures such as education and training, that the United Nations can implement to minimize the number of disputes that arise;

(v) Examine the functioning of the Office of the Ombudsman and, if needed, present models to provide services tailored to responding to the needs of the Organization;

(vi) Examine and develop the criteria to be used in the categorization of cases;

(vii) Review the functioning of the United Nations Administrative Tribunal and examine the further harmonization of its statute and that of the International Labour Organization Administrative Tribunal with a view to further professionalizing the United Nations Administrative Tribunal;

(viii) Examine the possibility of an integrated judicial system with a two-layer structure of first and second instance, taking into account existing structures;

(ix) Examine the legal representation of the Secretary-General in the system of administration of justice;

50. *Decides* that the panel shall start its functions no later than 1 February 2006 and shall submit its findings and recommendations by the end of July 2006;

51. *Requests* the Secretary-General to transmit the report and recommendations of the panel to the General Assembly as a matter of priority;

52. *Also requests* the Secretary-General to submit his comments on the recommendations contained in the panel's report, along with the estimate of time and resources needed for their implementation, to the General Assembly at the first part of its resumed sixty-first session;

53. *Decides* that activities requested above that would give rise to additional resource requirements during the biennium 2004–2005 should be included in the proposed programme budget for the biennium 2006–2007.

91st plenary meeting 13 April 2005

ANNEX IX

United Nations ST/SGB/2005/8

Secretariat

13 April 2005

Secretary-General's bulletin

Organization of the Department of Management

The Secretary-General, pursuant to Secretary-General's bulletin ST/SGB/1997/5, entitled "Organization of the Secretariat of the United Nations", as amended by ST/SGB/2002/11, as well as for the purpose of streamlining the organizational structure of the Department of Management, promulgates the following:

Section 1
General provision

The present bulletin shall apply in conjunction with Secretary-General's bulletin ST/SGB/1997/5, entitled "Organization of the Secretariat of the United Nations", as amended by ST/SGB/2002/11.

Section 2
Functions and organization

2.1 The Department of Management formulates policies and procedures and provides strategic guidance, direction and support to all entities of the Secretariat, including the offices away from Headquarters, in three broad management areas, namely, finance and budget, human resources, and physical resources (support operations and services). The specific functions and organization of the Offices of Programme Planning, Budget and Accounts, Human Resources Management and Central Support Services are described in separate Secretary-General's bulletins.

2.2 The present bulletin sets out the structure of the Office of the Under-Secretary-General for Management and describes the functional linkage and supervision of the work relating to the capital master plan (see A/57/285 and Corr.1 and General Assembly resolution 57/292 of 20 December 2002).

2.3 The Department is headed by the Under-Secretary-General for Management, who is supported by the Executive Management Group, comprising the Assistant Secretaries-General of the three offices mentioned in section 2.1, the Executive Director for the Capital Master Plan and the Director of the Office of the Under-Secretary-General for Management.

2.4 The Under-Secretary-General, the Assistant Secretaries-General and the officials in charge of each organizational unit, in addition to the specific functions set out in the present bulletin, perform the general functions applicable to their positions, as set out in Secretary-General's bulletin ST/SGB/1997/5, as amended by ST/SGB/2002/11.

Section 3
Under-Secretary-General for Management

3.1 The Under-Secretary-General for Management is accountable to the Secretary-General.

3.2 The Under-Secretary-General is responsible for the formulation of the Organization's management policies and has overall responsibility for the management of the financial, human and physical resources of the Organization. He or she also directs and manages the activities of the Department of Management, in accordance with the Secretary-General's delegation of authority, including as set out in the Financial Regulations and Rules of the United Nations.

3.3 The Under-Secretary-General formulates policies and provides policy guidance, coordination and direction for the preparation and review of the proposed strategic framework and the biennial budget and provides policy guidance, coordination and direction on management reform issues to programme managers of the Secretariat.

3.4 The Under-Secretary-General represents or ensures the representation of the Secretary-General on management matters in relation to governing bodies, agencies in the common system and administrative advisory bodies and monitors emerging management issues throughout the Secretariat by interacting with the executive committees.

3.5 The Under-Secretary-General is responsible for the overall supervision of the internal system for the administration of justice.

3.6 The Under-Secretary-General is responsible for providing strategic and management direction and coordinating relations with the host country relating to management and facilities issues. He or she also has overall responsibility for the management of facilities and the assignment of office space in the United Nations.

3.7 The Under-Secretary-General is responsible for maintaining close liaison with host-country authorities and Member States on all substantive aspects relating to financial, budgetary, personnel and common services support matters.

3.8 The Under-Secretary-General provides strategic guidance and management oversight concerning the implementation of the capital master plan project.

Section 4
Executive Director for the Capital Master Plan

4.1 The Executive Director for the Capital Master Plan reports to the Secretary-General through the Under-Secretary-General for Management.

4.2 The Executive Director is responsible for the management and implementation of the capital master plan project (see General Assembly resolution 57/292) and, to that end, relies on the Secretariat's services and facilities to carry out the functions and responsibilities related to that project.

Section 5
Secretariat of the Administrative and Budgetary (Fifth) Committee of the General Assembly and of the Committee for Programme and Coordination

5.1 The secretariat of the Fifth Committee of the General Assembly and of the Committee for Programme and Coordination is headed by a Secretary who is accountable to the Under-Secretary-General for Management.

5.2 The core functions of the secretariat of the Fifth Committee and the Committee for Programme and Coordination are:

(a) Providing substantive and technical services to the work of the Fifth Committee and the Committee for Programme and Coordination;
(b) Planning and organizing activities and services related to sessions of the Committees, and advising the chairpersons of the Committees, Member States, and offices and units of the Secretariat in all matters relating to the work of the Committees.

Section 6
Office of the Under-Secretary-General for Management

6.1 The Office of the Under-Secretary-General for Management is headed by a Director, who is accountable to the Under-Secretary-General and is responsible for providing support to the Under-Secretary-General on the executive direction and management of the Office and ensuring efficient coordination and monitoring of the delivery of the programmatic mandates of the Department. The Director also serves as the ex officio Secretary of the Executive Management Group.

6.2 The core functions of the Office of the Under-Secretary-General for Management are as follows:

(a) Advising on and promoting departmental policies and guidelines dealing with specific management issues and problems;
(b) Ensuring the issuance of periodic and ad hoc reports to Member States and addressing their interests and concerns relating to management and oversight matters in the Organization;
(c) Consulting, negotiating and coordinating with other departments and offices, and the funds and programmes of the United Nation system, on matters of mutual concern and providing concerted leadership to inter-agency forums, such as the High-level Committee on Management and other inter-agency bodies;
(d) Providing executive direction and management coordination to ensure the efficient functioning of the Office of the Under-Secretary-General for Management, including managing all offices and units within the Office of the Under-Secretary-General for Management;

(e) Establishing and maintaining administrative policies and procedures for the effective functioning of the internal justice system;
(f) Providing guidance and supervision to the Secretaries of the Joint Appeals Board, the Joint Disciplinary Committee, the Panel on Discrimination and Other Grievances and the Panel of Counsel regarding the operational aspects of their functioning.

Section 7
Principal Office

The Principal Office is headed by a Principal Officer, who is accountable to the Director of the Office of the Under-Secretary-General for Management. The Office is responsible for providing support to the Under-Secretary-General in the coordination of information and activities in the Department. The core functions of the Principal Office are:

(a) Assisting the Under-Secretary-General in the implementation of the Department's priorities and tasks, in particular those related to management reform objectives, through policy and strategy development;
(b) Monitoring and coordinating departmental activities in order to streamline the work products of the offices within the Department;
(c) Liaising with the host country, non-governmental organizations and other external entities on management-related issues;
(d) Conducting and monitoring special projects in the areas of productivity strategy, streamlining of processes, and dissemination of best practices in management.

Section 8
Office for Oversight and Internal Justice

8.1 The Office for Oversight and Internal Justice is headed by a Chief, who is accountable to the Director of the Office of the Under-Secretary-General for Management, and comprises the Administration of Justice Unit and the Oversight Unit.

Administration of Justice Unit

8.2 The Administration of Justice Unit is headed by a Senior Legal Adviser, who is accountable to the Chief of the Office for Oversight and Internal Justice. The core functions of the Administration of Justice Unit are:

(a) Establishing administrative policies, procedures and machinery for the efficient and effective functioning of the internal justice system, including taking swift action, as necessary and appropriate, to deal with staff grievances;
(b) Providing legal advice on the disposition of appeals, staff grievances, disciplinary matters, and the implementation of judgements of the United Nations Administrative Tribunal.

Oversight Unit

8.3 The Oversight Unit is headed by a Senior Management Analyst, who is accountable to the Chief of the Office for Oversight and Internal Justice. The core functions of the Oversight Unit are as follows:

(a) Liaising with and following up on the implementation of the recommendations of the United Nations Board of Auditors, the Office of Internal Oversight Services and the Joint Inspection Unit;

(b) Coordinating internal and ongoing responses and preparing the appropriate parliamentary documentation on the status of implementation of recommendations made by the oversight bodies and providing analysis of the decisions made by the internal justice bodies;

(c) Supporting the accountability activities by reporting on the implementation of recommendations made by the oversight bodies and providing analysis of the decisions made by the internal justice bodies;

(d) Administering internal control and the administration of requests for exceptions to the standard of accommodation for air travel and reporting to advisory and legislative bodies in a timely manner.

Section 9
Secretariats of the Joint Appeals Board, the Joint Disciplinary Committee, the Panel on Discrimination and Other Grievances and the Panel of Counsel

9.1 The secretariats of the Joint Appeals Board, the Joint Disciplinary Committee, the Panel on Discrimination and Other Grievances and the Panel of Counsel are each headed by a Secretary or Coordinator, who are accountable to the Director of the Office of the Under-Secretary-General for Management with respect to the operational aspects of their functions. They are independent with respect to the substance of their work.

9.2 The functions of the secretariats are to provide analytical and technical services, including assistance in processing appeals, conducting investigations, providing legal advice and conducting legal and administrative research.

Section 10
Executive Office

10.1 The Executive Office is headed by an Executive Officer, who is accountable to the Director of the Office of the Under-Secretary-General for Management.

10.2 The core functions of the Executive Office are set out in section 7 of Secretary-General's bulletin ST/SGB/1997/5.

Section 11
Final provisions

11.1 The present bulletin shall enter into force on 15 April 2005.

11.2 The Secretary-General's bulletin of 21 November 2003, entitled "Organization of the Department of Management" (ST/SGB/2003/15) is hereby abolished.

(*Signed*) Kofi A. **Annan**
Secretary-General

ANNEX X

United Nations ST/IC/2005/19

Secretariat

24 March 2005

Information circular*

To : Members of the staff
From : The Under-Secretary-General for Management

Subject: **Reporting of suspected misconduct**

I. Introduction

1. As international civil servants, United Nations staff members are required to adhere to the highest standards of efficiency, competence and integrity. The concept of integrity enshrined in the Charter of the United Nations includes all aspects of behaviour of an international civil servant, including such qualities as honesty, truthfulness, impartiality and incorruptibility. Staff members have often expressed the view over the years that they regard integrity as the most important among the core values of the Organization, together with professionalism and respect for diversity.

2. As part of the organizational integrity initiative launched in 2003 at the Secretary-General's instruction, a United Nations organizational integrity survey was conducted last year, in which staff emphasized the importance that they attach to integrity. In his letter of 4 June 2004 to all the staff, the Secretary-General indicated that staff members would be reminded of the means available to them for reporting suspected misconduct.

3. The present circular provides information on the mechanisms that currently exist within the United Nations system for reporting suspected misconduct. It also provides information on other mechanisms available to staff who may need advice when they are unsure of how they should proceed. All these mechanisms continue to be reviewed, developed and strengthened, as necessary. For instance, the policies and procedures to be followed in cases of harassment, including sexual harassment, will be reviewed at the next meeting of the Staff Management Coordination Committee.

* The present circular will be in effect until further notice.

4. Reports of suspected misconduct are handled with the utmost discretion. No retaliatory action is permitted against a staff member for submitting in good faith a report of suspected misconduct or for cooperating with investigations subsequent to such a report. A policy on whistle-blower protection is currently under preparation and will be issued after staff consultations. Staff members are reminded that the submission of information or reports with knowledge of their falsity or with wilful disregard for their veracity would be inconsistent with the concept of integrity.

II. Mechanisms for reporting cases of suspected misconduct

5. Staff members have the duty to report cases of suspected misconduct either to a higher-level official, whose responsibility it is to take appropriate action, or to the Office of Internal Oversight Services. All staff members are entitled to make reports directly to the Office of Internal Oversight Services without the need for prior consultation with their supervisor or the head of department (see ST/SGB/273). "Misconduct" is defined by staff rule 110.1 as failure by a staff member to comply with his or her obligations under the Charter of the United Nations, the Staff Regulations and Staff Rules or other relevant administrative issuances, or to observe the standards of conduct expected of an international civil servant. The mechanisms for reporting misconduct are outlined below.

A. Heads of departments and offices

6. A staff member who has knowledge that another staff member in his or her department or office has engaged in conduct for which a disciplinary measure may be imposed should report this information to the head of the department or office concerned and provide as much detail as possible. Should the matter concern a staff member from another department or office, the staff member should inform his or her supervisor or human resources officer, who has the duty to review the information and transmit it through appropriate channels to the department or office of the staff member suspected of misconduct. The staff member may also report suspected misconduct to the Office of Internal Oversight Services.

7. Under administrative instruction ST/AI/371, the head of department or office has the responsibility and the obligation to review the information and, where there is reason to believe that a staff member has engaged in misconduct, to undertake a preliminary investigation and fact-finding. If the preliminary investigation appears to indicate that the report of misconduct is well founded, the head of department or office has the duty to report the matter immediately to the Assistant Secretary-General, Office of Human Resources Management, giving a full account of the facts and attaching documentary evidence. Heads of departments also have the right to report such information directly to the Office of Internal Oversight Services for review and action.

B. Office of Internal Oversight Services

8. The Office of Internal Oversight Services was established in 1994 to undertake evaluation, audit, inspection, compliance monitoring and investigation functions. The functions and responsibilities of the Office are set out in General Assembly resolutions 48/218 B and 54/244 and Secretary-General's bulletins ST/SGB/273 and ST/SGB/2002/7.

9. The Investigations Division of the Office of Internal Oversight Services is staffed by professional investigators who investigate allegations of misconduct, abuse of authority, mismanagement and waste of resources. In recent years, the Investigations Division has investigated a wide range of cases, including those involving refugee smuggling, sexual exploitation and abuse, sexual harassment, travel fraud, theft of United Nations-owned equipment, conflicts of interest and fraudulent education grant claims.

10. As provided by General Assembly resolutions and Secretary-General's bulletin ST/SGB/273, the Investigations Division of the Office of Internal Oversight Services has procedures to protect individual rights and the anonymity of staff members and others and to provide due process for all concerned and fairness during any investigation, as well as protection against reprisals. The Investigations Division protects the confidentiality of those who make reports in good faith, whether the investigation substantiates the report or not. Unauthorized disclosure by Office of Internal Oversight Services investigators of information provided and received may constitute misconduct for which disciplinary measures may be imposed. Where the Investigations Division has determined that retaliatory action has been taken against staff or others for disclosing information to or cooperating with Office of Internal Oversight Services investigators, such retaliatory actions may constitute misconduct for which disciplinary measures may be imposed.[1]

11. The web site of the Office of Internal Oversight Services is at http://www.un.org/Depts/oios. Staff and others are encouraged to report information regarding wrongdoing to the Investigations Division of the Office through any means preferred by the reporting person. Several options have been developed by the Investigations Division for that purpose.[2] The contact information for the Investigations Division is as follows:

New York

Location:	One UN Plaza, DC-1, Room 734, New York, NY 10017
Telephone:	1-212-963-1111
Facsimile:	1-212-963-7774

---

[1] Further details about the protection of anonymity and confidentiality are set out in ST/SGB/273 and ST/AI/397.

[2] Further details about reporting inappropriate use of United Nations resources are provided in ST/AI/397.

Postal address:	Reporting Facility Dag Hammarskjöld Convenience Centre 884 Second Avenue PO Box 20114 New York, NY 10017
Director:	Barbara Dixon
Telephone:	1–212–963–5663

Vienna

Location:	Investigations Division United Nations Office at Vienna "D" Building, 7th Floor, Vienna International Centre Vienna, Austria
Head:	Francis Montil
Telephone:	43–12–6060–5420

Nairobi

Location:	Investigations Division United Nations Office at Nairobi "U" Block, United Nations, Gigiri Nairobi, Kenya
Head:	Jesse Ngari
Telephone:	254–2–64–4086

C. Special procedures for sexual harassment, sexual exploitation and sexual abuse

12. Administrative instruction ST/AI/379[3] defines the term "sexual harassment" as any unwelcome sexual advance, request for sexual favours or other verbal or physical conduct of a sexual nature, when it interferes with work, is made a condition of employment or creates an intimidating, hostile or offensive work environment. The instruction lists a number of informal approaches that may be used in such cases. If informal resolution is not appropriate or has not been successful, the aggrieved individual should make a written complaint to the Assistant Secretary-General for Human Resources Management, who is responsible for conducting the initial investigation in sexual harassment cases.

13. The contact information for the Assistant Secretary-General for Human Resources Management is as follows:

Telephone:	1–212–963–9518
Facsimile:	1–212–963–1944

[3] The procedures for dealing with sexual harassment are currently under review. Until new procedures are issued, ST/AI/379 remains applicable.

E-mail: mccreery@un.org
Postal address: Assistant Secretary-General
Office of Human Resources Management
Room S-2527 A
United Nations
405 East 42nd Street
New York, NY 10017

14. Secretary-General's bulletin ST/SGB/2003/13 defines the term "sexual exploitation" as any actual or attempted abuse of a position of vulnerability, differential power or trust for sexual purposes, and the term "sexual abuse" as actual or threatened physical intrusion of a sexual nature, whether by force or under unequal or coercive conditions. Unlike sexual harassment, sexual exploitation and sexual abuse do not necessarily take place in the work environment. Sexual exploitation and sexual abuse constitute acts of serious misconduct.

15. Heads of departments, offices and missions are required to appoint an official to serve as a focal point to receive reports on cases of sexual exploitation and sexual abuse. Staff members who develop concerns or suspicions regarding the commission of sexual exploitation or sexual abuse may report such concerns to the focal point established for their department, office or mission. They may also report their concerns to the Office of Internal Oversight Services.

III. Additional mechanisms and resources

16. If staff members have information indicating that misconduct or a breach of integrity and ethical conduct may have occurred and are not sure how to proceed, they may wish to avail themselves of the additional mechanisms and resources set out below.

A. The Ombudsman

17. The Office of the Ombudsman was established in 2002 to make available the services of an impartial and independent person to address the employment-related problems of staff members, including matters pertaining to conditions of employment, administration of benefits and managerial practices, as well as professional and staff relations. In the performance of her duties, the Ombudsman is independent of any United Nations organ or official. The terms of reference for the Ombudsman are set out in Secretary-General's bulletin ST/SGB/2002/12.

18. The Ombudsman, as a designated neutral, does not assume the role of advocate for any party. The Ombudsman advises staff of their various options and facilitates conflict resolution, using any appropriate means, with a view to avoiding recourse to the formal grievance process.

19. The Ombudsman maintains strict confidentiality concerning matters brought to her attention and will not divulge the identity of a staff member who seeks the assistance of the Office without the authorization of that staff member. All interactions

with the Ombudsman are voluntary. A staff member who brings a matter to the attention of or provides information to the Ombudsman shall not be subject to reprisals for doing so.

20. The web site of the Ombudsman is at http://www.un.org/ombudsman and contains a secure contact form. The contact information for the Ombudsperson is as follows:

Telephone: 1–917–367–5731
Facsimile: 1–917–367–4211
E-mail: ombudsman@un.org
Postal address: Office of the United Nations Ombudsman
PO Box 4136
Grand Central Station
New York, NY 10163

B. Staff Counsellor's Office

21. Staff counsellors are available at a number of duty stations to provide counselling, information and assistance to staff on issues that may have an impact on their welfare and productivity, such as stress management and conflict resolution. In cases requiring conflict resolution, a staff counsellor may assist by referring the staff member to other offices, providing general information on options that are available to staff members and providing advice and consultation as part of efforts to find an informal solution.

22. The web site of the Staff Counsellor's Office in New York is at http://iseek.un.org/m210.asp?dept=132. The contact information for the Staff Counsellor's Office is as follows:

Telephone: 1–212–963–7044 1–917–488–5142 (for emergency consultation, seven days a week)
Facsimile: 1–212–963–4399
Postal address: Staff Counsellor's Office
Room S-505, United Nations
New York, NY 10017

C. Panel of Counsel

23. The Panel of Counsel is composed of a group of serving and retired staff members who have volunteered to represent their colleagues in various stages of appeals and in disciplinary and other claims. Their work is supported and administered by the Office of the Coordinator, Department of Management, at United Nations Headquarters in New York and by the respective Coordinators at a number of other duty stations.

24. Members of the Panel of Counsel may represent staff members initiating formal appeals before the Joint Appeals Board, replying to charges of misconduct

and defending themselves against those charges in a hearing before the Joint Disciplinary Committee. Members of the Panel of Counsel may also advise or assist staff members in proceedings before the Administrative Tribunal or other appeal mechanisms. While members of the Panel of Counsel provide counsel in formal recourse mechanisms, the Coordinator may also be approached for preliminary consultations before initiating the formal appeals process.

25. The web site of the Panel of Counsel is at http://www.un.org/staff/ panelofcounsel. The contact information for the Coordinator of the Panel of Counsel is as follows:

Telephone: 1–212–963–3954
Facsimile: 1–212–963–0252
E-mail: poc-1@un.org
Postal address: Room S-1B-1 A, United Nations
New York, NY 10017

D. Office of the Focal Point for Women in the Secretariat

26. The Office of the Focal Point for Women in the Secretariat is within the Office of the Special Adviser on Gender Issues and Advancement of Women. The Focal Point is mandated to monitor the improvement of the status of women in the Secretariat. The goals of the Office include policy formulation for issues related to the status of women and intervention in recruitment, promotion and placement processes to ensure that more women are recruited, promoted and retained. The Office also provides grievance redress, counselling, referrals and responses to enquiries of women staff members on issues affecting their career development or conditions of service.

27. The Focal Point is assisted in her work by the departmental focal points for women appointed for each department, office or regional commission, pursuant to Secretary-General's bulletin ST/SGB/1999/19, who may provide counsel and advice to women on issues affecting their career development or conditions of service.

28. The web site of the Office of the Focal Point for Women in the Secretariat is at http://www.un.org/womenwatch/osagi/fp.htm. The contact information for the Office of the Focal Point is as follows:

Telephone: 1–212–963–6828
Facsimile: 1–212–963–9545
Postal address: Two United Nations Plaza, East 44th Street, 12th Floor
New York, NY 10017

E. Staff representative bodies

29. Pursuant to staff regulation 8.1, staff representative bodies are established at the United Nations Headquarters in New York, at the United Nations Offices at

Geneva, Vienna and Nairobi and at the headquarters of the regional commissions (Addis Ababa, Bangkok, Beirut and Santiago). International staff serving in missions are represented by the Field Staff Union, which is currently located at Brindisi, Italy. Staff may bring individual cases to the attention of members of the Staff Committee or staff representatives in their office, who can assist them in addressing issues informally or formally.

ANNEX XI

United Nations ST/SGB/2005/1 (extract)

Secretary-General's bulletin

Amendments to the 100 Series of the Staff Rules (ST/SGB/2002/1)

The Secretary-General, pursuant to staff regulations 12.2, 12.3 and 12.4 and staff rule 112.2 (a), hereby promulgates the text of the amendments to the 100 Series of the Staff Rules promulgated in Secretary-General's bulletin ST/SGB/2002/1. The text of the amendments is attached to the present bulletin.

Section 1
Purpose

1.1 The text of the Staff Rules listed below is amended for the reasons set out below in relation to each rule:

(a) Rule 105.1 (c), Annual leave, is provisionally amended to establish a new annual leave cycle from 1 April through 31 March, which will begin on 1 April 2005;

(b) Rule 106.2 (e), Sick leave during annual leave, is amended to clarify that sick leave during annual leave may be approved only if the period of sickness exceeds five consecutive working days;

(c) Rule 107.1 (c), Official travel of staff members, is amended to clarify that on separation of a staff member the Organization will pay the travel expenses of staff member to the place of home leave if the staff member has a probationary appointment or an appointment of two years or longer or has completed two years of continuous service;

(d) Rule 110.4 (d), Due process, is amended to reflect that matters pertaining to financial responsibility for gross negligence will be considered by a Joint Disciplinary Committee under rule 110.5, as amended, and to clarify that subsequent appeals shall be submitted directly to the United Nations Administrative Tribunal;

(e) Rule 110.5, Joint Disciplinary Committees, is amended by adding a new paragraph (c) to include matters pertaining to financial responsibility for gross negligence in the competence of the Joint Disciplinary Committee at Headquarters;

(f) Rule 110.6, Composition of Joint Disciplinary Committees, is amended by adding a new paragraph (i) to specify that when the advice of the Joint Disciplinary Committee at Headquarters is sought in a matter pertaining to financial responsibility for gross negligence, the level of the members constituting the panel should be at least the same as the level of the staff member whose financial responsibility may be engaged;

(g) Rule 110.7, Joint Disciplinary Committee procedure, subparagraph (d), is amended to ensure consistency with rule 110.4, as amended, to implement the decision taken by the General Assembly in its resolution 57/307 of 15 April 2003, and a new paragraph (e) is added to specify the participation of the Office of

Legal Affairs, in an advisory capacity, in matters pertaining to financial responsibility for gross negligence;

(h) Rule 112.3, Financial responsibility, is amended to clarify that staff members are to be held responsible for financial loss resulting from their gross negligence and to ensure consistency with the wording of the other amendments necessary to establish the existence and the extent of the financial responsibility of staff members for financial loss suffered by the Organization.

1.2 Attached for insertion in the printed copy of ST/SGB/2002/1 are the new pages containing the amendments to the Staff Rules and the changes in the Staff Regulations and their annexes, and in the appendices to the Staff Rules.

Section 2
Final provisions

2.1 Unless otherwise indicated, the amendments introduced in the present bulletin shall enter into force on 1 January 2005.

2.2 The following bulletins are hereby abolished:

- ST/SGB/2004/14, entitled "Amendments to staff rules 110.4, 110.5, 110.6, 110.7, 112.3, 212.2 and 312.2"
- ST/SGB/2004/16, entitled "Annual leave cycle".

(*Signed*) Kofi A. Annan
Secretary-General

Rule 110.4

Due process

(a) No disciplinary proceedings may be instituted against a staff member unless he or she has been formally notified, in writing, of the allegations against him or her and of the right to seek the assistance of counsel in his or her defence at his or her own expense, and has been given a reasonable opportunity to respond to those allegations.

(b) No staff member shall be subject to disciplinary measures until the matter has been referred to a Joint Disciplinary Committee for advice as to what measures, if any, are appropriate, except that no such advice shall be required:

(i) If referral to the Joint Disciplinary Committee is waived by mutual agreement of the staff member concerned and the Secretary-General;
(ii) In respect of summary dismissal imposed by the Secretary-General in cases where the seriousness of the misconduct warrants immediate separation from service.

(c) In cases of summary dismissal imposed without prior submission of the case to a Joint Disciplinary Committee in accordance with subparagraphs (b) (i) and (ii), the staff member or former staff member concerned may, within two months of having received written notification of the measure, request that the measure be reviewed by such a Committee. A request shall not have the effect of suspending the measure. After the advice of the Committee has been received, the Secretary-General shall decide as soon as possible what action to take in respect thereof. An appeal in respect of such a decision may not be submitted to the Joint Appeals Board.

(d) An appeal in respect of a disciplinary measure considered by a Joint Disciplinary Committee pursuant to either paragraph (b) or (c), or in respect of financial responsibility for gross negligence pursuant to rule 110.5, shall be submitted directly to the United Nations Administrative Tribunal.

Rule 110.5

Joint Disciplinary Committees

(a) A standing Joint Disciplinary Committee is established and shall be available to advise the Secretary-General at his or her request in disciplinary matters at Headquarters; comparable standing committees may be established in the United Nations Office at Geneva, the United Nations Office at Vienna and such other offices as may be designated by the Secretary-General.

(b) The Secretary-General may also establish ad hoc Joint Disciplinary Committees at these or other duty stations for a particular case or series of cases, or may substitute an alternate procedure that conforms to the requirements of due process at duty stations or missions where there is no established staff representative body.

(c) The Joint Disciplinary Committee at Headquarters shall also be available to advise the Secretary-General at his request in matters pertaining to financial responsibility for gross negligence.

Rule 110.6

Composition of Joint Disciplinary Committees

(a) Each standing Joint Disciplinary Committee shall be composed of:

(i) Chairpersons, appointed by the Secretary-General after consultation with the staff representative body or bodies at the duty station at which the Committee is established;
(ii) Members appointed by the Secretary-General;
(iii) Members elected by the staff at the duty station at which the Committee is established.

(b) If necessary, additional members may be selected at any time in the same manner as indicated in paragraph (a).

(c) The chairpersons and members of the Joint Disciplinary Committee shall be appointed or elected for two years, shall be eligible for reappointment or re-election and shall remain in office until their successors are appointed or elected as long as they are staff members assigned to the duty station of the Committee.

(d) A chairperson may be removed from the Joint Disciplinary Committee by the Secretary-General after consultation with the staff representative body or bodies at the duty station at which the Committee is established. The members appointed by the Secretary-General may be removed by him or her. The members elected by the staff may be recalled by a majority vote of the staff at the duty station at which the Committee is established, taken at the initiative of any staff representative body at that duty station.

(e) The Secretary-General shall, in consultation with the staff representative body or bodies at the duty station at which a Joint Disciplinary Committee is established, appoint a Presiding Officer from among the panel of chairpersons.

(f) For the consideration of each case, a panel of the Joint Disciplinary Committee shall be constituted by the Presiding Officer as follows:

(i) A chairperson;
(ii) A member from among those appointed by the Secretary-General;
(iii) A member from among those elected by the staff.

The Presiding Officer, at the request of either party, may disqualify the chairperson or any member from the consideration of a specific case if in the opinion of the Presiding Officer the action is warranted by the relation of that member to the staff member whose case is to be considered or by any possible conflict of interest. The Presiding Officer may also excuse any member at that member's request from the consideration of a specific case.

(g) Ad hoc Joint Disciplinary Committees shall be composed as follows:

(i) At duty stations where there is an established staff representative body or bodies, ad hoc Joint Disciplinary Committees shall be composed, by the Secretary-General or an official designated by him or her, in a manner similar to that of standing Joint Disciplinary Committees, except that staff-appointed members may be substituted for staff-elected members. If no appointments are made within a period set by the Secretary-General, the designated official may make the appointments after consultation with the staff representative body or bodies;

(ii) At duty stations or missions where there is no established staff representative body, the head of office or mission, after reporting the matter to the Secretary-General, shall constitute a panel from among staff present at the duty station to investigate the allegations and to recommend what, if any, disciplinary measure should be imposed. The panel members shall be selected with a view to ensuring that the rights of all parties are respected.

(h) Any case relating to a staff member serving at a duty station where a standing Joint Disciplinary Committee is established shall be referred to that Committee, unless the Secretary-General considers there is a good reason to refer the case to a standing Committee at a different duty station or to an ad hoc Committee at the same or another duty station.

(i) When the advice of the Joint Disciplinary Committee at Headquarters is sought in a matter pertaining to financial responsibility for gross negligence, the level of the members constituting the panel shall be at least the same as the level of the staff member whose financial responsibility may be engaged.

Rule 110.7

Joint Disciplinary Committee procedure

(a) In considering a case, the Joint Disciplinary Committee shall act with maximum dispatch and shall make every effort to provide its advice to the Secretary-General within four weeks after the case has been submitted to it.

(b) Proceedings before a Joint Disciplinary Committee shall normally be limited to the original written presentation of the case, together with brief statements and rebuttals, which may be made orally or in writing, but without delay. If the Committee considers that it requires the testimony of the staff member concerned or of other witnesses, it may, at its sole discretion, obtain such testimony by written deposition, by personal appearance before the Committee, before one of its members or before another staff member acting as a special master, or by telephone or other means of communication.

(c) Each standing Joint Disciplinary Committee shall adopt its own rules of procedure, which shall be consistent with these Staff Rules and with any applicable administrative instructions, as well as with the requirements of due process. An ad hoc Committee shall apply the rules of procedure of the Headquarters Joint Disciplinary Committee, except to the extent that it decides, consistent with the requirements of due process, to apply other such rules.

(d) A Joint Disciplinary Committee shall permit a staff member to arrange to have his or her case presented before it by counsel, at his or her own expense, at the duty station where the Committee is established.

(e) A representative of the Office of Legal Affairs shall participate in an advisory capacity in the deliberations of the Joint Disciplinary Committee at Headquarters on an ex officio basis when the advice of the Committee has been requested in a matter pertaining to financial responsibility for gross negligence.

Article XI

APPEALS

Regulation 11.1

The Secretary-General shall establish administrative machinery with staff participation to advise him or her in case of any appeal by staff members against an administrative decision alleging the non-observance of their terms of appointment, including all pertinent regulations and rules.

Regulation 11.2

The United Nations Administrative Tribunal shall, under conditions prescribed in its statute, hear and pass judgement upon applications from staff members alleging non-observance of their terms of appointment, including all pertinent regulations and rules.

Chapter XII

GENERAL PROVISIONS

Rule 112.1

Gender of terms

In the French text of these Rules reference to staff members in the masculine gender shall apply to staff members of both sexes, unless it is clearly inappropriate from the context.

Rule 112.2

Amendment of, and exceptions to, Staff Rules

(a) Subject to regulations 12.1, 12.2, 12.3, 12.4 and 12.5, these Rules may be amended by the Secretary-General in a manner consistent with the Staff Regulations.

(b) Exceptions to the Staff Rules may be made by the Secretary-General, provided that such exception is not inconsistent with any staff regulation or other decision of the General Assembly and provided further that it is agreed to by the staff member directly affected and is, in the opinion of the Secretary-General, not prejudicial to the interests of any other staff member or group of staff members.

Rule 112.3

Financial responsibility

Any staff member may be required to reimburse the United Nations either partially or in full for any financial loss suffered by the United Nations as a result of the staff member's gross negligence or of his or her having violated any regulation, rule or administrative instruction.

Rule 112.4

Liability insurance

In accordance with General Assembly resolution 22 (E) (I) of 13 February 1946, staff members who own or drive motor cars shall carry public liability and property damage insurance in an amount adequate to insure them against claims arising from injury or death to other persons or from damage to the property of others caused by their cars.

Rule 112.5

Staff member's beneficiaries

(a) At the time of appointment, each staff member shall nominate a beneficiary or beneficiaries in writing in a form prescribed by the Secretary-General. It shall be the responsibility of the staff member to notify the Secretary-General of any revocations or changes of beneficiaries.

(b) In the event of the death of a staff member, all amounts standing to the staff member's credit will be paid to his or her nominated beneficiary or beneficiaries, subject to application of the Staff Rules and of the Joint Staff Pension Fund Regulations. Such payment shall afford the United Nations a complete release from all further liability in respect of any sum so paid.

(c) If a nominated beneficiary does not survive, or if a designation of beneficiary has not been made or has been revoked, the amount standing to the credit of a staff member will, upon the staff member's death, be paid to his or her estate.

Rule 112.6

(Cancelled)

Rule 112.7

Proprietary rights

All rights, including title, copyright and patent rights, in any work performed by a staff member as part of his or her official duties, shall be vested in the United Nations.

Rule 112.8

Effective date and authentic texts of rules

Except as otherwise indicated and subject always to the provisions of regulations 12.1, 12.2, 12.4 and 12.5, rules 100.1 to 112.8 as published in the present edition (ST/SGB/2002/1) shall be effective 1 January 2002. The English and French texts of these Rules are equally authoritative.

ANNEX XII

United Nations ST/AI/2004/3

Secretariat

29 September 2004

Administrative instruction

Financial responsibility of staff members for gross negligence

The Under-Secretary-General for Management, pursuant to section 4.2 of Secretary-General's bulletin ST/SGB/1997/1 and for the purpose of implementing the provisions of staff rules 112.3, 212.2, and 312.2, and the provisions of financial rule 101.2, hereby promulgates the following:

Section 1
General

1.1 The present instruction defines the conditions for implementing staff rules 112.3, 212.2, and 312.2, under which staff members may be required to reimburse the United Nations either partially or in full for any financial loss suffered by the United Nations as a result of the staff member's gross negligence or of his or her having violated any regulation, rule or administrative instruction. It also defines the conditions for implementing financial rule 101.2, under which any staff member who contravenes the Financial Regulations and Rules or corresponding administrative instructions, may be held personally accountable and financially liable for his or her actions.

1.2 The provisions of the present instruction are based on the Organization's established policy to maintain a clear distinction between:

(a) Instances where a financial loss suffered by the Organization results from an inadvertent error, oversight or simple negligence, or inability to foresee the negative consequences of a chosen course of action, in which case no financial recovery against staff members shall be undertaken and any deficiencies on the part of the officials involved shall be addressed through performance management mechanisms; and

(b) Instances where a financial loss results from gross negligence, as defined in section 1.3 below. Financial responsibility in such instances shall be established in accordance with the provisions set out in the present instruction.

1.3 For the purposes of the present instruction, "gross negligence" is negligence of a very high degree involving an extreme and wilful or reckless failure to act as a reasonable person in applying or in failing to apply the regulations and rules of the Organization.

1.4 Cases where losses result from gross negligence as defined above may also give rise to disciplinary proceedings under chapter X of the Staff Rules.[1] In order to ensure consistency of findings and protection of the due process rights of the staff members involved, disciplinary action and recovery action for financial losses shall be consolidated wherever grounds exist to initiate both actions.

Section 2
Scope

2.1 The present instruction shall apply to cases of gross negligence in the application of the Staff Regulations and Rules and of the Financial Regulations and Rules, as well as Secretary-General's bulletins and administrative instructions implementing those Regulations and Rules.

2.2 The present instruction shall not apply to:

(a) Recovery from staff members of overpayments made to them in excess of their entitlements. Such recovery is governed by the provisions of administrative instruction ST/AI/2000/11;

(b) Loss, damage or other discrepancy regarding the property of the United Nations, which shall be considered by a property survey board in accordance with financial rule 105.21. For purposes of the present instruction, "property" shall mean supplies, equipment, building and land belonging to or entrusted to the charge of the United Nations.

Section 3
Preliminary investigation

3.1 When the head of a department or office has reason to believe that the gross negligence of a staff member may have led to financial loss by the Organization or receives credible allegations to that effect, the head of department or office concerned shall immediately inform the Controller and the Under-Secretary-General, Office of Internal Oversight Services (OIOS), and take the necessary steps to secure available evidence. The head of department or office shall initiate a preliminary investigation of the facts to determine whether there was gross negligence and a resulting financial loss, unless OIOS or the Controller advises the head of department or office within two weeks that the matter will be investigated by the respective department or office.

3.2 Allegations of gross negligence resulting in financial loss by the Organization and pertaining to a head of department or office shall be reported to the Controller and to the Under-Secretary-General for OIOS. Unless OIOS advises the Controller that it intends to investigate the matter, the preliminary investigation shall be conducted by officials designated by the Controller.

[1] The procedures applicable in disciplinary cases are set out in administrative instruction ST/AI/371 of 2 August 1991.

3.3 The investigation shall be conducted promptly and shall normally be completed within six months unless extraordinary circumstances arise, which would justify completion at a later stage.

3.4 If the allegations are of such nature and gravity that suspension may be warranted, or if there is a risk of evidence being destroyed or concealed, the investigating authority shall recommend suspension pending investigation to the Assistant Secretary-General for Human Resources Management, giving reasons. Suspension shall normally be with pay, unless the Under-Secretary-General for Management, on behalf of the Secretary-General, decides that exceptional circumstances warrant suspension without pay. Suspension with or without pay shall be without prejudice to the rights of the staff member.

3.5 If the staff member under investigation separates or is due to separate from service before the conclusion of the proceedings under section 4 below, the Assistant Secretary-General for Human Resources Management, at his or her own initiative or at the request of the Controller, may authorize withholding of final separation payments until the proceedings have been concluded.

3.6 The investigation report, together with supporting evidence and a computation of the amount of the financial loss involved shall be submitted to the Controller and to the Assistant Secretary-General for Human Resources Management.

Section 4
Action following preliminary investigation

4.1 After analysis of the investigation report, together with supporting evidence and a computation of the amount of the financial loss involved, the Assistant Secretary-General for Human Resources Management, after consultation with the Controller, shall decide whether the allegations of gross negligence appear to be substantiated. If the allegations are not substantiated, the staff member, the department or office concerned and OIOS shall be informed in writing that the case for recovery is closed and that the evidence does not support recovery action and/or the allegations of gross negligence.

4.2 If the allegations appear to be substantiated, a designated official of the Office of Human Resources Management shall:

(a) Inform the staff member in writing of the allegations of gross negligence and resulting financial loss, and of his or her right to respond;
(b) Provide the staff member with a copy of the documentary evidence of the gross negligence, a computation of the resulting financial loss, which the Organization proposes to recover, and an explanation of the basis on which the computation was made; and
(c) Notify the staff member of his or her right to counsel.

4.3 The staff member shall be given a specified time to answer the allegations and produce countervailing evidence, if any. The amount of time allowed shall take into account the seriousness and complexity of the matter. If more time is required, it shall be granted upon the staff member's written request for an extension, giving cogent reasons why he or she is unable to comply with the deadline. If no response is submitted within the time limit, the matter shall nevertheless proceed.

4.4 The entire dossier shall be submitted to the Assistant Secretary-General for Human Resources Management who, in consultation with the Controller, shall take one of the following actions, as appropriate:

(a) Decide that the case should be closed and inform the staff member and the department or office concerned to that effect; or

(b) Refer the matter to the Joint Disciplinary Committee at Headquarters, which shall consider it in accordance with chapter X of the 100 series of the Staff Rules and part III of administrative instruction ST/AI/371, with the following adjustments:

(i) As required by staff rule 110.6 (i), the level of the members constituting the panel shall be at least the same as the level of the staff member whose financial responsibility for gross negligence may be engaged;

(ii) As required by staff rule 110.7 (e), a representative of the Office of Legal Affairs shall participate in the deliberations of the Committee on an ex officio basis in an advisory capacity; and

(iii) The report of the Joint Disciplinary Committee shall set out the allegations of gross negligence and of resulting financial loss, the response of the staff member, a statement of the proceedings, the findings of the Committee on each allegation and the advice of the Committee to the Secretary-General on the proposed recovery, taking into account any relevant aggravating or mitigating factor. The report should also include any dissenting or separate opinion of the Committee members;

(c) Transmit the report of the Joint Disciplinary Committee with maximum dispatch to the Secretary-General through the Under-Secretary-General for Management. The decision on the Committee recommendation shall be taken by or on behalf of the Secretary-General. Any recourse against the decision shall be submitted to the United Nations Administrative Tribunal.

4.5 The staff member may, at any time during the investigation and before submission of the report of the Joint Disciplinary Committee, decide to waive his or her right to having the case decided in the light of the report of that Committee and agree in advance to recovery by the Organization of a specified amount established by the Assistant Secretary-General for Human Resources Management in consultation with the Controller. The staff member shall be assisted by counsel in deciding on the waiver, unless he or she specifically declines such assistance. Should the allegations against the staff member be based on misconduct as well as gross negligence, the waiver should, whenever possible, encompass both the disciplinary and the financial recovery aspects of the case. Should the waiver be limited to either misconduct or gross negligence charges, the case before the Joint Disciplinary Committee would proceed on the charges for which no waiver has been made. The terms of the waiver shall be recorded in writing.

Section 5
Final provision

The present administrative instruction shall enter into force on 1 October 2004.

(*Signed*) Catherine **Bertini**
Under-Secretary-General for Management

ANNEX XIII

United Nations ST/SGB/2005/13

Secretariat

5 May 2005

Secretary-General's bulletin

Management Performance Board

The Secretary-General, for the purposes of strengthening accountability in the Secretariat, and taking into account the provisions of relevant General Assembly resolutions, has decided to discontinue the Accountability Panel established by ST/SGB/2000/14 and replace it with a Management Performance Board, with strengthened and expanded functions. He promulgates the following:

Section 1
Functions of the Management Performance Board

1.1 The Management Performance Board shall assume an advisory role to the Secretary-General and shall perform the following functions:

(a) Review the findings and recommendations of the high-level follow-up mechanism to be established in accordance with General Assembly resolution 59/272 of 23 December 2004; and ensure that the Secretariat addresses the serious managerial issues identified by its oversight bodies and acts upon the recommendations of these bodies in a timely manner;

(b) Monitor the manner in which senior managers exercise all aspects of the authority that has been delegated to them, including their performance in achieving the objectives contained in human resources action plans;

(c) Review the outcome of the administration of justice proceedings in the Secretariat for management accountability purposes.

1.2 The Management Performance Board shall also put into place a system of peer review to ensure adherence to acceptable standards of managerial conduct.

1.3 In order to discharge its functions, the Management Performance Board may assess the functioning of individual departments and offices and the manner in which senior managers in those departments and offices discharge their responsibilities. Where problems are identified, the Management Performance Board shall consider the management policy implications and hold senior managers accountable by recommending appropriate corrective action to the senior managers, reviewing the action taken and deciding on any further measures necessary.

1.4 The Management Performance Board may request at any time the information it finds necessary for the discharge of its functions.

1.5 Based on its findings, the Management Performance Board may recommend appropriate remedies. Recommendations shall be communicated to the Secretary-General and the concerned programme manager. The Management Performance Board shall monitor implementation of any decision taken by the Secretary-General, or agreement made between the Secretary-General and the concerned programme manager.

Section 2
Composition

2.1 The Management Performance Board shall consist of a chairperson, who shall be the Deputy Secretary-General, two members at the Under-Secretary-General level and a member who shall be an external expert in public sector management.

2.2 The Management Performance Board shall invite, as appropriate, representatives of any department or office in the Secretariat to advise on substantive questions.

2.3 The members of the Management Performance Board shall be appointed by the Secretary-General for a two-year period, which may be renewed.

Section 3
Final provisions

3.1 The present bulletin shall enter into force on 13 May 2005.

3.2 ST/SGB/2000/14, entitled "Accountability Panel", is hereby abolished.

(*Signed*) Kofi A. **Annan**
Secretary-General

ANNEX XIV

Decision of the Secretary-General Concerning the Policy to Prevent and Combat Harassment

Preventing and Dealing with Harassment at the OECD Policy and Guidelines

1. All OECD staff members have the right to be treated with dignity and respect and to work in an environment which fosters professional respect and courtesy. Harassment of any kind at work, or in connection with work performed on behalf of the Organisation, will not be tolerated and may give rise to disciplinary action.

2. All staff, regardless of their grade and contract status, share the responsibility for preventing harassment and maintaining a harmonious working environment. This implies that, in accordance with the standards of conduct expected in the relevant provisions of the Organisation's staff rules, they shall treat each other with respect and due regard for individual dignity so as to ensure that the workplace is free of intimidation, hostility or offensive behaviour and, in particular, of any form of harassment. In an international environment like the OECD we must all be aware of the fact that our own cultural norms and values may not be shared by colleagues and be sensitive to misunderstandings or differences of opinion based on those differences of culture. But these differences cannot be used as an excuse for harassing behaviour.

3. Managers at all levels have a key role and bear special responsibility for preventing the occurrence of any form of harassment. They should foster a positive working environment and, in their leadership, display a willingness and ability to deal effectively with harassment when it does occur, in particular by being responsive to and supportive of any staff member who complains about such conduct. They must set a good personal example and pay attention to signs of a deteriorating work atmosphere. They shall ensure that the Organisation's policy and guidelines on harassment are communicated to and understood by all their staff, and that they are applied in the workplace.

4. Any retaliation or threat of retaliation against individuals making formal or informal complaints of harassment, or participating in the investigation of such complaints (for example, as witnesses), will be considered a violation of acceptable standards of conduct and will result in disciplinary action. At the same time, any accusation or complaint shown to be made in bad faith will also be considered a violation of acceptable standards of conduct and will be treated in the same manner.

5. This policy will regularly be reviewed in order to ensure its effectiveness.

Personal harassment

6. Personal harassment is any repeated behaviour or pattern of behaviour that is reasonably regarded as aimed at creating a hostile work environment. It maybe perpetrated by an individual or by a group. It includes behaviour which, in violation of the right to dignity at work, demeans, belittles or causes humiliation or embarrassment to an individual, or unfairly compromises the individual's career prospects.

While an isolated incident of such behaviour may infringe the right to dignity at work, personal harassment takes the form of an accumulation of incidents, even when each incident, taken in isolation and out of context, could be seen as trivial.

7. Even though there may be "grey" situations, personal harassment should be distinguished from other types of behaviour that may be detrimental to another individual's working conditions, but that are manifestly unintentional, or are attributable solely to poor management skills. For example, the behaviour of a manager or colleagues who fail to keep staff informed of important business developments as a result of poor organisation would not, *prima facie*, be considered personal harassment. On the other hand, the behaviour of a manager or colleagues who sabotage an individual employee's work by deliberately withholding information that is required to fulfil a task, and who do so repeatedly, would, *prima facie*, present the characteristics of personal harassment.

Sexual harassment

8. Sexual harassment is any sexual advance, request for sexual favour, or other type of conduct of a sexual nature, whether verbal, physical or otherwise, which is offensive and unwelcome, which interferes with work, is made a condition of employment or advancement, in other ways adversely influences, or tries to influence, the career of the person subjected to it, or which creates an intimidating, hostile or offensive environment.

Harassment and abuse of power

9. When harassment is engaged in by an official or group who is in a position to influence the career or employment conditions of the victim (including through recruitment, assignment, contract renewal, performance evaluation or promotion), it constitutes an abuse of a position of power which in itself will be regarded as serious misconduct.

How to respond in case of possible harassment

10. The Organisation encourages employees who may feel they are being harassed to follow the steps listed below:

- Do not be afraid to speak up.
- Do not assume that the behaviour will stop if you try to ignore it.

- Do not hesitate to ask for help, as harassment is neither trivial nor a personal matter between staff members.

11. If you witness what may be the harassment of a colleague or if someone confides in you that he/she is being harassed, do not ignore it and do not hesitate to offer your help. Some people may be reluctant to defend themselves because they are not aware of the OECD policy and guidelines on harassment. Others, even if they are aware of them, may require support from a third party before being able to react.

Practical steps

12. The first thing to do if you believe that you are being harassed is to inform the person concerned immediately and unambiguously of the unwelcome nature of his or her behaviour and ask that it cease. If you find it difficult to speak with the person concerned directly, you may prefer to write a short letter which describes the behaviour – and records the fact that you find it unacceptable and wish it to stop. Some people may be unaware of the effect of their behaviour and will stop it when asked.

13. Keep a detailed written record of the instances of offensive conduct, indicating the time, place, and nature of the behaviour and, if possible, witnesses to it.

Informal procedure

14. If dealing directly with the person concerned fails to put a stop to such behaviour – or if you feel unable, for whatever reason, to raise the matter directly with him or her or your management – you can consult one or more of the following persons on a confidential basis. They will meet with you privately, discuss the situation with you and make suggestions as to how to deal with it. They will explain the difference between an "Informal procedure" and an "Enquiry". These people may also be available to provide mediation and resolution of the situation on an informal basis with the agreement of the different involved parties. Any informal procedure must be conducted promptly.

- the Social Advisers;
- the Organisation's doctors;
- the Human Resource Advisers;
- the OECD Mediators;
- the Staff Association.

15. If the matter cannot be resolved informally or sufficiently quickly, any of the people above can forward the matter to the Head of Human Resource Management, but only upon receipt of a written request from you outlining your complaint. The request should state your readiness to co-operate in the enquiry which may follow.

Enquiry

16. The Head of Human Resource Management will examine the information that is submitted and if appropriate will immediately initiate an enquiry. The enquiry should be completed within 30 days from the date that the Head of Human Resource Management receives the written version of the complaint.

17. The enquiry will be conducted with due respect for the rights of both the complainant and the person accused. Specifically, the alleged harasser will be given the opportunity to answer the allegations and to produce evidence to the contrary. The enquiry may also involve a meeting between the alleged harasser and the complainant, if so requested and agreed upon by all involved parties.

18. Depending on the circumstances of the case and the conclusions of the enquiry, the Head of Human Resources management will take appropriate measures. These may include initiating a disciplinary action under Staff *Regulation 21.*

Index

L'Institut International des Sciences Administratives

IISA: Que sommes-nous?

L'Institut international des Sciences administratives existe dans le but de faire progresser l'étude et la pratique de l'administration publique et de la gestion publique. Il fonctionne à un niveau global et est financé par les Etats et Membres qui proviennent du monde entier, tout en gardant son autonomie vis-à-vis d'eux. Il se veut, grâce à sa relation avec les Nations Unies, d'être le plus objectif possible en apportant un message et une vision neutre, et en répondant à des besoins réels.

IISA: Quel est notre rôle?

Bien que l'Institut existe depuis plus de soixante-dix ans (à partir de 1930), son regard est assurément tourné vers le futur. Comment pratiquer la gouvernance et l'améliorer; de quelle manière les lois administratives sont appliquées et comment les réformer; par quelles méthodes la gestion des affaires publiques est conduite et comment l'améliorer ? Voilà quelques questions qui reflètent à juste titre ses activités.

IISA: Quelles sont nos valeurs?

La *responsabilité* est une valeur primordiale de l'Institut. Les personnes qui exercent l'autorité doivent faire preuve d'un usage irréprochable de leur pouvoir à l'égard des citoyens. L'Administration publique est l'activité centrale qui relie les gouvernements au peuple. Nous considérons que l'exécution des tâches, dans ce domaine, doit être bien organisée, de manière efficace et économique. Nous sommes pour une *gouvernance moderne* et une *administration publique saine* et affirmons que cette approche gouvernementale doit être réalisée de façon équilibrée tout en respectant la diversité, l'identité et les convictions des citoyens.

IISA: Comment fonctionne l'Institut?

Une petite équipe dynamique et bilingue assure le Secrétariat à Bruxelles sous le contrôle du Comité Exécutif qui est lui-même supervisé par un Conseil d'Administration représentatif. Le Président et le Directeur général gèrent et dirigent l'Institut pour ses membres. Chaque année l'IISA organise trois conférences dans trois pays distincts à travers le monde; accueille plus de 700 participants; publie quatre numéros de sa prestigieuse *Revue internationale des Sciences administratives* (en français, anglais et arabe); gère un budget d'approximativement 1 million d'euros; conduit et dirige les activités de ses quatre-vingt dix Etats Membres et Sections Nationales.

L'Institut comprend deux associations spécialisées, l'Association internationale des Ecoles et Instituts d'administration (AIEIA) et le Groupe Européen d'administration publique (GEAP) qui organisent respectivement des études, recherches et activités de réseaux.

L'Institut possède une bibliothèque spécialisée qui comprend plus de 15.500 livres et revues d'Administration publique en plusieurs langues afin de refléter les connaissances et expertises de ses membres. Le site web de l'Institut reçoit des milliers de visiteurs par mois et offre un panorama complet de nos activités présentes et futures.

The International Institute of Administrative Sciences

IIAS: What is it?

The IIAS exists to advance the study and practice of public administration and public management. It operates at a global level and is funded by states worldwide; but is independent of any of them and, through its links with the United Nations, seeks to develop a voice and a vision that is neutral, as objective as possible and grounded in the exigency of the fact.

IIAS: What is it for?

Although it has existed for over seventy years (since 1930), the Institute's focus is on the present and the future. How governance is done and how it could be done better; how the law of administration applies and how it might be applied more correctly; and how the management of public affairs is conducted and how it might be best done—all of these reflect its activities.

IIAS: What are its values?

Accountability is a core value for the Institute. Those who exercise authority must account for its use to those on whose behalf they use it. Public Administration is the key activity that connects between the power-holders and the citizen. We believe it should be effective, efficient and economical in its execution of the duties and rights of the state. We support *modern governance* and *proper public administration* and believe these should be carried out in a way that actively acknowledges *diversity*, that is *respectful* of identity and serious belief and that reflects *balance.*

IIAS: How does it work?

A small-dedicated bilingual secretariat in Brussels serves the Executive Committee, which is in turn accountable to a fully representative Council of Administration. The President and Director General lead and manage the Institute for its members. Each year IIAS holds three conferences in three different countries around the world; is host for seven hundreds-plus delegates; publishes four issues of its prestigious *International Review of Administrative Sciences* (in three editions English, French and Arabic); manages a budget of approximately 1 million Euros; leads and coordinates activities among its ninety Member States and National Sections

The Institute has two specialised bodies: the International Association of Schools and Institutes of Administration (IASIA) and the European Group of Public Administration (EGPA); each of which conducts study, research and networking.

The Institute has a distinguished library of 15,500 public administration books in several languages to reflect the accumulated wisdom and experience of its members; and a Website, which receives many thousand 'hits' per month about what it is doing now and what it will do in the future.

NIJHOFF LAW SPECIALS

1. D. Campbell: *Abortion Law and Public Policy.* 1984 ISBN 90-247-3107-0
2. J. Pictet: *Development and Principles of International Humanitarian Law.* 1985 ISBN 90-247-3199-2
3. J. van Houtte: *Sociology of Law and Legal Anthropology in Dutch-speaking Countries.* 1985 ISBN 90-247-3175-5
4. C.D. De Fouloy: *Glossary of NAFTA Terms.* 1994 ISBN 0-7923-2719-5
5. H.L. Zielinski: *Health and Humanitarian Concerns.* Principles and Ethics. 1994 ISBN 0-7923-2963-5
6. K.S. Foster and D.C. Alexander: *Prospects of a US-Chile Free Trade Agree-ment.* 1994 ISBN 0-7923-2885-X
7. F.J.M. Feldbrugge (ed.): *Russian Federation Legislative Survey.* June 1990-December 1992. 1995 ISBN 0-7923-3243-1
8. R. Platzöder (ed.): *The 1994 United Nations Convention on the Law of the Sea.* Basic Documents with an Introduction. 1995 ISBN 0-7923-3271-7
9. D. Warner (ed.): *New Dimensions of Peacekeeping.* 1995 ISBN 0-7923-3301-2
10. M. van Leeuwen (ed.): *The Future of the International Nuclear Non-Proliferation Regime.* 1995 ISBN 0-7923-3433-7
11. E.-U. Petersmann: *International and European Trade and Environmental Law After the Uruguay Round.* 1995 ISBN 90-411-0857-2
12. V. Gowlland-Debbas: *The Problem of Refugees in the Light of Contemporary International Law Issues.* 1996 ISBN 90-411-0085-7
13. A. Kaczorowska: *International Trade Conventions and Their Effectiveness. Present and Future.* 1995 ISBN 0-7923-3362-4
14. T.F. Acuña: *The United Nations Mission in El Salvador. A Humanitarian Law Perspective.* 1995 ISBN 90-411-0123-3
15. H. Wiggering and A. Sandhövel (eds.): *European Environmental Advisory Councils.* 1996 ISBN 90-411-0873-4
16. E.A. Ankumah: *The African Commission on Human and Peoples' Rights.* Practice and Procedures. 1996 ISBN 90-411-0130-6
17. B. de Rossanet: *Peacemaking and Peacekeeping in Yugoslavia.* 1996 ISBN 90-411-0192-6
18. A. Webster and K. Packer (eds.): *Innovation and the Intellectual Property System.* 1996 ISBN 90-411-0907-2
19. H. Bocken and D. Ryckbost (eds.): *Codification of Environmental Law.* Draft Decree on Environmental Policy. 1996 ISBN 90-411-0911-0
20. K. Lescure and F. Trintignac: *International Justice for Former Yugoslavia.* The Working of the International Criminal Tribunal of the Hague. 1996 ISBN 90-411-0201-9
21. G. de Nooy (ed.): *The Role of European Naval Forces after the Cold War.* 1996 ISBN 90-411-0227-2
22. M. Bertrand and D. Warner (eds.): *A New Charter for a Worldwide Organisation?* 1997 ISBN 90-411-0286-8

NIJHOFF LAW SPECIALS

23. E.-U. Petersmann: *The GATT/WTO Dispute Settlement System.* International Law, International Organizations and Dispute Settlement. 1996 ISBN 90-411-0933-1
24. G. de Nooy (ed.): *Cooperative Security, the OSCE, and its Code of Conduct.* 1996 ISBN 90-411-0316-3
25. M. Bertrand: *The United Nations.* Past, Present and Future. 1997 ISBN 90-411-0337-6
26. D. Dijkzeul: *The Management of Multilateral Organizations.* 1997 ISBN 90-411-0356-2
27. G. de Nooy (ed.): *The Role of European Ground and Air Forces after the Cold War.* 1997 ISBN 90-411-0397-X
28. M. Hilaire: *International Law and the United States.* Military Intervention in the Western Hemisphere. 1997 ISBN 90-411-0399-6
29. D. Warner (ed.): *Human Rights and Humanitarian Law.* The Quest for Universality. 1997 ISBN 90-411-0407-0
30. J.C. Hathaway (ed.): *Reconceiving International Refugee Law.* 1997 ISBN 90-411-0418-6
31. G. de Nooy (ed.): *The Clausewitzian Dictum and the Future of Western Military Strategy.* 1997 ISBN 90-411-0455-0
32. Canadian Council on International Law and The Markland Group (ed.): *Treaty Compliance: Some Concerns and Remedies.* 1997 ISBN 90-411-0732-0
33. B. de Rossanet: *War and Peace in the Former Yugoslavia.* 1998 ISBN 90-411-0499-2
34. C.M. Mazzoni (ed.): *A Legal Framework for Bioethics.* 1998 ISBN 90-411-0523-9
35. M. Marín-Bosch: *Votes in the UN General Assembly.* 1998 ISBN 90-411-0564-6
36. L. Caflisch: *The Peaceful Settlement of Disputes between States: Universal and European Perspectives.* Règlement pacifique des différends entre Etats: Perspectives universelle et européenne. 1998 ISBN 90-411-0461-5
37. R. Wazir and N. van Oudenhoven (eds.): *Child Sexual Abuse: What can Governments do?* A Comparative Investigation into Policy Instruments Used in Belgium, Britain, Germany, the Netherlands and Norway. 1998 ISBN 90-411-1034-8
38. E.M. Barron and I. Nielsen (eds.): *Agriculture and Sustainable Land Use in Europe.* 1998 ISBN 90-411-9691-9
39. K. van Walraven (ed.): *Early Warning and Conflict Prevention.* 1998 ISBN 90-411-1064-X
40. S. Shubber: The International Code of Marketing of Breast-milk Substitutes. An International Measure to Protect and Promote Breast-feeding. 1999 ISBN 90-411-1100-X
41. G. Prins and H. Tromp (eds.): *The Future of War.* 2000 ISBN 90-411-1196-4
42. Choung Il Chee: *Korean Perspectives on Ocean Law Issues for the 21st Century.* 2000 ISBN 90-411-1301-0
43. K. Idris and M. Bartolo: *A Better United Nations for the New Millennium.* The United Nations System – How it is now and how it should be in the future. 2000 ISBN 90-411-1344-4

NIJHOFF LAW SPECIALS

44. E. McWhinney: *The United Nations and a New World Order for a New Millennium*. Self-determination, State Succession, and Humanitarian Intervention. 2000
ISBN 90-411-1371-1
45. C.Y. Pak: *Korea and the United Nations*. 2000 ISBN 90-411-1382-7
46. G. Prins and H. Tromp (eds.): *The Future of War*. 2000 ISBN 90-411-1399-1
47. V. Gowlland-Debbas, H. Hadj-Sahraoui and N. Hayashi (eds.): *Multilateral Treaty-making*. The Current Status of Challenges to and Reforms Needed in the International Legislative Process. 2000 ISBN 90-411-1448-3
48. G. Simpson (ed.): *Detainees Denied Justice*. 2001 ISBN 90-411-1552-8
49. C.A. Magariños, G. Assaf, S. Lall, J.D.-Martinussen, R. Ricupero and F. Sercovich: *Reforming the UN System*. UNIDO's Need Driven Model. 2001
ISBN 90-411-1669-9
50. K. Wellens (ed.): *Resolutions and Statements of the United Nations Security Council (1946-2000)*. A Thematic Guide. 2001 ISBN 90-411-1722-9
51. P. Soar (ed.): *The New International Directory of Legal Aid*. 2001
ISBN 90-411-1718-0
52. C.M. Mazzoni (ed.): *Ethics and Law in Biological Research*. 2002
ISBN 90-411-1742-3
53. I. Omar: *Emergency Powers and the Courts in India and Pakistan*. 2002
ISBN 90-411-1775-X
54. M. O'Flaherty: *Human Rights and the UN: Practice Before the Treaty Bodies*. 2002
ISBN 90-411-1788-1
55. Y. Beigbeder: *Judging Criminal Leaders*. The Slow Erosion of Impunity. 2002
ISBN 90-411-1815-2
56. Marianne van Leeuwen (ed.): *Confronting Terrorism: European Experiences, Threat Perceptions, and Policies*. 2003 ISBN 90-411-1960-4
57. Ralf Bredel: *Long-term Conflict Prevention and Industrial Development: The United Nations and its Specialized Agency, UNIDO*. 2003 ISBN 90-04-13619-3
58. Raphael Walden: *Racism and Human Rights*. 2004 ISBN 90-04-13651-7
59. Monique Leyenaar: *Political Empowerment of Women: The Netherlands and Other Countries*. 2004 ISBN 90-04-14099-9
60. Sjurdur Skaale (ed.): *The Right to National Self-Determination: The Faroes and Greenland*. 2004
ISBN 90 04 14207 X
61. Edward McWhinney: *The September 11 Terrorist Attacks and the Invasion of Iraq in Contemporary International Law: Opinions on the Emerging New World Order System*. 2004
ISBN 90 04 14143 X
62. Bertrand G. Ramcharan (ed.): *The Protection Role of National Human Rights Institutions*. 2005 ISBN 90 04 14526 5
63. Chris de Cooker (ed.): *Accountability, Investigation and Due Process in International Organizations*. 2005 ISBN 90 04 14793 4

MARTINUS NIJHOFF PUBLISHERS – LEIDEN / BOSTON

www.ingramcontent.com/pod-product-compliance
Lightning Source LLC
Chambersburg PA
CBHW031321230926
51848CB00001B/42
9789004147935